UNIVERSITY ADMINISTRATION
Global Challenges in the 21st Century

UNIVERSITY ADMINISTRATION

Global Challenges in the 21st Century

P.N. GAUTAM

DEEP & DEEP PUBLICATIONS PVT. LTD.
F-159, Rajouri Garden, New Delhi - 110 027

UNIVERSITY ADMINISTRATION
Global Challenges in the 21st Century

ISBN 978-81-8450-212-1

Typeset by RAHUL COMPOSERS
358, Pocket-B, Phase-II, Sector-16B, Dwarka, New Delhi - 110 075

Printed in India at MAYUR ENTERPRISES
WZ Plot No. 3, Gujjar Market, Tihar Village, New Delhi - 110 018

Published by DEEP & DEEP PUBLICATIONS PVT. LTD.,
F-159, Rajouri Garden, New Delhi - 110 027 • Phone : 25435369, 25440916
E-mail : ddpubs@gmail.com • ddpbooks@yahoo.co.in
Showroom :
2/13, Ansari Road, Daryaganj, New Delhi - 110 002 • Telefax : 23245122

Contents

Preface

Shouting of slogans like "P.N. Gautam Murdabad", "P.N. Gautam Go Back", "P.N. Gautam Nahin Chalega" and burning of the effigy of the Vice-Chancellor who later died of heart attack due to unbearable stress from many groups, corners and quarters made me to ponder over the phenomenon through which our higher education especially university education is passing these days. Posted as the Director of the Himachal Pradesh University Regional Centre at Dharamshala with no powers and resources, left entirely at the mercy of the neighbouring Government College Dharamshala to provide life support system, provided me with many situations of helplessness and at the same time gave me opportunities to use my ingenuity to tackle some of the present problems and challenges being faced by higher education in India. Retirement after a short stint as a Chairman of the Department of Public Administration back in the University campus at Shimla and UGC fellowship provided ample time to think over the challenges clamouring for early solution.

As I went through the literature on university administration, scanned various reports on higher education, glanced through the news papers, observed the students' agitations fraught with acrimonious scenes, abusive slogans (Remove *Chore* VC), and aggressive postures, I became more and more cynic and fast developed a feeling that I cannot do more than a post-mortem of higher education. I may give some suggestions, but who is going to accept them what to speak of practicing them. However, my observations during my visits to the universities of the sample, analysis and interpretation of data collected through the questionnaires, and insight gained into the challenges to the university administration through case studies and interviews revealed that the situation is not beyond redemption, there were many silver linings in the dark clouds and if we make sincere efforts things can be improved.

Undoubtedly, universities play a pivotal role in the development of a country. University administration in India is afflicted with many problems and weaknesses and naturally is not in a position to face the challenges it is surrounded with. Good governance is urgently needed for making the universities efficient and effective and meeting the challenges. For the sake of good governance in universities we need a many pronged strategy with a great political will and administrative skill. Suggestions made in the study are worth trying. Scholars, politicians, educationists, administrators, economists, NGOs and other enlightened citizens can make significant contributions in this regard. Educational administrators, teachers, students, non-teaching employees and all those interested in the future of the country have to sit together, join heads and work collectively for the success of the university administration. Delay in this concerted action will be detrimental to their interests and to those of the country.

I am highly obliged to the University Grants Commission for providing the financial assistance to me for the major research project without which this work would not have been possible. My sincere thanks are also due to the authors whose books helped me to understand the challenges to university administration, to the scholars who guided me at all the stages of the study, to my colleagues in the Department of Public Administration in H.P. University, Shimla, to the scholars who helped me in the collection of data in all the universities of the sample, and to Sh. Ajay Sharma, a my Project Assistant in the study whose penetrating observation has proved a great asset to me. Last but not the least, I am highly obliged to my daughter, Varda, for the help she rendered to me in the completion of the study and to my wife, Mrs. Shashi Gautam, who as usual suffered patiently and managed almost single-handedly the affairs of the family during the period of the study.

I may kindly be excused if any of my observations, remarks or conclusions hurt the feelings of any person. I have written every word with malice towards none and love only for higher education regarding it crucial for the development of the country. I shall feel sufficiently rewarded if my observations and suggestions help in the amelioration of the conditions of higher education in general and university education in particular.

P.N. GAUTAM

Abbreviations

ABVP	Akhil Bharatiya Vidyarthi Parishad
AERA	Agro-Economic Research Centre
AICTE	All India Council of Technical Education
AIR	All-India Radio
AIU	Association of Indian Universities
ASC	Administrative Staff College
CAGI	Comptroller and Auditor General of India
CBSE	Central Board of Secondary Education
CET	Common Entrance Test
CoE	Controller of Examination
CPMT	Combined Pre-Medical Test
CSIR	Centre for Scientific and Industrial Research
DCC	Directorate of Correspondence Courses
DCI	Dental Council of India
DDE	Directorate of Distance Education
DMC	Detailed Marks Card
DST	Department of Science and Technology
DU	Delhi University
EC	Executive Council
Ed.	Editor
FIST	Fund for Improving Infrastructure in Science and Technology

GNDU	Guru Nanak Dev University
HEIs	Higher Educational Institutions
HODs	Heads of Departments
HPCPMT	Himachal Pradesh Combined Pre-Medical Test
HPU	Himachal Pradesh University
HRD	Human Resource Development
ICAR	Indian Council of Agricultural Research
ICDEOL	International Centre for Distance Education and Open Learning
ICHR	Indian Council of Historical Research
ICMR	Indian Council of Medical Research
ICSSR	Indian Council of Social Science Research
IGMC	Indira Gandhi Medical College
JRF	Junior Research Fellowship
JU	Jammu University
KAS	Kashmir Administrative Service
KU	Kurukshetra University
LAD	Local Audit Department
NAAC	National Assessment and Accreditation Council
NET	National Entrance Test
NRI	Non-Resident Indians
NSUI	National Students Union of India
NTS	Non-Teaching Staff
OHP	Over-Head Projector
OMR	Optical Mark Reader
PET	Pre-Engineering Test
PMET	Pre-Medical Entrance Test
PMT	Pre-Medical Test
PRC	Population Research Centre
PU	Panjab University
PVC	Pro-Vice-Chancellor
SAP	Special Assistance Programme
SCA	Students' Central Association

SFI	Students' Federation of India
SLP	Special Leave Petition
TQ	Total Quality
UGC	University Grants Commission
UNESCO	United Nations Education and Socio-Cultural Organisation
UP	Uttar Pradesh
VC	Vice-Chancellor

CHAPTER

1

Introduction

"University administration is a very complex job since it calls for running a system which consists of diverse groups and which has several masters."[1] The Vice-Chancellor as the head of the organization has to manage the whole show. He is responsible for generating sufficient funds in these difficult days of perennial resource crunch. The students, teachers, and other employees, who otherwise are his supporting staff, press for their different demands which, to the ultimate analysis, entail lot of financial involvements. Strikes by the teachers, employees and especially violent ones by the students cause a great strain on the Vice-Chancellor and some other senior officers concerned with administering a university. Politics has entered the university administration in a much more intricate and vigorous way than it has done in any other field of administration. This has resulted in splitting the three powerful groups, i.e. students, teachers and employees both horizontally and vertically. The masters of these groups outside university who hold the strings would not allow them to remain peaceful and cooperate with the university administration. Internal politics of senior officers add more intricate dimension to the already complex scenario.

Extremely powerful position of a Vice-Chancellor in the University Administration perhaps makes him weak and vulnerable. He is the Chairman of the Executive Council (called Syndicate in some universities) and the Academic Council. These are the highest decision-making bodies in all academic and administrative matters of a university. In the matter of recruitment, his powers are immense, absolute and unchallengeable. He can very easily influence the selection committees. In almost all the universities he has been given special powers in the name of smooth and efficient administration of a university which empower him to keep all the University Acts, Rules, Regulations and Ordinances at bay. In all the daily routine matters he has been equipped with formidable powers which make his position vulnerable to the various striking groups who adopt the 'gun on the head policy' of 'do it or leave'. University Acts, Rules, Regulations, and Ordinances which could otherwise serve as shields for the protection of a Vice-Chancellor are violated by him for some expediency. Interested parties, thus pressurize the Vice-Chancellor to use his special powers in their favour making it difficult to run the administration based on sound principles. This position is perhaps the root cause of all maladministration, favouritism, and nepotism in a university.

There is utter lack of public confidence in the quality of education imparted to the students and the research conducted therein, the capability, sincerity and impartiality of the teachers and administrators. Students and society both are fast getting disillusioned. J.D. Sethi in his book, "*The Crisis and Collapse of Higher Education in India*" has pointed out, "It is well known that about one-third of the colleges and even universities remain closed at one time or another because of disturbances. Arson and violence have become a common occurrence in most universities. The police continue to exercise a presence in several universities but the moment they are withdrawn the trouble flares up again. The university administration is unable to function both due to internal dissensions and perversion of the role of teachers, students, vice-chancellors and *karamcharis*, and to the intervention of the external political and coercive factors."[2] Intelligent and industrious students with their gold medals and degrees are not sure of getting the jobs they deserve.

Teachers have little role to play in evaluation of their students. They may help them in getting a degree but not a job. For getting a job they have to depend upon their own contacts and resources. Naturally this state of affairs is lowering down the morale and motivation of teachers as well as that of students.

Talk of university autonomy seems totally unrealistic in the present scenario. We cannot think of university autonomy when the highest functionary, the vice-chancellor, achieves his position after a lot of lobbying using and abusing caste, religion, region, political affiliation, and all the imaginable possible factors at his command. Even after achieving his position he finds it very difficult to retain it. During the whole term of three or five years, whatever may be the case, he is always worried about his next extension. For this he is to keep the Chief Minister, Governor who is Chancellor of the University in case of state universities, other important political heavy-weights always in good humour. To earn their pleasure, he has to play to their tunes at the time of appointments, giving plum posts and many other many benefits to some officials. This does not stop here. Dr. Amrik Singh has rightly pointed out: "The government has whole armoury of weapons at its disposal which it can use to subdue and control the universities and, as the things are developing, it has no compunction in using them. Universities have to deal with the Government for various things: in other words, there are limitless possibilities for the Government to harass a university should it so desire."[3] Funds are his Achilles heel. Talk of university autonomy seems a great farce when the Finance Officer of a University is rushing to the State Government Secretariat every month and approaching many petty officials there for release of even much promised grants.

Talk of university autonomy or academic freedom seems mainly for the vice-chancellors or learned professors sitting in their ivory towers. For the common masses who want their wards to be well educated and then well placed in life, regarding education as an investment in human resources, want teachers to teach well in the classes, examinations conducted and results declared quiet well in time, question papers properly evaluated, fellowships, library, laboratory, computers, transportation, health, and all others facilities efficiently and effectively managed, and so on. They are feeling not only concerned with daily *gheraos*, strikes, slogans, violence, etc. but disturbed also with the fast deteriorating academic life and standards in the university campuses. Whole of the situation, thus, need to be studied deeply and thoroughly, if we have to provide answers to the satisfaction of all, i.e., students, teachers, non-teaching officials, administrators, and to the society as a whole.

Realising the gravity of the situation, the present researcher has taken a problem which can be worded as follows:

Statement of the Problem,
Challenges to University Administration in India: A Study of the North-Western Universities, and
Importance of the Problem.

Importance of such a study can hardly be over exaggerated. It has rightly been said that future of a nation is shaped in its classrooms and 'if you want to change a nation, you must change its system of education.' Education is the most valuable investment for the future of a nation. Only well trained motivated and committed citizens make a nation great and strong. Educational institutions, thus, in general and universities in particular are crucial for the all round development of a nation. Such important institutions are thus needed to be governed and developed properly. Inefficiency or maladministration in such institutions is going to cost dearly to a nation. Universities, thus, need to be studied in all seriousness and defects, shortcomings and hindrances in their effective governance removed to avoid further loss.

Role of knowledge and information is critical in today's global world. We are living in a highly competitive world. We have to work not only hard but smart also to survive and succeed in such a world. Knowledge has thus to be created and information properly managed. University is a place which provides and should provide all the facilities and opportunities to accomplish this task. Naturally, good governance of the universities is a mantra for national development and survival.

Importance and role of universities in the development of a nation can be pointed out as follows by citing the ideas of some great men and authorities:

Pandit Jawaharlal Nehru in his convocation address to the University of Allahabad in 1947 summing up the basic objectives of the University which is regarded as the symbol of citadel of higher education remarked: "A university stands for humanism, for tolerance, for reason, for the adventure of ideas and for the search for truth. It stands for the onward march of the human race towards even higher objectives. If the universities discharge their duties adequately, then it is well with the nation and the people". These valuable and meaningful words highlight the very fundamental truth that universities and colleges have a significant role to play in the national life for promoting welfare and strength of the people.

The Education Commission (1966), popularly known by the name of its chairman Dr. D.S. Kothari as Kothari Commission, has enunciated the following functions of the universities which distinctly reflect the objectives of higher education (274-75) :

(a) to seek and cultivate new knowledge, to engage vigorously and fearlessly in the pursuit of truth and to interpret old knowledge and beliefs in the light of new needs and discoveries;
(b) to provide the right kind of leadership in all walks of life, to identify gifted youth and help develop their potential to the full by cultivating physical fitness, developing the powers of the mind and cultivating;
(c) to provide society with competent men and women trained in agriculture, arts, medicine, science and technology and various professions, who will also be cultivated individuals, imbued with a sense of social purpose;
(d) to strive to promote equality and social justice and to reduce social and cultural differences through diffusion of education; and
(e) To foster in the teachers and students and through them in society in general, the attitudes and values

needed for developing the good life in individual and society.

Words of Professor Federico Mayor, the Director-General of UNESCO during an international conference in Caracas in April 1991 deserve to be quoted to describe the role of a university in present times:

> "A university is for the training at a high level of citizens capable of acting efficiently and effectively in their various functions and activities, including the most diverse, up-to-date, and specialization; for the life long and intensive education of all citizens who so wish; for the updating of knowledge; for preparing teacher trainers; for identifying and addressing great national issues; for contributing to the analysis and solution of the major problems affecting and concerning the whole planet; for cooperating with industry and the service sectors in the progress of the nation; for forging attitudes of understanding and tolerance; for providing governments with the scientifically reliable information required for decision-making on such important areas as the environment, in the context of the progressive "scientification" of political decision-making."[4]

In the words of A. Gnanam, formerly Vice-Chancellor of Pondicherry University: "In educational system of a nation, universities occupy a pivotal position as the most important producers of knowledge and as instruments of human resource development. They function as the focal centers of higher education rendering varied functions—teaching, research, consultancy and extension. By imparting and inculcating values and morals in young minds, universities help create useful citizens. The intellectual dynamism, resourcefulness and economic prosperity of the nation reflected in the quality of university education which provides political, scientific, social and professional leadership to the country. By producing men of talent and scientific temper, universities contribute to the cultural, economic and social development of the nation. The ideological life required for a better quality of life and pace of development is created by the universities and the intelligentsia nurtured by them. Universities supply a wide range of trained manpower which is needed in the industry, agriculture, administration and services, besides scholars, doctors, lawyers, engineers, diplomats, scientists, historians, educationists and economists. Thus the role of universities in societal formation, nation-building and scientific development is immense and pervasive."[5]

Significance of the universities for the national development in this highly competitive world naturally calls for their good governance. However, "the universities are facing pressures from two contradictory directions and are in the midst of a crisis. The first emanates from globalization and economic liberalization which puts higher education in the market to be traded as a commodity for profit. The other flows from concern with human and social development and their links with education. Emphasis on development raises the expectations that universities will play a critical role in social development. These contradictory expectations have raised questions about the traditional functions of the universities, namely, generation of knowledge and service to society."[6]

Crises in the governance of universities—who hold key for the development of a nation-naturally call for immediate and sincere efforts for their revitalization and reform. Thus, the present study which has discussed various aspects of administration of the universities in India in general and in the north-western part of the country in particular by pointing out the challenges being faced by them and by suggesting for turning the challenges into opportunities will, thus, be of great importance not only to students, teachers, administrators, and planners but to all those interested in the development of the country.

SURVEY OF RELATED LITERATURE

Many books have been published and studies conducted in the field of university administration, some of which may be mentioned below:

Asha Gupta, *Education in the 21st Century: Looking Beyond University*, Delhi, Shipra Publications, 2008.

This book looks beyond the traditional concept of university to be able to grasp not only the drastic changes taking place at higher education systems worldwide due to the emergence of knowledge-based and technology-driven economies, new internationalism, information age and faster means of communication and massification of higher education. It also traces the causes and consequences of the same. The author stressed that earlier the universities acted as the handmaids of the nation state but today they are required to promote global ethos transcending cultural and linguistic differences beyond the nation state.

Aruna Goel and S.L. Goel, *Encyclopaedia of Higher Education in the 21st Century*, New Delhi, Deep and Deep Publications, 2005.

This is the most exhaustive encylopaedia on higher education giving latest and detailed information in three volumes. First volume discusses organization, administration and functions of higher education. The second volume deals with quality and excellence and the third one with extension education services. The first volume dealing with organization, administration and functions of higher education contains very useful information for the present study.

Amrik Singh, *Fifty Years of Higher Education in India*, New Delhi, Sage Publications, 2004.

In this book the author has discussed the role played by University Grants Commission in higher education for the last 50 years since its establishment on the 28th December, 1953. This book, as pointed out by the author himself, "is not a research piece on the history of the UGC. Instead it is a piece of critical assessment."[7] Again to quote the author about the functioning of UGC ". . . their indifference to how universities are run at the state level and how policy decisions are at the central level is perhaps the basic reason for why the educational policy is being implemented as it is and why the UGC has not performed better than this. This had to be said. Neither the Ministry of Human Resource Development (HRD) nor the UGC feel answerable to anyone."[8] Last two chapters of the book contain his ideas about student assessment of teachers and teacher leadership.

Karuna Channa (Ed.), *Transforming Links between Higher and Basic Education: Mapping the Field*, New Delhi, Sage Publications, 2004.

The contributors to this volume start from the premise that universities have a social obligation and that extension programmes are a way of fulfilling them. In this context, they explore various important and fundamental issues, such as:

- The role of higher educational institutions (HEIs) in fulfilling the larger goals of the society.
- The possibilities of firmly linking HEIs with grassroots efforts at promoting and spreading basic education.
- The nature of these linkages, as also the ongoing efforts to forge such transformative links.

The contributors map the diverse efforts made in these directions at the theoretical and policy levels as well as the field level. They set out the empirical contours of the grassroots work which establishes the interface of the universities with societies. In doing so the volume spells out the different dimensions of the kinds of linkages between higher and basic education.

Jagannath Mohanty, *Current Trends in Higher Education*, New Delhi, Deep and Deep Publications, 2003.

This book is a comprehensive compendium covering all aspects of higher education. It consists of six parts in all. (A) Philosophical and sociological trends, (B) Psychological and pedagogical trends, (C) Trends in planning and management, (D) Trends in new media and modes, (E) Trends in finance and budgeting, and (F) Trends in evaluation and accountability.

Jandhyala, B.G. Tilak (Ed) *Financing Education in India*, New Delhi, National Institute of Educational Planning and Administration, 2003.

This book provides a detailed review of the pattern of financing education at the center and in different states and critically examines the pros and cons of the changing approaches to financing education. It makes a significant contribution to a wider discussion on several issues of financing education, and contributes to sound and effective policy-making in education.

Fauzia Khan, *Development of University Administration in India,* Delhi, Abhijeet Publications, 2003.

This thesis is a study undertaken to examine the factors facilitating and hindering the process of administration of central and state universities. A comprehensive questionnaire has been used to collect data on operational part of administration and staff development. The study covers nine state and six central universities. The authoress has discussed many defects of university administration, like absence of forward planning, grouping of unrelated activities, lack of clarity in duties and responsibilities, lack of decision-making at all levels, practice of old methods, ineffective leadership, lack of delegation of authority, faulty staffing procedure and lack of motivation and coordination. The authoress has also made valuable suggestions for the improvement of university administration.

Bhim S. Dahiya, *The University Autonomy in India: The Idea and The Reality,* Shimla: Indian Institute of Advanced Study, 2001.

This study has been conducted under the aegis of Indian Institute of Advanced Study, Shimla by Prof. Bhim S. Dahiya, a former Vice-Chancellor of Kurukshetra University. The learned author, making good use of his practical knowledge and wisdom, has made a brilliant analysis of how "Indian Universities have, over the years, derailed these institutions from their assigned social role of producing healthy human resource for the spiritual as well as material advancement of the nation. Making a free and frank review of reports of various Education Commissions and showing an unsparing attitude to the politico-bureaucratic meddling in the affairs of the universities, it offers new ideas on the subject of structural management of higher education. The book offers both short-term remedies as well as long-term solutions to the burning problems of eroding autonomy and sinking standards in the dominion of the dons."

Anirudh Prasad, *University Education Administration and the Law*, New Delhi, Deep and Deep Publications, 2000.

This book presents the study of university administration and its ailments from a quite different angle with a tone of socio-legal realistic outlook. It also discusses performance and failure of different segments of the educational fraternity.

M.S. Jeremiah, *Deteriorating Quality of Higher Education: Owing to Poverty of Resources*, Jaipur, ADB Publishers, 1998.

This book speaks on poverty of resources, determinants of quality in higher education, growth of higher education in India, Gujarat and South Gujarat University, State Grants, Central Grants, UGC Grants, internal and external income of the educational institutions, and their expenditure. The topics discussed in this book are of great relevance to the educational administrators, leaders, planners, scholars, and students.

Ralph, G. Lewis and Douglas, H. Smith, *Total Quality in Higher Education*, New Delhi: Vanity Books International, 1998.

The book provides a framework for implementing TQ principles in college or university environment. It includes case studies and articles that give the reader a thorough understanding of the subject. It presents a unique chapter on ISO 9000 in training and education.

Roger, G. Noll (Ed.), *Challenges to Research Universities*, Washington, D.C.: Brookings Institution Press, 1998.

Contributors of various papers of the book assess the

prospects of research support from government, industry, profits from university medical centres, and conclude that the future does not appear bright in these cases. They also examine the methods used by the federal government to pay for university research, and they propose changes that would make both universities and federal government better off by reducing the administrative costs of federal grants.

M.V. Mathur, Ramesh, K. Arora, and Meena Sogani (Eds.), New Delhi, Wiley Eastern Limited, *Indian University System*, 1994.

This volume contains thirty five papers contributed by well known authors in the field of higher educational system. These papers present a comprehensive picture of various aspects of higher education. Some papers give new and radical ideas. Well-known ideas have also been restated, but which according to the editors, "need to be executed with greater rigour and vigour."

K.V. Subbaram, *Indian Universities and Systemic Ailments*, New Delhi: Harman Publishing House, 1993.

This book contains the text of the draft report released by the Association of Indian Universities (AIU) based on the findings of Committee of Elders constituted by the AIU regarding the malaise afflicting university system in states of Bihar, Orissa, and Madhya Pradesh and the country at large. The book also includes some pertinent questions on and answers to some important issues such as: establishment, structure and role of universities, mode of appointment of vice-chancellors and terms and conditions of appointment; governor-chancellor dichotomy; role of the state governments, the central government, the state assemblies, and parliament and of national organizations like UGC and AIU itself in contributing to a professional and purposeful working of universities in the country.

M.V. Mathur and Ramesh K. Arora (Eds.), *The Vice-Chancellors Remember*, New Delhi, Associated Publishing House, 1992.

This volume gives a first hand lively account of the reminiscences and reflections of twenty-six Vice-Chancellors who collectively have left an imprint on the university system in India. This book—fairly representative of the broad spectrum of Indian universities—covers twenty institutions of higher education. Among the twenty-six contributors are distinguished scientists, social scientists, educational administrators, civil servants and men of eminence from the fields of judiciary, international administration, management sciences and social work. The recollections included in the book are intense, warm, and scintillating, while at places, they manifest poignancy and pathos. No doubt, the tenure of a Vice-Chancellor has moments of ecstasy as well as agony. Lucid and forthright account of such moments made this book highly useful for the present researcher.

Monis Raza, (Ed.), *Higher Education in India: Retrospect and Prospect*, New Delhi: Association of Indian Universities, 1991.

This comprehensive volume having overview of higher education in India was edited by Monis Raza and released on the occasion of the Conference of Executives of Commonwealth Universities held in New Delhi in January, 1991. Distinguished scholars have presented the entire panorama of Indian higher education from ancient to the present times. They made a critical analysis of its strong and weak points as well as its successes and failures.

J.N. Kaul, *Governance of Universities: Autonomy of the University Community*, New Delhi: Abhinav Publications, 1988.

Author has discussed autonomy of the university community, its concept and historical development; governance of modern Indian higher education; national development, and social change. The author has raised the question: Is autonomy precedent to universities discharging their duties and obligations? After surveying the history and present conditions of universities in India and some important countries of the western world, he suggests that there cannot be autonomy for autonomy's sake just as there cannot be a university for university's sake. The study has raised a number of questions, including the question of aims and uses of the universities.

J.D. Sethi, *The Crisis and Collapse of Higher Education in India*, New Delhi, Vikas Publishing House Pvt. Ltd., 1983.

In this book the author has observed that about one-third of colleges and even universities remain closed at one time or another because of disturbances. The university administration is unable to function both due to internal dissensions and perversion of the role of teachers, students, vice-chancellors and *karamcharis*, and to the intervention of the external political and coercive factors.

Champa Tickoo, *Indian Universities: A Historical, Comparative Perspective*, Bombay, Orient Longman, 1980.

This book is a revised and abridged version of the doctoral dissertation submitted by Champa Tickoo to the University of London. Starting from the description of universities in British India, the authoress has discussed the growth of universities in free India, undergraduate university education, post-graduate education and research, student life in the universities, governance of Indian university and has made suggestions for planning a new university system.

Anil Baran Ray, *Students and Politics in India: The Role of Caste, Language and Religion in an Indian University*, Delhi: Manohar, 1977.

This is a published Ph.D. thesis. Here the author discusses the movement for a Hindu university. He also discusses politicization of the students of the Banaras Hindu University.

D.M. Nanjundappa, *Working of University Finances*, New Delhi: Sterling Publishers, Private Ltd., 1976.

Author examines the structure of university finances in

relation to its cost and performance, financial relations between universities and UGC and between universities and government. He argues that there is a gap between the cost of higher education and the fees charged. He questions the appropriateness of the direct method of financing university education by means of grants and advocates an indirect system whereby a portion of public funds is transferred to the students as loans to cover the full cost of education, subject to a contract to pay the loan out of their future earnings. Such a system, according to the author, preserves the autonomy of a university better.

S.C. Malik, (Ed.), *Management and Organisation of Indian Universities*, Shimla: Indian Institute of Advanced Study, 1971.

The volume includes papers by many eminent writers on topics like, the problem of numbers and pressures on the system; relevance of courses of study with regard to emergent social realities and necessary processes of change; structures and channels of authority with the university *vis-à-vis* UGC, IUB and Government; faculty and departmental organization; relation between teaching and administrative staff; evaluation and planning for development; standardization of methods of teaching and student management; and such other papers of importance.

S.R. Dongerkery, *University Education in India*, Bombay: Mamaktalas, 1967.

In this book the author has covered a wide range of topics starting from university education in ancient India to the present day. He has discussed landmarks in university education, types and constitutions of Indian universities, university autonomy, role of teachers in university education, students' life in universities, teaching and research, and many other important aspects which are of importance for the present study.

A.B. Shah, (Ed.), *Higher Education in India*, Bombay: Lalvani Publishing House, 1967.

The editor has included many papers from eminent academicians and administrators on the topics: higher education and problems of expansion, university and the government, foundations of university, modernization of courses, the pursuit of excellence, higher education-myths—old and new, governance of university, university and research, youth unrest, and the like.

To sum up, the researcher has scanned the relevant literature published during the last four decades. There are some more studies about universities which have not been mentioned here because of time and space. These have, however, been included in the bibliography. All these studies have no doubt added depth and new dimensions to the present study. However, the present study is a first of its own kind in the following ways:

(i) No study so far has been conducted on the north-western universities;
(ii) Most of the studies though written by renowned academicians and administrators, who were vice-chancellors themselves, have naturally been influenced by their subjective experiences. Perceptions of vice-chancellors and others are bound to differ and reality may, thus, be different;
(iii) All the studies, including a couple of Ph.D. dissertations, have used only secondary sources for data collection, analysis and interpretation and none has used primary source like a questionnaire in his/her study; and
(iv) Even the most of secondary data drawn from the reports of various commissions and committees may not have remained relevant for presenting the present day reality.

Above mentioned reasons, thus, justify the need for the present study which has employed primary sources of data collection in addition to assimilating information and wisdom from the secondary sources like books and reports of various commissions and committees.

AIMS AND OBJECTIVES

Present research aims at discussing various problems of University Administration by employing empirical methods and thereby suggesting the ways and means to improve it.

The study aims at making an in-depth analysis of the following:

1. Challenges being faced by the universities.
2. Working of the universities.
3. Management of finances of the universities.
4. Politics of various groups comprising a university.
5. Academic activities and performance.
6. To offer suggestions for enabling the universities to play their role effectively for increasing global competitiveness of India.

SCOPE

Present study has covered all the four North-Western states of India, namely, Haryana, Himachal Pradesh, Jammu and Kashmir, and Punjab, and one union territory, i.e., Chandigarh. It has studied the universities in the above states and the union territory. The sample for the study is purposive one, i.e., one university each from a state and the union territory. Union territory Chandigarh has only one university, i.e., Panjab University. This is a central university. All the states included in the sample have their own state universities. Thus, present sample will be quite rich and enable the researcher to make a comparative study of central and state universities also.

The groups with whom the present researcher has interacted include students, teachers, non-teaching staff and high officers like the Chancellor, Vice-Chancellor, Pro-Vice-Chancellor, Registrar, etc. Unions and Associations of the above groups and officials have also been included in the present study. Their views and opinions have been taken through interviews and questionnaires.

METHODOLOGY

Usual empirical research methodology has been adopted in the present study. The researcher has laid his hands both on secondary and primary sources. The secondary sources included Ordinances, Handbooks, Rules, Regulations, Reports, routine files, news paper reports, Ph.D. dissertations, books, etc. The primary sources were observation, questionnaires, and interviews. Observation has been done by visits to the Universities of the sample by the researcher as well as by the research associate engaged for the purpose. Observation was done by using Observation Sheet designed by the researcher (Appendix 2). Questionnaires have been prepared to be got filled from the Vice-Chancellors, Pro-Vice-Chancellors, Registrars, Deans, Head of the Departments/other high officers, teachers, non-teaching staff and students (Appendix 1). It was estimated that the five universities of the sample had a combined strength of 1,800 teachers, 2,150 non-teaching staff, and 21,500 students. The present researcher took a sample of one-sixth of the total strength in each category. Thus, sample covered through the questionnaires was 300 teachers, 350 non-teaching staff, and 3500 students. Quantitative information collected through questionnaires has been supplemented with qualitative information in the form of case studies. Information about the case studies has been collected during the visits to the universities of the sample by interviewing the officials, through official records, and news papers reports.

As for interviews, these were confined to the Chancellor of Himachal Pradesh University, Vice-Chancellors of Himachal Pradesh and Kurukshetra Universities, Registrars, selected Deans and Heads of Departments, office-bearers of various organizations, associations/unions of the students, a few teachers, non-teaching staff, and students of all the universities of the sample. Interviews included formal as well as informal talks on various occasions.

CHAPTERISATION

The study contains following chapters:

1. Introduction
2. Challenges
3. Sample: Profile of the Universities
4. Working of the Universities
5. Some Case Studies
6. Comparative Study
7. Conclusions
8. Suggestions

   Bibliography

Appendix: Questionnaires and Observation Sheet.

First chapter in addition to pointing out the complexities of university administration, importance of the present study, survey of the related literature, aims and objectives, etc. also discussed the methodology by which the present study has been conducted. The second chapter discussed various challenges being faced by the Indian universities. Third one discussed the rationale of selecting the sample of the present study and also presented the profile of all the universities included in the sample. The fourth one discussed the actual working of the universities different than what has been mentioned in the formal statutes, rules and regulations, and also described the intricate web of politics involving students, teachers, non-teaching staff, high officers including registrar, pro-vice-chancellor, and vice-chancellor. The fifth chapter contains some case studies about the universities included in the sample which throw a light on the actual state of affairs of the university administration. The sixth chapter makes a comparative study of the universities included in the sample mainly on the basis of the data collected through questionnaires. The last two deal with conclusions and suggestions, respectively.

Notes and References

1. Prof. Naresh, G. Mathur, University Administration and Transparency, in *ASC Bulletin*, Vol. VII, No. 1, Academic Staff College, H.P. University, Shimla, December, 1997, p. 38.
2. J.D. Sethi, *The Crisis and Collapse of Higher Education in India*, New Delhi, Vikas Publishing House Pvt. Ltd., 1983, p. 2.
3. Amrik Singh, Universities and the Government, A.B. Shah (Ed.), *Higher Education in India*, Bombay: Lalvani Publishing House, 1967, p. 69.

4. Professor Federico Mayor, the Director General of UNESCO as quoted in Dahiya, Bhim, S. *The University Autonomy in India*, Shimla: Indian Institute of Advanced Study, 2001, pp. 81-82.
5. A. Gnanam, Holistic Approach to Reform, M.V. Mathur, Ramesh K. Arora and Meena Sogani, *Indian University System: Revitalization and Reform*, New Delhi, Wiley Eastern Limited, 1994, p. 63.
6. Karuna Channa (Ed.), *Transforming Links Between Higher and Basic Education: Mapping the Field*, New Delhi, Sage Publications, 2004, p. 14.
7. Amrik Singh, *Fifty Years of Higher Education in India*, New Delhi, Sage Publications, 2004, p. 9.
8. *Ibid.*, p. 9.

CHAPTER

2

Challenges to University Administration

With the expansion of educational institutions the challenges to University Administration have increased manyfold. The situation has reached the nadir where even to perform normal duties like conducting of examinations or routine classroom tests, ensuring minimum lecture attendance, holding of Executive Council/Senate meetings, etc. have become a challenge. Politicisation, lack of commitment to the professional ethics by the teachers, inefficient work culture of the supporting staff, lack of urge for academic excellence on the part of students, commercialisation and greed for making money and not imparting education by the authorities have made our universities and colleges highly unmanageable and incompetent to impart, what to say of quality education, even any education worth the name. Present impoverished academic climate with malfunctioning administration is not capable of meeting the highly competitive and powerful global challenges we are facing. Let us discuss the educational scenario and the potent challenges our University Administration is facing these days.

1. POOR PUBLIC IMPRESSION

Public confidence and appreciation so essential for the success of an organization is woefully missing in case of our institutions of higher education. General public may not know about the quality of education imparted in the classrooms, and usefulness or originality of research conducted in the libraries and laboratories, but they certainly get disturbed by the frequent strikes, slogan shouting, presence of police, *lathi* charges, murders, hooliganisms, and other such activities very common in the so-called temples of higher learning. Campuses and hostels in the vicinity are now being considered as nuisance by the people. General public marched many a time through the streets to the office of the Vice-Chancellor of Himachal Pradesh University in Summerhill (Shimla) shouting slogans to protest against the construction of a students' hostel by the University in the vicinity of their village, Chaili and finally succeeded in getting site of the hostel shifted in 2001. *The Tribune*, the oldest daily of the north-western region published a feature in the year 2003, "State of Universities" covering twelve general, agricultural, horticultural, and technical universities of Punjab, Haryana, and Himachal Pradesh. The feature in unambiguous words painted the deteriorating picture of the universities. The letters to the editor followed by the feature also deplored the sad position of the universities of the region.

2. ADMINISTRATIVE INCOMPETENCE

Administrative structure right from top to bottom has become incompetent, weak and outmoded. Vice-Chancellor around whom the whole administration moves is himself an extremely weak person whose very appointment, continuation, success or failure depend upon the party in power and relationship with the Chief Minister if it is a State University, and with the Human Resource Minister or may be Prime Minister if it is a Central University. Extremely powerful position of a Vice-Chancellor in the University administration (as per Statutes) perhaps makes him weak and vulnerable. He is the Chairman of the Executive Council (called Syndicate in some universities) and the Academic Council. These are the highest decision-making bodies in all administrative and academic matters of a university. In the matter of recruitment, his powers are immense, absolute and unchallengeable. He can very easily influence the selection committees. In almost all the universities he has been given special powers in the name of smooth and efficient administration of a university which empower him to keep all the University Acts, Rules, Regulations and Ordinances at bay. In all the daily routine matters he has been equipped with formidable powers which make his position vulnerable to the various striking groups who adopt the 'gun on the head policy' of 'do it or leave'. University Acts, Rules, Regulations, and Ordinances which could otherwise serve as shields for the protection of a Vice-Chancellor are violated by him for some expediency. Interested parties, thus pressurize the Vice-Chancellor to use his special powers in their favour making it difficult to run the administration based on sound principles. This position is perhaps the root cause of all maladministration, favouritism, and nepotism in a university.

Next in the hierarchy comes the Pro-Vice-Chancellors who is appointed with the objective of assisting the Vice-Chancellor in his academic and administrative duties and taking care of the university in his absence as his deputy. However, in actual practice it is seen that PVC becomes anti-VC by developing another power centre in the university, always trying to find and use the weaknesses and shortcomings of the VC to usurp his place. These warring lords do a great harm to university administration by crippling it with their daily manoeuvres. Then is the Registrar who is the legal custodian of university administration. Appointment of a Registrar is done by one of the following methods: He is appointed amongst the Professors of the university, or by the Government from the administrative officers of the State cadre/Indian Administrative Service, or on full time basis by direct interview after due advertisement. At times *ad hoc* arrangements are also made by appointing some senior officer of the university.

Efficiency in the working of university administration can easily be judged from a recent report published in *The Tribune*: "Maharshi Dayanand University has set a record of sorts by functioning without a regular Vice-Chancellor, Registrar, Dean of Colleges, Director of Distance Education, Chief Librarian,

Executive Engineer and Finance Officer. With all the key posts lying vacant for years, the work culture in the university has touched its nadir. Long delays in the disposal of files, indiscipline and absenteeism have become hallmarks of the university over the years."[1]

University administration is not as simple as that of other public organizations. University officers have to face highly politicized organistions and groups of students, teachers, and *karamcharies*. Addition of a single element of students' politics, with their inclination and power of turning into violent agitations at the slightest provocation or lapse on the part of administration make university administration sensitive, intricate and cumbersome. In the matters of strikes and agitations teachers and *karamcharies* also follow the students making it very difficult for the administration to manage. They, thus simply mark time resulting into a listless style of working where no improvement is possible and only movement is downward.

3. FINANCIAL RESOURCE CRUNCH

Education in India is being financed by Central Government, State Governments, Local authorities and other sources like endowments, donations, scholarships, consultancy, voluntary contributions from the alumni and public. With the tremendous expansion in higher education, the need for greater funds has also increased for keeping the system running. "Simultaneously, due to successive reduction in private contribution its dependence on government for funds also increased. Consequently, the government contribution to educational finance increased from about 57% in 1950-51 to about 90-95% during 1990s. During the same period the contribution of students in terms of fees decreased from about 20% to less than 5%. Moreover, the allocation of funds for education over nine five year plans has not shown noticeable improvement, rather, in relative terms, it has been declining continuously".[2] Over all these years higher education is still greater sufferer. The relative share for higher education declined from 25% during Fourth Five Year Plan to 8% during the Eighth Five Year Plan to cater to the needs of universal primary education. The share of higher education, however, was increased to 12% during the Ninth Five Year Plan. Moreover, it is also a common knowledge that about 80 to 90% of the total funds of a college or university are spent on the payment of salaries of the staff only.

Paying for higher education has not been taken seriously in India. Medical and engineering education is the only exceptions. Middle class parents who spend huge amounts in paying for the education in convents and other 'public schools' want to pay only a token amount for the education of their wards in Government colleges and universities. Rising cost due to inflation and cost of living is not a consideration for them. Whenever there is a rise in the fees, the student unions resort to violent agitations and get the fee hike reversed.

In addition to the above factors, "it is felt that the financial hazards are mostly due to improper planning, inefficient management, indiscriminate expenditure and inadequate control on expenses".[3] It is also a common knowledge that huge amount of money from the UGC grants are not expended by the universities resulting in the lapse of money every year. At times utilization certificates are not issued by the universities to be able to claim another grant. Many a time, students and teachers are not properly informed about the funds available to them under various schemes for their benefit. Many of the teachers do not want to undertake UGC research projects to avoid the sufferings and harassment at the hands of university accounts branches and audit. Financial rules and regulations though made for proper maintenance of records and legal and prudent use of public money, stand in the way of utilizing even the insufficient funds allotted to the universities. This naturally results in the impoverished academic climate in the university.

4. INFRASTRUCTURAL INADEQUACIES

Concern about the poor infrastructure has been pointed out by the former Chairman of the UGC himself. "Prof. Arun Nigavakar, Chairman University Grants Commission, New Delhi yesterday expressed his deep concern over the mushrooming of a number of universities which promises higher education without having infrastructure. His specific reference was Chhattisgarh where 97 universities have been established under the State Act without proper infrastructure and qualified faculty. He said the UGC in recent past had inspected 47 universities in Chhattisgarh and found only four actually operating. He said most of these universities had given addresses in Chhattisgarh but operating from Delhi".[4]

Financial crunch is naturally leading to infrastructural inadequacies. Libraries are poorly equipped to provide latest information to the students and teachers. Knowledge is expanding at a very high speed. New researches are being conducted in the different branches. Administrative reforms are being taken in every department. Financial rules and regulations are being changed to meet the emerging demands of the society. New statistics are being collected and produced in all the fields, but the university libraries in many cases have the information which is one decade and may be two decades old. A decade back, when the present researcher, a representative of the Himachal Pradesh University Teachers' Association, complained to the then Vice-Chancellor about the miserable position of the HPU Library, the Hon'ble Vice-Chancellor cleverly dodged by saying "Soon we are going to have internet facilities in the library with connection to all the Departments and you can easily have the latest information." This assurance has not been fulfilled so far and perhaps may take another decade for becoming a reality. Even where the internet facilities have been extended, proper working still needs to be ensured. Websites of most of the universities are not found to be up to date. Hostel facilities, especially for the girl students are awfully lacking. Teachers are sticking to old lecture methods. Audio-visual aids, like overhead projector, slide-projector, whereever available, are used very rarely.

5. PRIVATISATION

Teaching or imparting education was considered as a pious and sacred duty according to Indian cultural traditions. With the advent of the British, education became a paid activity wherein schools, colleges and universities were set-up and Government grants were provided. After Independence, there was a rapid and haphazard growth of educational institutions. This growth in the size made it difficult for the Government to finance it. This financial position is a worldwide phenomenon. Because of certain socio-economic changes it has become difficult for Governments of all the countries to provide liberal financial support to higher education. Governments all over the world, consider investment in primary education of greater social value than in higher education. Moreover, the demands of the market economy require introduction of skill-oriented courses which need still higher investments. This socio-economic situation accelerated the pace of privatisation of higher education.

Economic reforms stressed on reducing the subsidies and outlays in the social sector and also meaning thereby that government's role in the socio-economic activities of the countries should gradually reduce and the private sector should take over the responsibilities towards the social sector including education. In its Report 'Higher Education: Lessons of Experience' (1994), the World Bank declared higher education as a 'non-merit good' whereas school education was put into the category of 'merit goods'. It then advised the governments of developing countries to rethink the policy of subsidizing higher education. Following this, the Ministry of Finance, Government of India, prepared the Paper on Government Subsidies in India (1997) which sought to drastically reduce the state funding of higher education. It proposed that over a period of five years, the subsidy should be brought from 90% down to 25%.

Another development in this direction was "A Policy Framework for Reforms in Education" prepared by some Indian industrialists in 2002. This report, popularly known as Ambani-Birla Report since Mukesh Ambani, an eminent industrialist, was its convener, recommended that the Government's role should be 'maximum' in the sphere of primary education but 'minimum' in higher education. This report has further recommended, "A Private Universities Bill should be legislated to encourage the establishment of new private universities." The report was of the view that "a redefinition of Government role in higher education would call for major changes in university education system in India."

Professor Yashpal, an eminent scientist and the former Chairman of University Grants Commission, filed Writ Petition

No. 19 of 2004 under Article 32 of the Constitution by way of public interest litigation for declaring certain provisions of The Chhattisgarh *Niji Kshetra Vishwavidyalaya (Sthapana Aur Viniyaman) Adhiniyam*, 2002 as *ultra vires* and for quashing of the notifications issued by State of Chhattisgarh in the purported exercise of power conferred by Section 5 of the said *Adhiniyam* for establishing various universities. The other petitioner, who joined in the petition, was a resident of Chhattisgarh and was concerned with the quality of education in his State. The respondent No. 1 to the petition was the State of Chhattisgarh, respondent No. 2 was the University Grants Commission and respondent Nos. 3 to 94 were the private universities established by the State of Chhattisgarh under the aforesaid *Adhiniyam*.

The Chhattisgarh Legislature enacted the Chhattisgarh *Niji Kshetra Vishwavidyalaya (Sthapana Aur Viniyaman) Adhiniyam*, 2002 (for short 'the Act') which was published in the Gazette on 4.2.2002 to establish self-financed private universities for higher education. Under Section 5 of the Act, the State has been empowered to incorporate and establish a university by issuing a notification in the Gazette and Section 6 permits such university to affiliate any college or other institution or to set-up more than one campus with the prior approval of the State Government. The main averments in the petition were that after coming into force of the Act, the State Government simply by issuing notifications in the Gazette, established universities in an indiscriminate and mechanical manner without having slightest regard to the availability of any infrastructure, teaching facility or their financial resources. In a short span of about one year as many as 112 universities were established and many of them had absolutely no buildings or campus and were running from one room tenements. There was absolutely no regulation or supervision over them. The legislation was enacted in a manner which completely did away with any kind of control of UGC over these private universities. The guidelines issued by UGC on the courses to be taught and award of academic degrees, was given a complete go-by. The universities issued brochures for award of all kinds of degrees like "Member of the International Institute of Medical Sciences", "Fellow of the International Institute of Medical Sciences" and many other similar degrees. The universities were wholly incapable of imparting any education much less a quality education in absence of basic infrastructure like classrooms, libraries, laboratories or campus. Nevertheless by conferment of a legal status of a university, they were empowered to award degrees. The private universities were running professional courses without taking prior permission from regulatory bodies such as All India Council of Technical Education (AICTE), Medical Council of India (MCI), Dental Council of India (DCI), etc. The requirement of obtaining prior permission from the regulatory bodies was not been followed and the universities were not under the control of any authority and were at liberty to grant degrees, diplomas and certificates to gullible students. The State Government did not do any verification or checking of universities after issuance of notification in the Gazette, whether they fulfil any norms laid down by the statutory bodies, which was essential for recognition of the degrees, diplomas and certificates awarded by such universities. In absence of requisite permission from the statutory bodies, the degrees and certificates awarded by such universities would not be recognized by the professional organizations, as a result whereof the students studying in such universities and obtaining the degrees there from would suffer immense loss, both in terms of money and also the time spent in completing the courses. It was further averred that the University Grants Commission Act was made nugatory as private universities were offering courses without subscribing to the standards laid down by the UGC. Since there was no homogeneity of the course content, the degree awarded might not be of any value. The private universities were offering unheard of courses and degrees which were not part of the Schedule to the UGC Act, which was in clear violation of Section 22 of the aforesaid Act and the Schedule appended thereto. The minimum requirement of teaching staff as laid down in the guidelines of UGC was also been given a complete go-by. Young students were being misled in enrolling themselves in courses which did not have any substantive content and the degrees offered by such private universities would affect the standard of education at large which in turn would jeopardize the educational system of the whole country and not that of State of Chhattisgarh alone.

Some photographs were also filed which showed that a signboard mentioning the name of the University was put over small room or shop on first or second floor in some congested market area. That they were functioning from small premises which were sometimes a single small room in a commercial complex or a small tenement on the first or second floor of a building or an ordinary flat or MIG house was evident from their address.

Writ Petition (Civil) No. 565 of 2003 was filed by Gopal Ji Agarwal with the *same prayer, namely, that the Chhattisgarh Niji Kshetra Vishwavidyalaya (Sthapana Aur Viniyaman) Adhiniyam,* 2002 be declared as *ultra vires* being a violation of Constitution of India, and also contrary to the provisions of University Grants Commission Act, 1956, Indian Medical Council Act, 1956, All India Council for Technical Education Act, 1987 and Bar Council of India Act, 1956. A further prayer was made that a writ of prohibition might be issued restraining the private universities incorporated under the aforesaid Act from imparting any education and conferring any degrees or diplomas. The averments made in the writ petition were substantially the same as made in the writ petition filed by Prof. Yash Pal, that a large number of universities were incorporated by merely issuing gazette notifications though they did not have any kind of infrastructure or teaching facility and were functioning from one room tenement in a second or third floor in a residential or commercial building and without any teaching staff. The universities were established merely to confer degrees and they had on their own created a large number of degrees and diplomas which were totally unheard of. The universities issued advertisements for opening up study centres in different parts of the country for award of any number of degrees and diplomas. By way of illustration, copies of advertisements issued by some of the universities were filed. One of such university, namely, the Indian University, issued an advertisement inviting applications for Nodal Service Centres/ University Centres for awarding many post-graduate degrees and diplomas.

Several legal issues were also raised in the writ petitions and the principle was that the manner in which these private universities were functioning would result in creating a complete chaos in the system of higher education in the country and the expert bodies created by the Central Government like, UGC, MCI, AICTE, etc. for coordination and determination of standards in their own respective fields would not be able to perform their statutory duty and would make their functioning not only difficult but almost impossible.

In view of the discussions made above, Writ Petition (C) No. 19 of 2004 (Prof. Yashpal & Ors. *vs.* State of Chhattisgarh & Ors.) and Writ Petition (C) No. 565 of 2003 (Gopalji Agarwal *vs.* Union of India & Ors.) were allowed and provisions of Sections 5 and 6 of the Chhattisgarh *Niji Kshetra Vishwavidyalaya (Sthapana Aur Viniyaman) Adhiniyam,* 2002 were declared *ultra vires* and were struck down. As a consequence of such declaration, all notifications issued by the State Government in the Gazette in the purported exercise of power under Section 5 of the aforesaid Act notifying the Universities (including respondent Nos. 3 to 94) were quashed and such Universities ceased to exist.

Education is essentially a spending sector and it has a legitimate claim over the country's resources both for its survival and development. To leave it to the considerations and grace of the profit-oriented private sector does not seem to be a wise proposition in the long run. While efforts may be made to promote community contribution to educational funding, the government cannot absolve itself of its responsibility towards funding of the social sector in general and education in particular. In the interest of long-term gains, of both equity and efficiency, even higher education should not be left to the discretion of private sector funding alone. The present trend of arguments of populism, and of reducing subsidy or government's role in higher education need to be viewed with serious caution. Let the country not lose the game of educational development while winning few points of satisfying the populist claims. One should hasten to add here that the really able to pay should be made to pay for their education and community's contribution should also be mobilized. But, let there not be a blanket policy of withdrawal of government from educational funding and leaving the matter entirely to private sector.[5]

6. COMMERCIALISATION

Financial crunch is forcing the universities to generate their own resources by adopting even objectionable methods. For instance, in the name of earning money from the wards of Non-Resident Indians (NRI), much higher dues are being charged by the universities. Moneyed Indian parents are thus paying these dues for the education of their wards by giving a blow to merit in education. These spoiled rich youths, not taking their studies seriously, are doing much harm to the cause of education. Their only aim is to buy the degrees through money of their parents and not to earn them by dint of hard work.

An example of this commercialization can be seen in the following report: "Punjabi University has been accused of turning the holding of tests for admissions to professional courses, including the five-year BA-LLB course, into a profit-making venture by charging Rs. 5,500 for the test and counseling procedure. . . . The university is charging Rs. 500 for the prospectus, Rs. 1,000 as fee for the conduct of entrance test, Rs. 2,500 for the first counseling and Rs. 1,500 for the second counseling. Similar is the case of combined state level tests organized by the university for admission into the MBA and MCA courses. The Democratic Rights Association, Sangrur, has protested against this practice, alleging that the university was turning education into a business which was against the Supreme Court order forbidding turning education into a business venture. Meanwhile, the spokesman of the university, Dr. Baldev Singh Sandhu, said the university was generating its own resources due to lack of requisite financial support from the state government. He said this was needed to maintain the present infrastructure and ensure quality higher education service for the students of the institution".[6] Another example, "Not satisfied by multifold increase it has ordered in the fee for various services it provides to its students and alumni, Panjab University has now started making money out of postal and delivery charges it collects from applicants. In some cases, the university charges three to six times more than what it actually spends in sending those documents by registered or speed post".[7]

7. GLOBALISATION

Globalisation is a socio-economic, cultural and political process by which all the countries of the globe communicate, interact, and trade with one another and the rules and regulations ordained not by the individual countries but by mutually established international organisations. Since commerce and trade in all the countries is carried out by MNCs and TNCs and regulated by the international bodies like WTO, IMF, and World Bank, individual countries lose much of their sovereignty. Because of increased interaction and powerful impact of media and communication reinforced by the fast developing IT, national culture will be eroded by the hybridisation.

Like all other fields of human activity, education has also been influenced by the process of globalistion. Like other commodities, it is also being bought and sold transcending the national boundaries. With the advances in the fast communication, distances have got reduced making the whole world a small village. Globalisation of economy has also led to internalisation of higher education. Students with high academic and technical qualifications can get lucrative jobs in foreign shores. Foreign degrees too are helping in getting highly paid jobs in India and abroad. Many of the advanced English-speaking counties are luring the Indians and other Asian students. Higher education has, thus become an emerging market for the advanced countries. Many fake foreign universities too have come into the field of higher education just to make money.

Some recent efforts by foreign Universities to woo Indian students may be cited below:

> More than 10,000 students from Punjab got admission last year to courses like tourism and hospitality, information technology, business administration, mass communication, tourism and travel and allied areas not only in North America but also in Great Britain, Poland, Ukraine, Uzbekistan, China, Australia, New Zealand and Canada. Most of them got admission in one to three-year diploma courses with permission to work part-time. Each student is

required to spend between Rs. 3 lakh and Rs. 10 lakh a year, depending upon the subject and standing of the university in which he or she is admitted. Eighty per cent of the Indian students happen to be boys.

China has been a late entrant in the market and has been offering seats both in medical colleges and medical universities specially designed for foreign students, both Indian and of the Indian Diaspora. While most of the foreign universities are operating independently in the Indian market, four countries—Canada, Great Britain, Australia and New Zealand—have their Indian missions directly involved in holding education fairs in major Indian cities in which Chandigarh, Ludhiana, Jalandhar, Patiala and Amritsar figure prominently.

A record number of 47 Canadian institutions, including universities, university colleges and senior secondary schools have held their annual education fairs in different cities of the Punjab, as the Punjab and Chandigarh market continues to be the largest supplier of students to foreign universities. Besides the Canadian fair, other nations, including—Australia, New Zealand and England, have been sending their international education marketing experts to India in general and Punjab in particular for admitting students. Other target areas for foreign educational institutions have been Delhi, Bangalore, Chennai and Mumbai.

While most of these education fairs were till recently organised by foreign universities independently, of late they have got official recognition with the involvement of the diplomatic missions and their respective education centres. For example, both the British and Canadian High Commissions have their Education Centres which assist their respective universities, university colleges and colleges in holding their admission fairs here. For example, the Ministry of Training Colleges and Universities, Ontario, and Manitoba International Education, Manitoba, Canada, have taken special interest in India as a destination. . . . The courses being offered are degrees as well as diplomas in business studies, engineering and computer science, biotechnology, animation, multimedia, new media, hospitality & tourism, and media and communication.

The one-day education fair, says a spokesperson of the Canadian High Commission, is a once-a-year opportunity for students and their parents to meet representatives from many Canadian educational institutions. The Canadian Education Centre-India was opened in June, 1997, by the Government of Canada to provide information and counselling services to Indian students interested in studying abroad.[8]

Another example of foreign universities wooing the Indian students with the help of their governments is cited below: Sir Michael Arthur, the British High Commissioner to India, announced the launch of a tri-city Education UK Initiative for Punjab on September 21, 2005. The initiative compromised informative road-shows, a study UK exhibition and a series of seminars. Addressing a press conference at the British Library, Chandigarh, Sir Arthur said 16,000 Indians went to study in the *UK* every year and the number was expected to increase to more than 26,000 by 2010. He said one of the reasons for the increasing popularity of the British courses in Punjab was the short duration of the courses and also the flexibility of the courses being offered. "The UK is known for its high standard of education and UK qualifications are internationally recognized and respected all over the world."

Challenges posed by globalization can be put in the words of C.P.S. Chauhan, "The globalization of knowledge and consequently of education, is going to pose serious threats before the conventional system of higher education in all developing countries including India. In the emerging international knowledge market, our universities have to compete with the foreign players. This situation leaves no option before our universities except improvement of quality of education imparted, so as to make it comparable to international standards, failing which their very survival will be in danger. It is said that knowledge is expanding so fast that it doubles itself every three years. This makes the learner increasingly selective in making choices to learn what is relevant for him. The universities have to redesign their programs so as to make them flexible, cost-effective, and relevant to the market economy. If our universities have to survive in the global market, we have to abandon the traditional mindset of making compromises in curricular reforms, conduct of examinations, admission of students, and selection of teachers."[9]

Higher education requires a very high investment. On the contrary, due to financial crunch and restrictions put under GATS, the developing countries cannot afford high investment in higher education. 'Structural adjustment' programmes in developing countries, insisted upon by the IMF-World Bank, have led to fiscal restraints and emphasized the need for private investment and initiative in education, especially in higher education. Government in India has allowed almost unrestricted entry of the private sector in higher education. As a natural sequel to this private initiative and investment, higher education is going to become a real commodity and a commercial venture. 'Borderless education' will give an overall jerk to the existing mode of educational system, especially in higher education. GATS will make higher education a commodity. The degrees, certificates, diplomas, trainings, apprenticeship, etc. will all be sold to the highest bidders. The universities which were traditionally viewed custodians and lighthouses of knowledge would function like business houses looking for the customers not only for their very existence but also to earn profit. This situation has its own threats as well as opportunities which requires a careful examination before venturing for future planning. Private investment, motivated by profit motive, will lead to quality degradation.

As a consequence of ever-increasing marketization of higher education due to GATS, the basic disciplines like physics, chemistry, mathematics, languages, philosophy, history, geography, etc., will be ignored in the private institutions and universities. The private investment is oriented to the courses which market demands. The private colleges will, thus, offer courses mainly in Computer, Electronics and IT which are in great demand these days.

Though GATS provides equal opportunities to the developing countries also to set-up their institutions in the developed countries, in actual practice the trade in higher education will not only be highly skewed but unidirectional also. "For example, only in Dhaka, city of Bangladesh there are 42 centres of foreign universities but there is no such centre of any Bangladesh university in any foreign country. This may make higher education trade like what is software trade today; and then all benefits of GATS inclusion of Higher Education will go to the developed nations."[10]

Adoption of open economy after GATS and other WTO agreements will put many restrictions on investment in higher education. This will lead to reduced expenditure on higher education with consequent practices of appointing teachers on contact basis and spending less on badly needed R&D. This is bound to affect the quality of higher education in developing countries. Higher education is critical to the development of developing countries has been noted by the world declaration adopted by the 128 countries in 1998 at conference on higher education of UNESCO, "Without adequate higher education and research institutions providing a critical mass of skilled and educated people, no country can ensure genuine endogenous and sustainable development and, in particular, developing countries and least developed countries cannot reduce the gap separating them from the industrially developed ones".

Transnational Companies (TNCs) have immense power of purse. Some of them have gross incomes greater than the GDP of most of the countries. General Motors is bigger than Denmark and at least hundred largest corporations are larger than most member-countries of the United Nations. Nearly 70 per cent of the world trade is controlled by 500 largest corporations. The policies and programmes of WB, IMF, and WTO are favourable to TNCs which are concentrated in USA and Europe. Though measures are being taken to make business responsible to society, the profit motive of TNCs and their ability to buy and corrupt the authorities in the developing countries is well known. *Economic and Political Weekly* in its story, Failure of the Global University has rightly pointed out, "Early this year (2005), Yale University's president visited India in an exercise to promote his institution and the concept of the 'global university'. Absent from his rhetoric was the reality of Yale's historical roots and its contemporary complicity in corporate greed and social irresponsibility."[11]

The current realities of globalization reflect a highly skewed relationship between East and West. Of the total 794,000 foreign students currently studying in the United States, more than 64 per cent are from Asia. Seven of the top ten "sending countries" of international foreign students in the US are Asian, while not a single Asian country is represented among the top ten destinations for American students studying abroad. India alone accounts for more than 62,000 students in the US, compared to only 1007 who studied in India during the 2002-03 academic year. Worldwide student mobility data, complied annually by UNESCO confirm similar imbalances in student exchange between India and other industrialized countries.[12]

Dr. A.R. Padoshi opined that "The process of globalisation as it operated today, is more beneficial to the rich countries at the expanse of the poor countries. Hence, there is an urgent need to improve the governance of globalization to solve the problem of poverty in the world. The social context of the globalization must be improved in order to benefit the poor".[13] It may be added that American students rarely go out to other countries for long-term study courses. This may be because they have got excellent education system in their own country. However, to get an international experience they are going on 'Study Abroad' programmes. This is why, the number of students participating in short-term (less than eight week) programmes has increased from 1.7% in 1993-94 to 7.3% in 2001-02 (Organisation for Economic Cooperation and Development-2004).

Task Force of the Association of Indian Universities has also cautioned against the commoditization of higher education as designed and dictated by GATS. It prepared a Position Paper on "General Agreement on Trade and Services and its Implications on Higher Education". This paper was considered and approved by the General Body of the Association at its 79th Annual Meeting held at University of North Bengal, Rajarammohunpur on November 18-21, 2004. The Task Force noted: Education is considered to be a pious mission in India since the dawn of its civilization. No one concerned with education in general, and higher education in particular, can even dream to conceive that education is a tradeable commodity, a concept which is not in tune with the socio-cultural milieu of our nation.[14]

8. POLITICISATION

Virus of politics has entered all the spheres of our life and universities have become favourite and fertile grounds for this. Here politics has been used to imply use of outside extraneous factors like caste, creed, region, party affiliations, etc. for academic or some pecuniary benefits. Politics in this sense is being used, abused and misused by most of the persons from the Vice-Chancellor to a peon, students and teachers alike. The very appointment and continuation of a Vice-Chancellor depends upon his political or other connections. Such is also the position of other functionaries like Pro-Vice-Chancellor, Registrar, Deans of various faculties, Hostel Wardens, etc. Policy of "spoil system" can be seen in its worst form when the above functionaries are unceremoniously changed with the change of party in power. One students' organisation has very clearly justified politicisation by writing its motto, "When Politics Decides Your Career, You Decide Your Politics."

"Politics has become a pervasive phenomenon in the constitution and working of almost all the university bodies, academic and administrative, in the selection of candidates for appointments, in the allocation of funds for research and in the award of scholarships. Politics has been playing a disgraceful role even in the award of degrees and diplomas. Direct political interference is the tendency of the politically-oriented trade unions or associations or unions of teachers, students and non-teaching employees, who exploit even the minor problems in the campus to whip up trouble and disrupt the peaceful academic atmosphere. Things have come to such a pass that students, teachers, and non-teaching employees are sharply divided into different political camps, and issues confronting them are analysed and their approach moulded not on the merits of issues but on the basis of their political affiliations. Each political party in the country is guilty of collusion in this nefarious game which has brought almost all our universities to a pathetic plight."[15]

Observations of Vikram Chadha, Professor of Economics, Guru Nanak Dev University, Amritsar deserve to be quoted in this context. "While the universities replicate the universe of knowledge and wisdom our universities have also come to epitomize the subtleties and intricacies of complex political processes. The university academics are so intensely engaged in the power games that either they have become oblivious of their prime activity of academics and research, or these institutions have been relegated to secondary position. The university campuses have come to reflect the mirror image of the power dynamics and struggle characterizing the national polity. Instead of gaining prominence and power through academics and research, teachers' groups on the campuses have blatantly indulged in reinforcing their power by enlarging their fold of rank 'followers', either by promising them to extra trivial benefits or by charming them with an aura of their 'connections'. The 'followers' also show their eagerness to join the entrenched groups, perhaps to camouflage their reluctance to work. The leaders of such entrenched groups assume the role of bourgeois rent-seekers or power-brokers. Hence the erosion of work ethos and the pursuit of non-academic achievements in the campuses. The authorities continue to discriminate and mess up rule implementation, while the teaching community continues to remain bogged down at the low level of effort. The campuses degenerate and become cesspools of stagnant academic activity, but power brokering and rent seeking continues to snowball and become self-sustaining."[16] Professor Chadha has concluded: "Instead of rewarding and patting serious thinking and research, power brokers have come to rule the roost in the contemporary university campuses as in the muddied mainstream national politics. This speaks volumes for the absence of practical relevance of university education and instructions for national development."[17]

According to Professor Deepak Nayyar, formerly Vice-Chancellor of University of Delhi, they (our universities) are "in the sick bay". He summed up the causes of sickness rather lucidly:

> "Universities are not stand-alone islands. Nor they are immune from the law of averages. They simply mirror society. Our universities witnessed the same erosion of work ethic, the same dilution of values and morality, the same chipping away at norms that was experienced by polity and society. Nehru saw universities as temples of

learning. But they became arenas of politics. As the political process slowly but surely intruded into the day-to-day life of universities, their governance became a political balancing act. As competing interests strove for control, a system of sharing spoils and extending patronage emerged. The casualty was the teaching-learning process."[18]

Students' elections have had harmful effects on the academic atmosphere in the universities. Editorial of *The Tribune*, dated September 21, 2005, entitled "Campus elections SC suggestions for guidelines" deserves to be quoted here:

> The Supreme Court has rightly sought the Centre's opinion on the need to evolve appropriate guidelines on conducting the students' union elections in all the colleges and universities in the country. In the absence of guidelines, these elections have become a free for all today, with absolutely no check either on the contestants or on the expenditure incurred by them. Backed by various political parties, the students' union elections have affected academic discipline and vitiated the campus life. As in the elections to Parliament and state legislatures, in these elections too, the role of money and muscle power has increased manifold. The court has said that money spent in these elections is equivalent to the one spent in a parliamentary constituency!

The entry of "divisive and disruptive tendencies" in the colleges and universities has led to increasing campus unrest. The apex court aptly referred to instances of even Vice-Chancellors being locked up by the student leaders in support of their demands. One way of checking these tendencies, according to the court, is to screen the contestants in the elections. In most institutions, student leaders get admitted repeatedly in different courses so that they can keep contesting the elections. Surely, such things would not be possible if there are well-defined rules and regulations for funding and conduct of election campaigns".

But the larger question remains—who will enforce these rules so framed? Perhaps the educational authorities themselves may have to shoulder the responsibility. It may not be desirable to rope in the district administration in this task because that may amount to encroachment on the autonomy of the educational institutions. Ideally, these issues need to be examined at length by the UGC Chairman and the Vice-Chancellors during their regular conferences. The Supreme Court is forced to intervene in such matters owing to the failure of the educational authorities to stem the rot, but clearly it had no alternative but to do so.[19]

9. VIOLENCE IN THE CAMPUSES

Campus violence has developed as a natural consequence of politicisation. Intermixing of political and anti-social elements with the students' leadership has given rise to campus violence. "In all fairness, however, it needs to be admitted that during the last two and a half decades, life in many universities especially in North has been characterized by frequent disruption. A general atmosphere of violence has developed... This violence has become endemic on many campuses... Gangsters have developed and an average student or teacher avoids confrontation with these *dadas*.[20]

Babita Jaiswal has pointed out following types of violence:

- Eve teasing
- Ragging
- Group clashes
- Murder
- Destruction of University property

To these types one more may be added, threatening and manhandling of teachers by the students when they check cheating during examination, or do not yield to the students' demands for allowing illegal admission to some student activist or permit them to appear in annual examination by keeping all the rules for compulsory class attendance at bay or the like. Instigation by the political parties, callous, insensitive, inefficient administration waking and acting only to the blackmail of strikes, *bandhs, gheraos,* property destruction, etc., increasing unemployment, useless education, waning respect for authority, publicity of violence in the media, and perhaps many more factors can be attributed to the campus violence. Whatever the reasons, we are witnessing a lot of violence and undignified behaviour unbecoming to the educated persons. Nasir Khan (NSUI) and Kuldeep Dhatwalia (ABVP), two students-leaders, fell prey to this campus violence in the Himachal Pradesh University.

10. CRIMINALISATION

University campuses have degenerated into dens of crimes and corruption where degrees are being sold, persons getting degrees without any admission, shameless cheating in the examinations, answer-books being marked not by the teachers but by the students themselves engaged by the teachers on payment of paltry amount, marks increased in the marks-lists by getting illegal money, huge money amassed by the highest officers like Vice-Chancellors, Registrars, Controller of Examination, etc. for printing question papers, or buying some furniture or equipment, or constructing some building. All this is done with the shield of autonomy, or improving the academic climate.

Editorial of *The Tribune*, September 20, 2005, entitled, Rot in universities CMs should have no say in VC's selection deserves to be quoted here:

> Uttar Pradesh Governor T.V. Rajeswar has indeed struck a blow against corruption, nepotism and maladministration by summarily sacking four Vice-Chancellors of the universities at Bareilly, Jaunpur, Kanpur and Meerut. This comes close on the heels of the dismissal of two Vice-Chancellors earlier (Bundelkhand University, Jhansi, and CCS University, Meerut). What is happening in these universities today is the antithesis of the concept and values of higher education. The four Vice-Chancellors sacked were running unauthorised and illegal franchising of centres all over the country. They were distributing degrees such as M.Phil., M.Sc., MBA, M.Tech, and LLM

> through intermediaries called "facilitators" who coordinated the illegal transactions between the universities and the centres. Thousands of students paid between Rs. 15,000 and Rs. 30,000 per semester for various courses, not knowing that these were fake degrees. The Governor took the extreme step following an inquiry by two Principal Secretaries of the government. He has now aptly decided to seek their criminal prosecution.

"But then, Uttar Pradesh is not the only state where the incumbents have brought shame and disgrace to the exalted post of Vice Chancellor. The VC's: image has taken a beating in most universities in the country today because Chief Ministers handpick persons for the top post on grounds other than scholarship, integrity and respect they enjoy in the academic community. There is indeed a steady deterioration in higher education. How can a university's standards be improved if the Vice-Chancellor himself is corrupt and does not take care that nobody questions his personal qualities?

"The Manmohan Singh Government needs to take effective steps to restore the pre-eminent position of the Vice-Chancellor. Malcontents should have no place in the universities. Otherwise, the whole system down the ladder will stink and we will continue to watch incidents such as those in UP. Chief Ministers should have no say on the appointment of Vice-Chancellors. The recommendations of the Education Commission (1964-66) headed by Dr. D.S. Kothari and the UGC Committee on Appointment of Vice-Chancellors in Indian Universities (1991-93) need to be implemented in right earnest to regain the lost image of the universities."[21]

Some evidence may be cited for the above depressing facts. "A former Vice-Chancellor of Vishva Bharti, Dr. Dalip Sinha was arrested late last night from his Ballygune Palace residence in south Kolkata for his alleged involvement in the Tagore's Nobel Prize theft and various other illegal activities in the university."[22] "With the arrest of yet another former Registrar of Vishva Bharti, Prof. Dilip Mukharjee, and the Trinamool Congress's decision to file a case in court tomorrow against former Vice-Chancellor of Rabindra Bharti, Partibha Sarkar on his fake D.Phil. degree, the controversy in these two major educational institutions has come up again. Professor Mukharjee was arrested from his Ballygunge area residence in connection with his involvement in the fake mark-sheet and certificate racket. Former Vice-Chancellor Dilip Sinha and Ms. Mukti Deb, a mathematics lecturer, were also arrested in this case on June 25. "Dr. Sinha and Ms. Deb, who have been in jail, will be produced in the Bolpur court on July 21, where the arrested former Registrar will also be presented".[23] "Mr. L.N. Mishra, Special Judge, today remanded Mr. P.N. Bhardwaj, a deputy registrar of the Himachal Pradesh University who is the main accused in the Rs. 25 *lakh* question paper printing scam along with the former Vice-Chancellor, Dr. S.D. Sharma, in police custody".[24] "Sh. Jeet Ram, a Superintendent in the Academic Branch of the Himachal Pradesh University, was caught red handed by the Vigilance Department of the Government of Himachal Pradesh for accepting a bribe of Rs. 2000 from a student for increasing the marks.[25] There are number of such cases right from Kashmir to Kanya Kumari.

11. LACK OF QUALITY EDUCATION

With all the above weaknesses, the institutes of higher education are not in a position to provide quality education to the students. They find no interest in learning from the dull and dreary lectures where teaching-learning process has become a uni-polar process of covering the outdated syllabi. Attending classes regularly has become a practice of bygone days. When the examinations draw near, they start preparing only a few sure shot questions likely to be set in the examination or plan for some innovative scheme for cheating or adopt some other underhand methods. Instead of understanding and experimentation, cramming has become a better and handy method of passing examination. Position of extension centres, set-up by some universities for imparting education through the directorates of continuing education, is still worse. They lack all the resources like good faculty, library, and other essential infrastructure. They, thus, provide no education worth the name and have degenerating into money-minting shops for helping the students to get degrees without any knowledge and expertise. "The linkage of university education and manpower planning has remained weak resulting in the production of unemployed and some times, unemployable people by the universities."[26] Much respected and valued degree of the Doctor of Philosophy has also lost much of its shine. Plagiarism has become a normal practice not only with young students but with many grown up teachers also. The standards of the theses have come down to shameful levels. This degree, in many cases now, is being given because of the good connections of a supervisor and not because of good work of a candidate.

We have discussed the challenges to the university administration in the previous pages. An attempt has been made in the study to find solution to these challenges. Suggestions to meet the challenges have been given in the last chapter.

Notes and References

1. Raman Mohan, *The Tribune,* 25.8.2004, p. 7.
2. *Ibid.,* p. 5.
3. Jagannath Mohanty, *op. cit.,* 445.
4. *The Tribune,* 18-4-2004, p. 04.
5. P.R. Panchamukhi, Contribution of Private Sector to Financing of Education, In Nandhyala, B.G. Tilak, (Ed.) *Financing Education in India,* New Delhi, National Institute of Educational Planning and Administration, 2003, p. 282.
6. *The Tribune,* 26-6-2004, p. 6.
7. Prabhjot Singh, *The Tribune,* 15-6-2004, pp. 4, 11
8. *Ibid., The Tribune,* September 20, 2005, p. 13.
9. *University News,* 40 (17), April 29-May 5, p. 9.
10. B.B. Bhattacharya and C.T. Bhunia, Threats and Opportunities of Higher Education in the Context of GATS, Association of Indian Universities, *University News, A Weekly of Higher Education,* Vol. 43, No. 44, October 31-November 06, 2005, p. 16.
11. Ajay Gandhi, Tale and India, Failure of the 'Global University', *Economic and Political Weekly,* Vol. XL, No. 18, April 30, 2005, p. 1815.
12. P. Periyasamy and J. Venkatesh, Globalisation of Higher Education: Means for India, Association of Indian Universities, *University News,* Vol. 42, No. 40, October 04-10, 2004, p. 3.
13. *Ibid.,* p. 23.
14. GATS and its Implications on Higher Education, Association of Indian Universities, *University News, A Weekly Journal of Higher Education,* Vol. 43, No. 6, February 07-13, 2005, p. 2.
15. M.V. Pylee, Governance of Universities, In M.V. Mathur, Ramesh, K. Arora and Meena Sogani, *Indian University System: Revitalization and Reform,* New Delhi, Wiley Eastern Limited, 1994, p. 156.

16. Vikram Chadha, *The Tribune*, 29-8-2004, p. 12.
17. *Ibid.*, p. 12.
18. S. Parsuraman, Guest Editor, Editorial, Rescuing Education from Our Universities, *University News*, Vol. 43, No. 47, Nov. 21-27, 2005, p. 3.
19. *The Tribune*, 21-9-2005, p. 10.
20. Babita Jaiswal, Campus Violence: Causes and Possible Actions, *University News*, Vol. 42, No. 33, August 16-22, 2004, pp. 24-25.
21. *The Tribune*, September 20, 2005, Editorial, p. 10.
22. Subhrangshu Gupta, *The Tribune*, 26-6-2004, p. 2.
23. *The Tribune*, 19-7-2004, p. 2.
24. *The Tribune*, 1-7-2004, p. 8.
25. *Amar Ujala*, 15-7-2004, p. 1.
26. A. Gnanam, In M.V. Mathur, Ramesh, K. Arora and Meena Sogani, *op. cit.* p. 68.

CHAPTER

3

Sample : Profile of the Universities

Present study has covered all the four North-Western states of India, namely, Haryana, Himachal Pradesh, Jammu and Kashmir, and Punjab, and one union territory, i.e., Chandigarh. It has studied mainly the multi-faculty residential and affiliating universities in the above states and the union territory. This has been done for the sake of having a manageable uniformity in the study. The sample for the study is a representative and purposive one, i.e., one university each from a state and the union territory.

Union territory Chandigarh has only one university, i.e., Panjab University. This is a combination of a state as well as a central university. Similarly, Himachal Pradesh has also only one multi-faculty residential and affiliating university, i.e., Himachal Pradesh University at Shimla. So both the above universities were included in the sample.

As for Punjab, Haryana, and Jammu & Kashmir, they have two such universities each. These may be mentioned as follows:

- Panjab—Guru Nanak Dev University, Amritsar and Punjabi University, Patiala.

- Haryana—Kurukshetra University, Kurukshetra, and Maharishi Dayanand University, Rohtak.
- Jammu & Kashmir—University of Jammu, Jammu, and University of Kashmir, Srinagar.

From the above states the present researcher has selected one university from each state on the criteria that the university falling alphabetically first has been included in the sample. Thus, Guru Nanak Dev University, Amritsar, Kurukshetra University, Kurukshetra, and University of Jammu, Jammu have been selected.

Total sample, thus, consists of the following universities, to mention them in the alphabetical order:

- Guru Nanak Dev University, Amritsar.
- Himachal Pradesh University, Shimla.
- University of Jammu, Jammu.
- Kurukshetra University, Kurukshetra.
- Panjab University, Chandigarh.

Profile of all the universities of all the four North-Western states of India and union territory, Chandigarh all of which are multi-faculty residential and affiliating universities have been mentioned in the following pages:

GURU NANAK DEV UNIVERSITY, AMRITSAR

INTRODUCTION

Guru Nanak Dev University was established at Amritsar on November 24, 1969 to mark the 500th birth anniversary of Sri Guru Nanak Devji. The objectives enshrined in the Guru Nanak Dev University Act, 1969 emphasised that the new University would make provision for imparting education and promote research in the humanities, learned professions, sciences, especially of applied nature and technology. The motto of the University as engraved on its emblem "Guru's wisdom illumines all" speaks of the vision and idealism for which the university stands. National Assessment and Accreditation Council (NAAC) of UGC has given it the much coveted Five Star Level status.

Spread over a stretch of 500 acres, the University presents a picture of modern architecture. Traditional red brick geometrical blocks represents its regard for time honoured values and commitment to scientific advancement. Making its humble beginning in an annexe of the adjoining Khalsa College, the University today boasts of 30 full-fledged academic departments, two regional centres at Jalandhar and Gurdaspur, two constituent colleges (Jalandhar and Niari, Gurdaspur) and score of support service departments beside several administrative offices.

Admission to courses at all levels is made strictly on the basis of National, State and University level entrance tests. At present over 5000 students are studying on the campus, a very large number of them being girl students drawn from the neighbouring countryside.

Over the years, the University has built up an excellent academic infrastructure in the form of a well stocked computerised library, state-of-art laboratories, Academic Staff College, All India Service Training Centre, Physiotherapy Centre, Language Lab, Multimedia Centre, Botanical Garden and Green House, The Library has 24 hours Internet facility, Placement Unit, etc. To promote research among its faculty, almost all the Departments have been provided with independent computer facilities and departmental libraries.

In addition to the academics, the University has also created necessary facilities for recreation and all round development of its students and faculty in the form of Department of Youth Services, National Service Scheme, Public Relations Department, a 900 seat all purpose auditorium, half a dozen seminar and conference halls, a modern hi-tech sports complex, sports hostel, open air theatre, faculty club, students' centre, health centre, day care centre, two separate holiday homes at Dalhousie for teachers and students, working women's hostel along with on-campus residential facilities for large number of teachers and administrative staff.

Academic Disciplines

Being an affiliating University, it also performs the parenting role of directing and monitoring the academic programmes of 92 colleges located in the five districts of Amritsar, Jalandhar, Kapurthala, Nawanshehar and Gurdaspur some of which have a long and creditable history of imparting higher education since late nineteenth century.

Research Centres and Chairs

A good number of Research Centres and Chairs for focused studies have been established. These are Centre for Immigrant Studies, Centre for Studies of Punjab Politics and Centre for South-Central Asian Studies. The University has established the Namdhari Guru Ram Singh Chair, Guru Ravi Das Chair, Baba Budha Sikh Study Chair, and Bhagat Puran Singh Chair to undertake research on the life and philosophy of these great personalities. Computer Centre, Centre for Genetic Disorders, Media Centre and Physiotherapy Centre have been established as Centres for support services with public orientation.

School of Legal Studies

The University from the academic session 2002 has started a School of Legal Studies, an institution of its own kind in the whole Northern India, at its new Regional Campus, Ladhewali, Jalandhar to impart quality-based and socially relevant instruction in the B.A., L.L.B. (Hons.) Course. The duration of this course is five years, consisting of 10 semesters. The object of this School is to meet the new challenges in legal education by adopting latest teaching and research methodology, so as to compete with the national level Law Schools/Institutes in the country. Its aim is to cultivate the Science of Law, to promote advanced studies and research in law, so as to keep pace with the fast developing economic, political and social changes.

New Courses for Outstanding Students

New courses in B.A. (Hons. School) in Social Sciences have been specifically designed and meant for outstanding students, who after completing 10+2 wish to excel in social sciences for higher teaching and research or to prepare for competitive examinations. The existing under-graduate courses were primarily designed keeping in view the interests of average students. The talents of exceptionally brilliant students under the existing scheme remain under-utilised during their education in arts and social sciences. This course is being run by the School of Social Sciences on the university campus.

Sports

The University has gained national recognition because of its hi-tech sports infrastructure and excellent achievements at the inter-versity, national and international level. It organises special training camps and inter-college tournaments in about 70 to 75 men and women events and participates in inter-university tournaments in 50 to 55 games involving more than 7000 students. The sprawling sports complex houses an international quality Astro-turf hockey stadium, an Olympic standard swimming pool, with separate facilities for training, diving and competition, a newly constructed international level standard indoor multipurpose gymnasium and playgrounds for football, cricket, lawn tennis, basketball, handball, softball, kho-kho, and kabaddi, etc. It has also an open air gymnasium for providing physical fitness training. The University has so far produced three Padamshree and 25 Arjuna Awardees in various sports disciplines. The University also lifted three national level sports trophies : Dr. B.L. Gupta General Champion Trophy for twelve times, Osmania University Platinum Jubilee Trophy for six times, and also Kridamaharishi Shri Meghnath Nageshkar Trophy for six times.

The University won Inter-University National Youth Festival Overall Championship for the fourth time consecutively. The National Youth Festival was organised by the Association of Indian Universities, Ministry of Youth Affairs and Sports, Government of India, at Jiwaji University, Gwalior during the month of February, 2004. The University also won music trophy in this festival and maintained its supremacy in cultural field. The University won overall championship during North Zone Inter-University Youth Festival which was held at Kurukshtera University, Kurukshtera during the month of January, 2004. It won Music, Theatre, Fine Arts and Literary Trophies during this festival. Dr. S.P. Singh, Vice-Chancellor of the GNDU, received Maulana Abdul Kalam Azad Trophy from President APJ Abdul Kalam at Rashtrapati Bhavan in New Delhi on 29th August; 2005. The University has won the prestigious trophy for the 19th record time.[1]

University Grants Commission has sanctioned "Centre of Excellence in Sports Sciences" to GNDU for providing meritorious education in the field of sports in line with new developments and challenges. UGC has also sanctioned Rs. five crore for the development of this prestigious centre.

Centre for Genetic Disorders

This Centre is one of the leading Centres of North India providing diagnostic services to patients and families suffering from various genetic disorders and bringing about awareness among people regarding genetic diseases and their management. Set-up in 1990 with a grant from the Ministry of Science and Technology, the Centre has acquired some of the most sophisticated instruments like automatic karyotyping system, automatic metaphase finder, automatic DNA sequencer, etc. and has facilities for advanced cytogenetic and molecular work. It is also actively carrying out research related to identification of genes causing different genetic disorders and has collaboration with different institutions of India and Germany in different fields of human genetics.

Distance Education Programme

Distance education was started in this University from the session 2002-03. Under this programme, a number of technical, professional, and conventional courses which are run parallel to courses offered in conventional mode, have been introduced. Unrestricted mobility of students between distance and conventional mode of education is the merit of this distance education programme. Under this programme, ordinances, syllabus, examination, evaluation, etc. is the same as for regular students. In this programme, educational instructions are imparted through the use of modern educational technologies. Classroom teaching is also an integral part of this programme. Before the start of the session 2002-03, after close scrutiny of the magnitude and quality of the infrastructure by expert committee about 40 Associate Institutes were set up. To create enthusiasm amongst the students receiving education through distance education, SAF Madanjeet Singh Scholarships have been awarded to six students selected on the basis of the merit-*cum*-means basis from various "Associate Institutes". The University has been awarded 100 such scholarships for the students admitted to the distance education programme.

University Regional Campuses and Colleges

Regional Campus, Gurdaspur

The Regional Campus Gurdaspur was started in 1999 on the persistent demand of the area to create facilities for higher studies and professional courses. Teaching programme of the campus include L.L.B. (Five year course) and MBA. Within a short span of time, the campus has come up with a well equipped library. The campus has its own computer lab to impart training to the students. A placement cell has been formed to assist the students of MBA for summer training and final placement. Foundation stone of three-storey building of Information Technology (IT) Block costing Rs. 2 crores was laid on April 19, 2005.

Regional Centre, Jalandhar

The Centre runs courses M.A. in English, and Punjabi and L.L.B. The Centre is going to have its beautiful campus very soon.

G.N.D. University College, Jalandhar

G.N.D. University College, Jalandhar is one of the oldest educational institutions. This college caters to the needs of the poor students as it charges very nominal fees from them. Commerce, Computer and Arts courses are run leading to B.Com, B.A. degrees.

Niari College

Shaheed Ram Singh Pathania Memorial College, Niari has been established in educationally backward area of Gurdaspur District. This college is situated in the laps of hills and is providing conducive-ambience for studies. A computer lab has been established in the college which has been made accessible not only to the students of the college but to the general public also.

INFRASTRUCTURE AND ALLIED ACADEMIC ACTIVITIES

The University Library

The University Library, named as Bhai Gurdas Central Library, is well endowed in terms of specialized journals, back sets, Sikh reference books and rare manuscripts. Started in 1970 with a nucleus of 10,000 books, it has now steadily built its collection to more than 3.84 lakhs, which include 1510 manuscripts, 5119 rare books and 7790 theses and dissertations, and current research journals: Indian 280; Foreign 195; and 79,026 back volumes. The Library remains open on all the days of the year except on two national holidays, i.e., 26th January and 15th August. It has open shelf system and a seating capacity for 500 readers. The Library has an air-conditioned hall which remains open 24 hours for reading personal books. It has created special sections for manuscripts, rare books, dissertations, text books and history and culture of Punjab. It has also allocated a separate floor for the display and reading of research journals. The Library has its own computer centre and all its operations including cataloguing of new books and existing books are carried on with computers. It has also prepared five data bases of books and periodicals on different subjects. The Library also provides Internet services and is a member of INFLIBNET which is providing access to 2858 e-journals and some database. Faculty and students can secure information and can get prints of any specific subject available anywhere in the world. The Library also provides reprographic facilities and micro-film reading facilities. It has already transferred many rare documents on micro-films. Besides the main library, 20 departments have also set-up their additional departmental libraries. Another 6 departmental libraries are multi-departmental and cater to more than one discipline.

Hostels

The University provides accommodation for 1300 girls, and 950 boys in three girls hostels and two boys hostels respectively on the campus. In these hostels there are facilities for indoor games, Common Room, Stationary Shop, PC's, Canteen services, bathroom geysers, water coolers equipped with water purifier, etc. The messes of all these hostels are running on cooperative bases which are managed by the students' mess committees under the guidance of hostel wardens. The daily vernacular and national newspapers and reputed magazines are also made available in all these hostels. Two computer labs consisting of fifteen computers in each lab, connected with internet facility, have been installed in the hostels for the benefit of the hostlers. The facility of Punjab and Sind Bank Extension Counter and First Aid has also been provided in these hostels.

Health Centre

GNDU has set-up its own Health Centre. It provides free medical aid to all students, teachers, staff and their dependants and retired persons. The Centre has an Ambulance Van and is geared for emergency services for 24 hours and is equipped with all modern facilities and equipment. It has two senior Medical Officers, one Lady Medical Officer and one Dental Surgeon. The Health Centre also provides ayurvedic medical system in its Ayurvedic Dispensary, which has been set-up by state government under the charge of an Ayurvedic Medical Officer. In addition, there are six pharmacists-assistants, two staff nurses and three laboratory technicians with sophisticated instruments for all basic clinical tests. The Centre has three ECG Machines and an ultra sound system. The Centre is having an Operation Theater specially designed for all kinds of most modern equipments like Digitally Controlled Hot Air Ovens, autoclaves glass bead sterilizer, and complete rustication kit, electric suction machine for the management of emergency patients; and separate male and female wards for admitting patients. The Health Centre has a computer system for computerizing the stock of medicines, office record and lab and ultrasound reports. It has also been updated with latest medical software, e-mail and internet facility.

Physiotherapy Centre

The University has a full-fledged Physiotherapy Centre equipped with a Body Composition Analyser, Ultrasonic machines, motorized Tread Mill and Bogy Massager and other equipment for Microwave diathermy and Infra-Red Rays therapy besides all kinds of baths (Sauna, Turkish, etc.) facilities and exercise equipment. The Centre is providing special physiotherapy services to the sportspersons.

Computer Centre

The Centre set-up with an initial grant from the UGC has been substantially upgraded. At present, there are three labs out of which one lab is being specifically used for research purpose. Each lab is equipped with 25 computers with latest peripheral devices and computer software. Internet facility is available in all the laboratories.

Computer Centre staff is engaged in teaching work in various departments like Computer Science and Engineering, Commerce and Business Management. Students of about ten departments use the laboratories for practical training. The Centre also facilitates research for scientific calculations and statistical analysis. In addition to that, the Centre imparts training to Senior Assistants, Junior Assistants and Clerks.

Academic Staff College

The Academic Staff College of GNDU was established in June 1988 and is currently one of the 51 Academic Staff Colleges operating in the country. Linked to the professional and career development of the University and College teachers, it runs various programmes to cover different categories of teachers. On an average, 15-20 programmes are conducted in a year in which nearly 600 teachers are given training. The Academic Staff College has so far conducted 117 Refresher Courses and 63 GOCs since its inception. Besides, it has also organised a number of workshops for college principals and Heads of teaching departments. The courses are run on the lines of participative and interactive learning style. The ASC has over the years built up a reasonable infrastructure to provide residential and messing facilities to its outstation participants. It has also developed fully furnished conference halls with all modern audio-visual aids. It has an in-house library with a holding of approximately 3500 books and a dozen periodicals along with fully furnished computer lab.

College Development Council

College Development Council is a very important institution of GNDU. This institution came into existence in May 1981 and from the very first day of its formation, its main motive is to establish balanced relations between the colleges and the University and to guide the colleges for their continuous uplift and progress. This College Development Council is the only council in India which is having its own Auditorium and Guest House. The Auditorium has the capacity of 100 persons and the Guest House has got 11 rooms. This council also works for the cordial relations of the colleges with the University, UGC, NAAC and other institutions.

All India Services Centre

The Government of India established in 1982 an All India Services Pre-Examination Training Centre for the weaker sections in this University. The University on its own created another Centre for preparation for Competitive Examinations for the general category students in 1984. The coaching classes of both the Centres have been combined for extended interaction among the students of different communities. From 1982 to 1988, there were classes only for IAS Preliminary and Main Examination, but from 1989 additional classes for Banking and other Subordinates Services were also started. The Centre also prepares the students for UGC/NET examination. Since the inception of this Centre 32 students have made it to IAS and allied services. In the year 2003 out of 91 candidates selected by the UPSC for Punjab Civil Services (Executive), 21 were students of this Centre. In the year 2004, 3 students made it to IAS and Allied Services. Besides these achievements, many students of this Centre have been selected in Central Excise, Customs, Public Sector Units, BSF, Banks, LIC, etc.

University-Industry Linkages

The University adopted the University-Industry Linkage Programme of UGC in the year 1993. AICTE has recently sanctioned a grant of Rs. 8.0 lakhs for further strengthening of the industry-institute partnership cells. GNDU under this programme held different meetings with the local and nearby industrialists from wide spectrum of industries. During this period a number of seminars, workshops, awareness programmes including awareness in ISO 9000 series, patent regime, conservation of petroleum energy, eco-friendly dyes were arranged for the benefit of industry and the scientists and researchers working in various departments of the university.

In an effort to generate its own resources, the GNDU has also established a Directorate of Consultancy, for providing the consultancy services in the areas such as Town Planning, Architecture, Textile and Sociology and Food Processing.

Placement Unit

The University has created a separate Placement Unit with a full time Placement Officer. This unit looks after academic and career counselling of students and organises workshops relating to job opening in various sectors. For this purpose it establishes advance communication with prospective employers and arranges their visits to the campus for direct recruitment of its fresh graduates. Since 1998 after its establishment, 1028 students have been placed with national and multinational companies. In the academic session 2004-05, 246 students were selected for placement from different courses by campus/off-campus placements.

Seven placement brochures were published for courses of MCA and B.Tech. (Computer Science), B.Tech. (Electronics), MBA, B.Tech (Food Tech.), B.Tech. (Textile Chemistry), M.Sc. Applied Physics and MBE. Big names in IT industry like TCS, Satyam, Wipro, Quark, HPS, Compro, etc. conducted campus recruitment for batch 2005 in year 2004. In addition, MNCs like Ranbaxy, Eli-lilly, Dr. Reddy's Lab, etc. conducted campus recruitments for Chemistry, Applied Chemistry and Pharmaceutical students. In management courses (MBA, MBE, etc.), students were offered jobs by companies like Reliance,

HDFC, Kotak Mahindra, JCT, ICICI, etc. Almost all students from B.Tech. (Textile Chemistry) of batch 2005 have been selected by different companies. All six students of B.Tech (Sugar Technology) of 2006 batch have been selected through campus placements by Diftech Technologies, New Delhi.

Press and Publication Department

The Press and Publication Department was set-up in 1972 to cater to the publication needs of the University in terms of highlighting its academic achievements and providing quality textbooks to its students. The Department has so far published 133 general books in Punjabi, 116 in English, 24 in Hindi, 60 Text Books. The Department at present is publishing 14 journals. The Department has also set-up a retail outlet for the sale of its publications. To promote sale it takes part in Book Exhibitions and runs a book club. The members can purchase University publications at 50% discount plus 10% bonus in the shape of books.

Community Outreach

GNDU has set-up following orgaisations to establish relationship with the community:

Department of Adult, Continuing Education and Extension

Department of Adult, Continuing Education and Extension is providing appropriate knowledge and skills to the backward and deprived sections of the society. The efforts are made to increase the employability of the underemployed and unemployed men and women. Literacy programmes are conducted for the illiterates, while skill development training courses like Dress designing, Cutting and Tailoring, Textile Designing, Electronics and TV Maintenance-Service and Computer Education are made available to the needy youth of the local area. Discussions and talks related to family welfare, health and hygiene, nutrition, child care, population education, environment protection, AIDS and drugs, etc. are organised. Curative and preventive medical camps are organised for the rural sick and poor community. The programmes are conducted at the GNDU Campus, Regional Centre, Gurdaspur and the villages adopted for the out-reach activities.

Public Relations Department

The GNDU has a full-fledged Public Relations Department which deals with the publicity of the University on electronic and in print media. This department serves as an important link between the University and the general public. The Department also conducts the visits of VIPs to the historical places in and around the city and to Indo-Pak Wagha Border. The Information Centre of the Department also provides all types of information to the students and the visitors. It also publishes a quarterly news bulletin University Samachar.

Media Centre

This University is the only university in the Northern region which established a media centre. Keeping in view the fact that the world has become global village because of the meteoric pace of information technology, well established Media Centre would go a long way in assessing useful information developments occurring in any part of the world.

Punjabi Folklore Museum

To popularise Punjabi folklore and to ward it off against the lecherous distortions, a Punjabi Folklore Museum has been build up on the campus. The Museum provides a fairly desirable knowledge of the rich diversity of the Punjabi folklore which forms the true spirit of the rural Punjab, but which is at discount in the face of materialistic onslaughts. To preserve the rich heritage of the Punjabi culture, the University has set-up a heritage village on its own campus so as to resurrect consciousness among the younger generations.

UNIVERSITY ADMINISTRATION

Top hierarchy of the University consists of the following officers: Chancellor who is always the Governor of the State, Vice-Chancellor, Registrar, Controller of Examination, and Deans of various faculties including Deans Studies and Deans of

Students Welfare. Other officers of the University are Finance Officer, Planning and Development Officer, Librarian, Executive Engineer, and Medical Officer. In addition to it, University is run by various bodies like University Court, Executive Council, Academic Council, Finance Committee, etc.

The University administration comprises a strong team of 1800 employees, who look after the essential university services, predominantly belonging to finance management and conduct of examinations. The University budget for the year 2005-06 was over 79.74 crores, out of which 40.50 crores were provided exclusively to the teaching departments. The Syllabus, admission forms of various classes/courses and other information about the University are available on university website: www.gnduonlinc.org

Audit System

GNDU has a well laid system of auditing the accounts. The university has got two accounts branches. Papers/bills mooted through respected departments/centres are moved upward through these branches. Then there is a section known as Internal Audit which has about one hundred strong employees to man it. Internal Audit looks after salary and telephone bills. There is also external audit system which is done by an officer of the rank of Deputy Controller of the Local Fund Department of the Government of Punjab. The Deputy Controller and his staff get salary from their parent Department and official accommodation in the University campus from the University. There is 100% pre-audit for all the bills except those of the salary bills. Post-audit of the salary bills is done once a year. Last of all, there is an audit by the Accountant General also. It is done because the University gets grants from the Government.

Examination System

GNDU has annual system of examination. It has brought in many innovations in the conduct of examinations. Timely declaration of results in the last decade (the schedule has not been broken or delayed even once), introduction of single answer book, revised pattern of question papers based on UGC-NET and UPSC system, computerization of results, computerized printing of photographs of candidates on the detailed marks card, names of mother and father on the DMC/ Degrees are some of the examples in this context. The University has also taken initiative in affixing holograms and photographs on the various degrees. Results of examinations held in April-May are declared by June 30 every year and some have also been available on internet. Students can see their answer-sheets as well as of any other examinee for a payment. That lends transparency and faith in the examination system. This facility is not available in any other university of the sample.

Teachers and their Association

Teachers have their own association, known as Guru Nanak Dev University Teachers' Association (GNDUTA) to look after their interests. Election to this association is conducted on yearly basis. The teachers can be members of a political party. They can even contest Parliamentary or State Assembly election. However, the election to GNDUTA is not fought on party lines but on the basis of important issues of the university. This helps in keeping the university out of the din of the political influences.

Students and their Association

Students have their association which is known as Guru Nanak Dev University Students' Association. It is not formed on any political basis. In fact, national level organizations of various students' bodies do not exist here. The banners, slogans, and mottos of the various students' bodies are totally missing on the walls of the university. Only one small handbill which came to the notice of the present researcher read as "Guru Nanak Dev University Students' Association (GNDUSA) Welcomes the Refreshers".

Non-Teaching Staff and their Association

Non-teaching staff too has its own association. This also is not formed on any political basis. Employees fight election on the basis of university issues like their recruitment and promotion. Hand bills are printed and distributed but not pasted on the walls.

HIMACHAL PRADESH UNIVERSITY, SHIMLA

INTRODUCTION

Himachal Pradesh University, only multi-faculty, affiliating-*cum*-residential University of Himachal Pradesh was established on the 22nd July, 1970 at Summer-Hill, a suburb on the western end of Shimla at a distance of 4 km. from the main town Shimla. The campus is located at about five minute walk from Summer-Hill Railway station and 15 km. from the Jubber Hatti Airport. Famous Indian Institute of Advanced Studies, located in the Rashtrapati Niwas, earlier called Vice-regal Lodge from where the Government of Undivided India used to govern the whole sub-continent, is also situated in the vicinity of the University. Being a Hill University, it does not have a walled campus but is sprawled over an area of 200 acres of lush green spurs and valleys surrounded by tall deodars, pines, rhododendrons and oaks overlooking snow-peaked majestic mountain ranges. Bracing climate and serene surroundings of the university campus are ideally suited to pursue higher studies and research.

The University has not got well marked campus. Many private shops catering to the needs of the university students, teachers, staff and the general public are located in the campus. All the teaching departments are located in the campus. There is a central library, an auditorium, canteens, H.P.T.D.C juice shop, STD/ISD facilities, book-shops, stationary shops, photocopying shops, etc. Post office and a branch of the State Bank of India are also operating in the campus. For University guests, there is a faculty house in the campus quite near to Rajkumari Amrit Kaur Bhawan where Mahatma Gandhi stayed often when he visited Shimla during 1935-46. The University Executive Engineer and his establishment look after the construction and maintenance of the roads and buildings.

ACADEMIC DISCIPLINES

Presently, it has 12 faculties (8 are campus-based) which have 24 departments. About 4,250 students are studying in the campus. 250 teachers (84 Professors, 89 Readers, and 97 Lecturers) are teaching in the university. 1195 non-teaching employees (01 A category, 128 B categoty, 550 C category and 516 D category and technical) are providing the support for teaching including the conduct of examination, declaration of results, and award of degrees. International Centre for Distance Education and Open Learning (ICDEOL) is catering to the needs of the students spread in remote and tribal areas of the Pradesh and in other parts of the country by importing education at their doorsteps. Institutions maintained by the University are: UGC Academic Staff College, HPU Centre for Evening Studies, HPU Regional Centre, Dharmshala, Swami Vivekananda Study Centre, University College of Business Studies, Shimla, Agro-Economics Research Centre, University Institute of Information and Technology, Integrated Institute of Himalayan Studies, International Centre for Distance Education and Open Learning, Tribal Research Institute, and Population Research Centre. Professional Colleges affiliated to the University include IIIT College of Engineering, Kala Amb, IGMC, Shimla, Government Dental College and Hospital, Shimla, Himachal Dental College and Hospital, Sunder Nagar, Dr. Rajinder Prasad Government Medical College, Tanda, Kangra, MN DAV Dental College, Solan, Bhojia Dental College and Hospital, Budh. 25 Government colleges and 26 private colleges are affiliated to the University. Government College of Teacher Education, Dharmshala, National Institute of Education, Solan, and a private Colleges of Education at Nalagarh, Solan, is also affiliated to the University. Three Government Sanskrit Colleges at Nahan, Kiartoo (Shimla District), and Phagli (Shimla District) are also affiliated to the University.

University Grants Commission has granted the status of a Special Assistance Department to the following Departments: (i) History, (ii) Physics, and (iii) Chemistry. The research scheme in the Department of History has started from 22nd February, 2003 for the duration of five years in the first instance. The thrust area of the research scheme is "Cultural and Environmental History of Himachal Pradesh". Department of Physics is being helped under FIST (Fund for Improving Infrastructure in Science and Technology).

UNIVERSITY COLLEGE OF BUSINESS STUDIES, SHIMLA

University College of Business Studies has been set-up for BBA and BCA students. It is headed by a Director of the rank of a Professor. About 170 students are studying in the College which is located at the distance of about two km from the University campus.

HPU CENTRE FOR EVENING STUDIES

Established in 1962 by the Panjab University, the HPU Evening College caters to a varied class of students. When the HP University came up in 1970, the Evening College became its integral part. This institution is now known as the Himachal University Centre for Evening Studies. It is an undergraduate as well as postgraduate College. In the PG Section, classes for English, Hindi, Economics and M.Com. are conducted. There is an overall strength of about 1000 students in the Centre. Paucity of space is definitely a drawback but this is surely overshadowed by the excellent location of the campus which is in the heart of the town in a prime location. The faculty consists of 29 teachers with a principal, 2 professors, 13 readers, 6 selection grade lecturers, 3 senior grade lecturers and 4 lecturers. Library has got 30,000 books. There is an Assistant Librarian one Senior Professional Assistant and two library attendants for its management. The Centre publishes its annual magazine, the Evening Glory.

REGIONAL CENTRE, DHARMSHALA

Himachal Pradesh University Regional Centre was set-up on the 17th August, 1992 at Dharmshala to cater to the needs of the region. Himachal Pradesh constitutes a wide variety of geographical area from Shiwalik Hills to mid-Himalaya and high Himalaya. H.P. University with its campus only at Shimla is not accessible to the students of far flung areas especially that of the tribal areas of Lahul-Spiti, Pangi, Bharmour, etc. In order to give benefits of education to the students from Kangra, Hamirpur, Una, Chamba, Lahul-Spiti and Mandi, the H.P.

University set-up its Regional Centre at Dharmshala which is a centrally located place to cater to the educational aspirations of the above mentioned districts and areas of the Pradesh. At present, 614 students (314 boys and 300 girls) are receiving education in the Centre.

The Regional Centre has got nine postgraduate departments: Commerce, Economics, English, Geology, Hindi, Laws, Mathematics, Political Science and Public Administration. The Centre is headed by Director. There is one regular lecturer in Public Administration and four in Laws. For the rest of the teachers, the Centre has to hire the services of the teachers on contract basis and also those of the teachers from the local Government Degree College on lecture basis. The Centre has got a skeleton staff, one Assistant, one senior clerk, three clerks, one Security Guard, one Semi-Professional Assistant, one Junior Library Attendant, one Laboratory Attendant, two peons, one *chowkidar* and one sweeper. The post of a Section Officer and some other posts have been lying vacant since long. The Centre has no building of its own and is housed on borrowed buildings from the local college.

AGRO-ECONOMIC RESEARCH CENTRE

Agro-Economic Research Centre (AERC) at the Himachal Pradesh University was established in December 1972 by the Ministry of Agriculture, Government of India to carry out research and investigations in the field of Agricultural Economics in Western Himalayan Region consisting of Himachal Pradesh and Jammu and Kashmir. This is one of the 12 centres established by the Government of India.

The AER Centre, Shimla is maintained by the H.P. University and governed by the rules and regulations of the H.P. University, Shimla. The AERC has a faculty of nine persons engaged in research work. AERC has expertise in impact evaluation and economic feasibility studies for Agriculture, Horticulture, Animal Husbandry, Forestry and Rural Development-related activities. Besides studies assigned by Government of India, the AERC has conducted studies sponsored by the State Government Departments of Agriculture, Horticulture, Animal Husbandry, Forests, Rural

Development and Tribal Development. The impact evaluation and economic feasibility studies for World Bank, GTZ, USAID, ICIMOD, CIP, and NJPC have also been carried out by the AERC. Nearly 3000 farmers have been provided training on various aspects of commercial farming.

UNIVERSITY INSTITUTE OF INFORMATION AND TECHNOLOGY (UIIT)

UIIT was set-up in June, 2000 in order to impart training to the students in the state-of-art Information Technology. It is headed by a Director of the rank of a Professor of the University. A System Administrator also works in the UIIT to assist the Director. UIIT imparts instructions for Integrated Programme of Master of Technology in Information Technology (M.Tech.) and Bachelor of Technology in Information Technology (B.Tech). The duration of Integrated Programme of Master of Technology in Information Technology is five and a half years spread over 11 Semesters and that of Bachelor of Technology in Information Technology is of four years spread over 8 Semesters on full time basis.

The Institute has acquired a good collection of books related to Information Technology and allied areas. It has about a thousand books. A good reading space has been provided for the students. Library also subscribes to about 20 computer magazines/journals besides daily news papers. To provide a rich hands-on experience to the students a state of the art computer laboratory worth about 50 lakh rupees has been created. The hardware and software meet all the needs of the courses of the students. All the students of the UIIT got job placements in prestigious companies working in places like Noida, Parwanu.

INTEGRATED INSTITUTE OF HIMALAYAN STUDIES (IIHS)

IIHS, UGC Center for Excellence, was set-up in the University on 1st April, 2002. UGC made this selection on an all India competition basis under the UGC scheme of 'Identifying Universities with Potential for Excellence'. This autonomous center for excellence was given to the Himachal Pradesh University on the basis of its strength—teachers/researchers, courses being taught in the university, institutional network/ support system, advantage of locale and need of the State.

The mission of the IIHS is to create an integrated knowledge base and evolve strategies for the development of the Himalayan region and its people through research, academic courses, and service with a global perspective. Some of its achievements deserve mention here. The institute has prepared a bibliography of 4000 books published on the Himalaya. The institute has also completed an annotated bibliographic database on the Himalaya wherein compilation of over 4500 entries of books in English and 600 books in Hindi, 6000 research papers and 200 project reports are included. IIHS has completed about two dozen major and minor research projects, and organized a dozen expert lectures, seminars/workshops/ training programmes.

INTERNATIONAL CENTRE FOR DISTANCE EDUCATION AND OPEN LEARNING (ICDEOL)

ICDEOL was established in July 1971. Since then, it has been catering to the needs and aspirations of those who could not find opportunity to join institutions of formal education as whole time campus students. The University has played a pioneering role in launching the programme of distant education at postgraduate level. It was the first to impart instruction at postgraduate level in Social Sciences, Humanities, Commerce and teacher training through the mode of distance education over the years.

It is headed by a Director of the rank of a Professor and has got 37 teachers to look after various subjects. About 40,000 students are enrolled with the ICDEOL. It offers facilities for various undergraduate and postgraduate courses, i.e., B.A., B.Com., B.Ed., M.A. (English, Hindi, Sanskrit, History, Political Science, Public Administration, Economics, and Mathematics), M.Com., M.Ed., PDDPM & LW, PGDCA, MMC, PGDIT, MJMC, and M.Phil. Print material is the dominant mode of instruction through distance education. This material has been developed by the experts in the relevant areas. It is revised at regular intervals as per needs of the students. ICDEOL also conducts personal contact programmes of about one week duration in all the subjects where classroom teaching is done to clarify the topics which are not clear to the students by the written material supplied to them. The performance of the students has been quite impressive. They have topped the University examinations many a time. Some of the students have got selection in the civil services in the State. ICDEOL has got a library of its own to cater to the needs of its teachers and students. It has also got a hostel. It has an Information-*cum*-Guidance Office in New Delhi to ensure regular interaction with the students. It has been arranging for spot admission throughout Himachal Pradesh and many other parts of the country.

POPULATION RESEARCH CENTRE (PRC)

PRC was established by the Ministry of Health & Family Welfare, Government of India, New Delhi in 1989 at Himachal Pradesh University, Shimla for the study of population, health and social-welfare related issues in economic development of Himachal Pradesh. It is also coordinating the Post-Graduate Diploma in Women's Development Studies, a full time course programme of one-year (two semesters) duration consisting of four courses (five theory papers and one applied Project Report).

PRC has a team of 7 permanent researchers and four supporting staff consisting of Honorary Director, Deputy Director, Assistant Director, and four Research/Field Investigators. PRC has completed forty-six research studies since it came into existence during the year 1989.

BIOINFORMATICS CENTRE

This Centre was established in 1999 with the support of Government of India, Ministry of Science and Technology, Department of Biotechnology (DBT), New Delhi. The Centre provides support to teaching and academic activities in biotechnology and modern biology. It also organizes training/workshops to enhance skills of master degree students, research scholars, teaching faculty and research scientists in bioinformatics and computational biology. The Centre is involved in development of databases on bio-resources, traditional fermented foods and industrial enzymes. Its focus is also on finding structure and functional relationship of proteins with emphasis on nitride degrading enzymes. The Centre has trained about 150 professionals from various institutions, universities and organizations on various aspects of Bioinformatics, e.g., Sequence Analysis, Structure prediction, Biological data mining, Genomics, Structural and Computational Biology, and Drug Designing. The Centre has also trained more than 150 students and researchers of biological sciences and biotechnology in this region in basic tools and techniques of the bioinformatics.

SWAMI VIVEKANANDA STUDY CENTRE

Swami Vivekananda Study Centre was set-up in the University in February, 2002 with the financial assistance from the UGC with the aim of pursuing studies related to the thoughts and vision of Swami Vivekananda. The Centre is headed by a Professor of the University. It conducts seminars on the thoughts and visions of Swami Vivekananda.

CENTRE FOR CANADIAN STUDIES

This Centre has been set-up to promote understanding between India and Canada. The Centre has been actively organizing seminars to achieve this purpose. It organized a National Seminar on Women, Law and Social Change from March 30 to April 1, 2005 in the campus.

INFRASTRUCTURE AND ALLIED ACADEMIC ACTIVITIES

The Central Library

The library is housed in a multi-storeyed building designed to house the functions of a modern university library. It has a collection of 1,97,470 books as on 31-3-2005. The library subscribes to 117 foreign journals and 247 Indian journals. The library functions for 12 hours on working days and for 7 hours on holidays. A separate Himalayan Studies Section has also been set-up in the HPU Library. The library has got three photo copier machines installed in by a private firm to give better and efficient Xeroxing facility to the readers on nominal charges. Computerisation of the library services is in progress. Database of books in English language and all theses/dissertations/ project reports is complete. Facility of e-journals in Physical Sciences, Mathematics, Social Sciences and Humanities under UGC-Infonet programme through INFLIBNET, Ahmedabad is available in the Cyber Centre of the library. Users can assess full text of the journals in the Centre.

In addition to the Central Library, there are other libraries also. ICDEOL, Academic Staff College, Departments like Law, Public Administration, Political Science have their own libraries. Department of Public Administration has got Dr. PPS Gill Memorial Library developed by the books donated by the teachers and students of the Department and also collected from the personal collections of the deceased teacher of the Department Dr. PPS Gill in whose memory the library has been set-up.

Hostels

Himachal Pradesh University has twelve hostels, seven for boys and five for girls. These provide accommodation to about 700 boys and 480 girls. In all hostels, there are facilities of Common Room, T.V., Reading Room, Indoor games and Geysers. Each hostel has its own mess which is run on co-operative basis by the boarders. There is a Student Prefect for every fifty residents and a Common Room Secretary from each hostel to manage the common room. All hostel affairs are managed by a committee consisting of the Chief Warden, Wardens and Students' representatives.

University Health Centre

The University Health Centre, housed in a spacious building in the heart of the campus, is providing round the clock medical facilities to the students, teachers, employees and their dependants. This Centre has two medical officers, three paramedical personnel, a staff nurse, a laboratory technician and a dresser. Timings of the OPD during summer are 09.30 am to 12.30 pm and 2.00 pm to 5.30 pm and during winter 10.00 am to 01.00 pm and 3.00 pm to 5.00 pm. Even during Sundays and other holidays, it is open from 10.00 am to 12.30 pm. After 5.30 pm, a Medical Officer is available on call till 9.30 am next morning to provide medical aid in the Health Centre. Serious cases are sent to the nearby hospitals (10 km away from the University Campus) by University Ambulances which are available round the clock. Ambulance facilities are available on reasonable rates. Even patients from nearby villages are attended to and given medical aid.

There is also a clinical laboratory for routine tests like urine analysis- estimation of Albumin, sugar microscopic analysis and liver function tests detectable in urine. Examination of peripheral block count including ESR and bleeding time and clotting time are also carried out. Even blood sugar is done by Glucometer. ECG machine is also available for emergency cases.

Employment Information and Guidance Bureau

The Bureau registers graduates and all the students holding master's degree for employment assistance. It provides information on various occupations, training, admissions, competitive examinations, fellowship and financial assistance. It provides information about various courses of studies, syllabi with respect to higher studies in India and abroad. It also helps students in their educational and vocational planning.

Students' Placements

HPU has a placement cell headed by a Professor of the University. Institute of Management Studies, Departments of MTA, Physics, and Chemistry have got a good number of placements of their students. MTA Department invited various tourism organizations like Oberoi Group of Hotels, TCI, Holiday Makers, ORBIT Tours, Indo Asia, Cox & Kings, etc. for the campus interviews. Out of 20 students, 15 got jobs in these organizations. Many students of 2004-06 batch studying for MBA got jobs even before the declaration of their results.

Pre-Examination Coaching Centre

Pre-Examination Coaching Centre was set-up in January, 1998. The Centre prepares the students belonging to the Scheduled Castes/Scheduled Tribes/Other Backward Classes of Himachal Pradesh for various competitive examinations, viz., Central Civil Services, Himachal Pradesh Administrative Service, allied services, Banking Services, Pre-Medical and Pre-Engineering Tests. The sole objective of the Pre-Examination Coaching Centre is to help the deprived classes of society by improving their skills and capacities as also ensuring their rapid economic development and integration in the mainstream. However, under the latest scheme of Government of India, Ministry of Social Justice and Empowerment, New Delhi, the Centre has also introduced coaching courses for three month duration for NET/SET examinations.

The Centre is situated in the University Campus. The students pursuing higher studies can easily approach this Centre and can avail of the facility of various coaching programmes in addition to their regular studies in the University. The Centre is headed by a Director of the University who handles this job in addition to his normal teaching duties as a Professor in his own Department in the University. The Centre has built up a kit of hardware, including a computer, a Xerox Photo- Copier, etc. The Centre has a library with about 5,000 books on different subjects, mainly focusing on different competitive examinations.

Computer Centre

Computer Centre in the Himachal Pradesh University was established in 1986 with initial financial support of the University Grants Commission. It is equipped with latest hardware like Compaq Servers and Pentium-based nodes and latest software. It offers computing facilities to students of department of computer science as well as to students of other departments. It provides consultancy to various departments as and when required.

The Computer Centre developed various programs in FORTRAN as per the data analysis requirements of the research scholars. The Computer Centre has been, ever since its inception, helping the Accounts Branch of the University in the payroll processing. It has helped the Budget Branch in preparing consolidated annual reports and expense forecasting. The Computer Centre is actively involved in providing technical help to the University Library in the implementation of the INFLIBNET Programme. Besides this, it has been helping various sections of the University like the recruitment branch, the acquisition branch of the library, the library of the Academic Staff College, etc. in their software requirements of system developments.

UGC Academic Staff College

UGC Academic Staff College (ASC) of Himachal Pradesh University came into existence in June 1989. The ASC conducts following types of programmes: Orientation, refresher courses, programmes for principals, induction, short-term and special lectures. Ford Foundation selected this ASC for implementing a Campus Diversity Initiative Project. Under this project, the ASC has developed and implemented training modules with the aim of sensitizing teachers to diversity concerns, and equipping them with the teaching skills and discussing diversity issues in the classroom and through workshops, seminars and symposia. Feedback reveals the fact that the ASC successfully brought about change in the outlook and attitudes of teachers engaged in higher education. During previous three years it has conducted 22 workshops, one seminar, one symposium and two training programmes.

ASC has its own web site; ascshimla.org which contains variety of information including some useful resource material for reading. Main techniques used during the different programmes include lecturing, breaking the ice, teaching game, self-introspection, brain-storming, brain-trust, role playing, panel discussion, group discussion, SWOT analysis, fish fowl, work shop, quiz, debate, multi-evaluation, sensitivity training, active learning, etc. The participants of each programme are supplied with adequate and quality reading material in addition to the input provided to them during different formal and informal sessions. ASC has developed a package of reading material for the participants of orientation programmes. In this package, articles written by experienced educationists have been included keeping in mind the coverage of all components.

The ASC has an impressive infrastructure including two conference rooms, a library room, a computer room, and equipment room and adequate office complex. The ASC has built up a small but useful library for the use of the participants. It has 300 volumes and subscribes to 24 periodicals. The ASC utilises modern educational gadgets such as LCD (Video Projector), internet facilities, audio-visual facilities, conference system, tape recorder, OHPs, slide projector, computers, etc.

COMMUNITY OUTREACH

H.P. University has set-up following orgaisations to establish relationship with the community:

Public Relations Office

The University has a Public Relation Office especially to share information with the public. The flow of information from various sections, branches, departments, institutions, etc. of the University is mainly in the shape of advertisements, press notes-releases and developmental features and articles. This office maintains a liaison with the higher authorities about various activities and achievements of the University at the main campus. This office works towards projecting and promoting University's image and achievements in the media. The department compiles and collates clippings related to the University on educational field.

The annual reports to be put before various authorities of the University are also prepared by this office. Department also publishes a newsletter "Campus Vibes". Souvenirs are printed by this office on different occasions. The Public Relations Officer has come from the mainstream of journalism and professionally looks after the entire department. He is assisted by an Information Assistant, Junior Assistant, Professional Proof Reader and Photographer.

Adult Education Centre

Full name of the Centre is Centre for Adult, Continuing Education and Extension. This Centre was set-up in the year

1979. The Centre has a Director who is assisted by two Assistant Directors. The Centre implemented various programmes like Adult Literacy, Population Education, Mass Programme for Functional Literacy, Total Literacy Programme, etc.

Some of the activities of the Centre deserve mention here. A 15 day course on Beauty Treatment was organized in April, 2005 in the University for hostel-girls. A 15 day crash course in English speaking organized during April-May, 2005 in the University for hostel-girls. Ministry of Human Resource Development has nominated Himachal Pradesh University as Monitoring Agency for Sarva Shiksha Abhiyan of the State of Himachal Pradesh. Under this assignment, the Monitoring Team of the Centre visited Lahul & Spiti, Shimla, and Bilaspur districts for the supervision and monitoring. A training programme for the newly promoted Grade C non-teaching employees of the University was organized in the campus during June 16-21, 2005 in collaboration with Academic Staff College of the University. The objective of the programme was to improve efficiency and to provide the knowledge of various rules and regulations of the University. The Centre imparted one month training to the students of Master's degree in Rural Development and Management, MJP Rohailkhand University, Bareilly (UP) during June 7–July 7, 2005. Two groups of students were formed. One group studied the functioning and activities of Nari Niketan, School for Handicapped Children, Balika Ashram, Anganwaris in district Shimla and the other group studied the functioning and activities of HPMC.

The Centre organized a training programme in Organic Farming for the members of the Neem Panchayat in the Basantpur Block of Shimla District. This training was imparted with the help of National Consultant on Organic Farming. On the demand of the people of the Neem Panchayat, the Centre is running a Weaving Centre in collaboration with Khadi Village and Industry Commission (KVIC), Government of India. The Centre is working as a catalytic agent. The Centre did a very useful work by organizing a Two Day Workshop on Enhancing Youth Employability in Himachal Pradesh: University-Industry Partnership during 8-9 December, 2005 in the University Campus. The Workshop was organized with the active collaboration of the Confederation of Indian Industry, H.P.

Council. Participants represented the Engineering Colleges, Institutes of Technology, Industrial Training Institutes, Polytechnics, Colleges, and Universities. The Workshop prepared an action plan called Himachal Pradesh Youth Employability Plan. The main objective of the action plan is to prepare Himachali youth to actively participate in the industrial development process in the State.

ADMINISTRATION

Top hierarchy of the University consists of the following officers: Chancellor who is always the Governor of the State, Vice-Chancellor, Pro-Vice-Chancellor, Registrar, Controller of Examination, fifteen Deans, viz., Dean of Studies, Students' Welfare, Faculty of Education, Faculty of Commerce and Management Studies, Faculty of Languages, Faculty of Social Sciences, Faculty of Life Sciences, Faculty of Physical Sciences, Faculty of Performing and Visual Arts, Faculty of Dental Sciences, Faculty of Law, Faculty of Ayurveda, Faculty of Medical Sciences, Faculty of Engineering and Technology, and College Development Council. Other officers of the University are Finance Officer, Planning and Development Officer, Librarian, Executive Engineer, and Medical Officer. In addition to it, University is run by various bodies like University Court, Executive Council, Academic Council, Finance Committee, etc.

Accounts of the University are pre-audited by an officer of the H.P. Government Local Audit Department (LAD) of the rank of Joint/Deputy Controller Finance. The University has also got a system of Internal Audit by the officials of the University itself. The office of the Dean Students' Welfare carries out activities pertaining to the general welfare of the students. Its main aims and objectives are to provide all facilities that are necessary for the overall development and general welfare of the students such as admission of students under cultural quota to various courses, organizing co-curricular and cultural activities, providing and managing travel concessions for students to go on educational tours, and to participate in cultural and sports events within and outside the state.

Audit System

HPU has got four systems of audit. Firstly, Internal Audit, secondly, CAGI Audit, thirdly, LAD Audit, and fourthly, Special Audit. To these four systems has been added another system of audit which can be named as a different version of Internal Audit, i.e., audit by two Accounts Branches—Accounts-I and Accounts-II. Every bill has to be processed and got cleared through either of these branches depending upon the areas allotted to them. Internal Audit is done by the non-teaching employees of the Internal Audit Section of the University who have been given this task after a long battle between the non-teaching employees of the University and the officials of Local Area Department (LAD). Since the inception of the University, accounts of the University are being audited by the Comptroller and Auditor General, Government of India (CAGI). Audit of the accounts has to be done the CAGI, in as much as according to the Section 14 and 15 of the Comptroller and Auditor General Act, 1971, the Boards and Corporations getting more than 75% grant-in-aid from a State Government have to get their accounts audited by the CAGI. However, after the increase of the amount of grants, a system of 100% pre-audit by the Local Audit Department (LAD) of the Government was added on 1st April, 1981. This way, now the University has got double external audit system, 100% pre-audit by the LAD and some sample or special audit by AG.

Examination System

H.P. University has got semester system of examination, having two examinations in a year, first from the last week of November to first week of January and the second from last week of May to the first week of July. Examination branch remains busy throughout the year. Both paper-setting and marking is done by the external examiners, i.e. experts from other universities. Results are declared regularly by the examination branch. For entrance tests, objective type tests of four options are given. For other examinations, subjective type questions are set. Examination work is looked after by Controller of Examinations.

Teachers and their Associations

At present there are two teachers' associations in HPU. First is Himachal Pradesh University Teachers' Association (HPUTA) and the second is Himachal University Teachers' Association (HUTA). HUTA is a breakaway group consisting mainly of the pro-BJP Teachers. It was formed on March 22, 2005 because of the differences on the issue of termination of the services of three teachers. (This has been discussed in detail in the chapter relating to case studies.) Teachers are further divided on the basis of different party cells. There are cells of BJP, Congress and CPM parties in the University. Naturally, thinking and activities of the teachers are influenced by the party ideologies.

Non-Teaching Employees and their Associations

There is a statutory association of all the non-teaching staff known as HPU Non-Teaching Staff Association. Annual election to this association is fought on party lines. Then the non-teaching staff has other associations like the officers' association, class four employees' association, technical staff association, etc. looking after the interests of their particular groups. These associations also maintain their relations with different political parties.

Students and their Associations

There are about 2500 students in the University. Admission process to the new classes starts in the month of May and is completed by the end of July every year. The students have an elected body called Students' Central Association (SCA) to look after the interests of the students. Elections of the SCA are generally held in the month of August every year. These elections are keenly contested on party lines. In the alphabetical order, these are Akhil Bhartiya Vidyarthi Parishad (ABVP), National Students' Union of India (NSUI), and Students' Federation of India (SFI). The students belonging to above organisations publish their manifestoes, put huge banners in the campus, paste and hung posters in the campus, exhibit their badges on their shirts, hold public meetings, contact the students and adopt every possible means to canvass for the success of their respective candidates. On the day of election the whole campus bears a festive look. SFI has been dominating the scene for more than a decade by winning most of the seats in the university elections.

THE UNIVERSITY OF JAMMU

INTRODUCTION

The University of Jammu came into existence in 1969 vide Kashmir and Jammu Universities Act, 1969 following bifurcation of the erstwhile University of Jammu and Kashmir. It is primarily a research, teaching, affiliating and examining body involved in the promotion of arts, sciences and other branches of learning. Like all other universities of the country, it is also open to all classes and creeds with the sole objective to carry people from darkness to light. This University has been accredited as Four Star University by National Assessment and Accreditation Council of India.

The beautiful campus of the University of Jammu is located in the City of Temples—Jammu-Tawi. It has two campuses—New Campus at Bahu Wali Rakh, with an area of about 118-70 acres and another small old campus at canal road, having an area of about 10.5 acres. The New Campus is well laid and is well earmarked for different activities. It has residential accommodation for all types of University employees. The teaching departments are located in the main campus. There is a central library, an auditorium, canteens, a kiosk for photocopying, STD/ISD facilities and other stationery items. In the campus, there is a bookshop, a bank and a post office. There are canteens for refreshment at suitable places. For guests there is a well-maintained Guest House within the campus. A sports complex and grounds for different games and activities, constitute another important feature of the New Campus. A botanical and a cactus garden have since become star attraction on the campus. The University Executive Engineer and his establishment look after the construction and maintenance of the roads and buildings. There is a medical centre with outdoor services under the overall supervision of CMO.

Among the six universities in Jammu & Kashmir, the University of Jammu has emerged as the flagship of not only higher education, but also extracurricular activities. In 2005 it was certified as the first ISO campus in the country. At the international level, the university created a virtual classroom in collaboration with the University of North Carolina, USA, and also entered into a MoU with the British Council for setting up of the International Resource Cell. It became one of the 16 universities identified for promotion of Indian higher education abroad under the PIHEAD programme of UGC.

The vision document of the University envisages the creation of an institution that will compete with the best, nationally as well as globally. To gear up this challenge, the University of Jammu has empowered itself technologically by acquiring VSAT connectivity (128 kbps Bandwidth) from ERNET India.

Following beautifully written play-card has been put on the walls at many important points in the buildings as well as on the tables of all the high officials:

Quality Policy

To continually upgrade systems and process of admissions, teaching learning, examination, evaluation, research and extension in order to become globally recognized institution of academic excellence.

Dated April 28, 2004
Place : Jammu-Tawi

Sd-
AMITABH MATTU
Vice-Chancellor
University of Jammu
Jammu

ACADEMIC DISCIPLINES

In 1969, at the time of its inception, the University had eleven teaching departments at Post-graduate level. At present there are thirty-three teaching departments offering Master's degree, M.Phil. Ph.D. and D.Lit. in different disciplines, besides LL.B, B.Lib. and some diploma courses. The courses like Master's degree programme in Business Administration, Tourism Management, Computer Applications, Environmental Sciences, Electronics, Bio-Technology, Sociology, Psychology, Physical Education and Strategic and Regional Studies are, available in the University. Teaching at under-graduate level is imparted in affiliated colleges/institutions. There are B.Ed. Colleges, Medical Colleges, Engineering & Technology Colleges, Ayurvedic College, Institute of Music and Fine Arts, Oriental Institution besides colleges for Arts, Commerce and Science subjects. To provide education at the doorsteps of the learners, University of Jammu has a Directorate of Distance Education offering various professional and non-professional courses at under-graduate and post-graduate level. Centre of Adult, Continuing Education and Extension offers short-term job-oriented and professional courses. It conducts Adult Education programmes and Extension services, it besides provides special coaching for various competitive examinations to deprived sections of society and also to others. Guidance, Counseling and Employment Bureau and a Yoga Centre are also functioning in the University.

PHYSICAL EDUCATION

The Directorate of Physical Education conducts inter-collegiate Tournaments and also projects the teams to participate in Inter-University (Men and Women) Tournaments.

POST GRADUATION PROGRAMMES OF KASHMIR UNIVERSITY

An office of the Coordinator Post-graduate Programme of Kashmir University was set-up during 1991-92 at the University of Jammu for running the Post-graduate Programme of Kashmir University for migrant students in M.A., M.Sc., M.Com., LL.B. and B.Lib. courses. These courses are being managed through the teaching faculty and the available infrastructure in the University of Jammu. However, the State Government has made provision of special grants to meet the additional needs such as, library, laboratories and honorarium to be paid to the concerned teachers. This Programme takes care of the admissions of migrant students through entrance test, their enrolments in the departments, monitoring of courses, conduct of their examination, etc. Wherever required study tours and field tours are supported through this programme. Presently 18 classes of the post-graduate courses are running in the teaching departments of the University of Jammu which are as per Kashmir University Schedule/Syllabi.

CENTRE FOR STRATEGIC AND REGIONAL STUDIES (CSRS)

CSRS at the University of Jammu has been conceived and established keeping in view the fast changing and integrated security matrix-involving both internal and external facets-societal well-being, stability and socio-economic development of the region. The Centre aims to undertake focused and policy-oriented research on strategic issues, national security and regional strategic/security developments.

CENTRE FOR QUALITY ASSURANCE

The centre is a nodal agency for ushering in the era of total quality management by working out intervention strategies to enhance the quality in the institution in totality. The centre works for assuring all the stakeholders—students, parents, teachers, staff, funding agencies and society in general—of the accountability of institutions for their own quality and probity.

CENTRE FOR NEW LITERATURES

To improve chances of job placement for the students, short and long-term courses on Canadian, African, Australian and Caribbean Literature have been organised from time to time. Since the inception of the Department, 17 scholars have got themselves registered for Ph.D. in various topics in the field of New Literatures.

YOGA CENTRE

Yoga Centre was established in the University of Jammu on December 15, 1998. Yoga Centre has been offering various courses and a large number of persons including University teachers, students, scholars, citizens and professionals have successfully undergone these courses.

REGIONAL CENTRE FOR FIELD OPERATIONS AND RESEARCH ON HIMALAYAN GLACIOLOGY (RCFOR-HG)

The University of Jammu, realizing the all-encompassing importance of glacier studies in the development of the State, set-up a Regional Centre for Field Operations and Research on Himalayan Glaciology (RCFOR-HG) in the University of Jammu, Jammu on 29-7-2005. The RCFOR-HG is directing its efforts in Glaciological Research in J&K State in a more focused and purposeful manner. The Jammu Himalaya has a common ice fence with the glaciers in Zanskar Ranges (Ladakh) as well as with the glaciers in Kashmir Himalaya and Himachal Himalaya through Jhelum-Chenab ice fields. As such, setting up of the Centre (RCFOR-HG) in Jammu University sounds logical and more meaningful as it would cater to the glaciological research in Kashmir, Ladakh, Jammu and Himachal Pradesh.

DIRECTORATE OF DISTANCE EDUCATION

Motivated by the desire to provide education at the doorsteps of the learners, University of Jammu established the Directorate of Distance Education, (then known as Institute of Correspondence Education) in March 1976. The DDE is offering a number of post-graduate and under-graduate courses. Besides traditional courses, it is imparting professional courses such as Master of Education, Bachelor of Education and Post-graduate Diploma in Business Administration. In the current session, it has launched Post-graduate course in Fisheries. This is a job-oriented course, the first of its kind through distance mode of education in the country. Currently, the DDE has study centres one each in government degree colleges—Kathua, Poonch, Rajouri, Bhaderwah, Kishtwar and Doda. By these centres, the

DDE has truly brought the facility of higher education to the doorsteps of the distance learners of the remote rural, backward and inaccessible hilly areas of the Jammu region.

The Teaching Faculty

The teaching faculty in the University consists of scholars of national repute and international eminence. Many of them have received national and international recognition, honours and awards. They represent all parts of India and have regular interaction with institutions of higher learning, the world over. Many of them have foreign assignments in various prestigious institutes.

Centres of Excellence

The University has Centres of Excellence supported by national and international agencies and these can be cited as:

- High Energy Physics,
- Special Assistance Programme (SAP) in Political Science, and
- FIST Programme in Botany, Physics and Chemistry and Geology.

INFRASTRUCTURE AND ALLIED ACADEMIC ACTIVITIES

The Central Library

The Central Library of the University is the hub of academic activities where students sit from morning till evening everyday throughout the year. Its four storey building has spacious reading halls and compact stack areas. The Library has a collection of nearly 3.5 lakh volumes, rare as well as latest, and 250 current periodicals with back numbers. The Library possesses facilities like photocopiers, LCD projectors, INFLIBNET, CD-ROM databases and inter-connected computer terminals at selected sites. The specialized Jammu and Kashmir section is also there. In addition, the Library is linked to and supported by Departmental Libraries, Evening Study Centre and Directorate of Distance Education Library. The University

Library is centrally located and constructed on modular plan. It has a total area of about 9,300 square feet which includes a stack area of about 36,000 square feet. The Library has three main reading halls and additional reading areas in the Textbook section, Periodical section, Jammu and Kashmir section, Reference section, Private books reading hall, besides a reading space for newspapers near the exhibition area. These areas provide reading facilities for about 500 readers.

University Hostels

The University of Jammu has set up five hostels, out of which three are for boys and two for girls. Almost all the hostels are situated on the campus itself and within walk-able distance from teaching Departments/Central Library/Administration Block/Post Office/P.C.O./Dispensary/Cafeteria, etc.

The Hostels are neat, clean and possess all kinds of amenities for making the living of boarders recreational and enjoyable. The room of each hostel is well ventilated and airy. Few rooms in each hostel have single seated capacity and majority is double seated. Each hostel has a very big lush green sprawling lawn in front and in backyard. Each hostel has facilities like telephone, sports (T.T./Badminton/Chess etc) drinking water fitted with aqua-guard, refrigerators, water coolers, television, modern cooking gas plant, geysers, and economical and affordable mess charges. Inverters are fitted for acting as standby light arrangement in case of power-failure. Good reading rooms with latest career and information promoting magazines, local/national papers subscribed, well furnished guest room and desired first aid is also available in each Hostel.

The Doctor resides on the Campus and is available on call. The transport facility is available in each hostel for taking the students to the Hospital, if need be. The supporting staff is made available to each hostel. The day to day activities of the hostel are run by different committees of the Boarders. The University has set up kiosks near each hostel having the facility of PCO, Fax and stationery items. The University/Hostels have matador/Mini-Bus facility at a stone's throw distance from each hostel for visiting any part of the city. The Bus Stand, Railway Station and Airport are connected with public transport from each hostel of the University. The affairs of the hostels are managed by Wardens. All hostels are under the overall supervision of Provost.

University Health Centre

The Medical Aid Facilities are provided to the students, both boarders and day scholars, employees and their dependants of the University in the University Health Centre, under the supervision of Chief Medical Officer and Doctor. In addition to the above mentioned two doctors, the University Health Centre has got two pharmacists, one sanitary inspector, one laboratory technician, one senior assistant, two nursing orderlies, one driver, two peons, and 53 *safaiwalas*. Facilities like clinical laboratory and E.C.G. and Ambulance service, are also available. The health Centre is providing O.P.D and other health-related services to approximately 15,000 patients per annum.

Computer Centre

Way back in 1978 University of Jammu established a Computer Centre. A full-fledged independent Department of Computer Science came into existence in 1987 when PGDCA programme was started. In 1995, Department started MCA three year course. The Department has computer laboratories, Internet Access and E-mail. This computer centre also provides IT facilities to support teaching, learning, research and administrative activities of the University.

Placement Efforts

ADLABS, A part of Reliance Group has conducted the first round of interviews in campus and 9 students were selected. GENPACT, A GE ASSOCIATE, conducted campus interview. One student was selected and five students of M.Com. and MBA were short listed. ICICI Prudential for its office in Jammu has also offered summer projects for graduates and post graduates. The university initiated summer placement programme in collaboration with Centre for Civil Society, New Delhi.

THE WOMEN'S STUDIES AND RESEARCH CENTRE

The Centre conducted various studies on the topics like maternal health and female's literacy in J&K state, crime against women in Jammu region, perception regarding gender issues, action-oriented research to organize awareness building programmes for rural women, etc. The Centre organized a training of trainers programme entitled, "Capacity Building Programme for Women Managers in Higher Education," in which women managers from universities of north India participated. The Centre also organized two entrepreneurship development programmes for rural women empowerment. Counselling and training was also provided to women in vulnerable situations. Migrant women and destitute staying in different organizations were provided counselling and training through these programmes. The Centre also participated in a national level research study lead by Delhi University entitled "Attitudinal change toward girl child in the northern states of India".

COMMUNITY OUTREACH

University of Jammu has following organizations to have contacts with the community:

Centre of Adult, Continuing Education and Extension

This Centre is headed by a Director who is assisted by five faculty members. The Centre arranges following programmes on self-supporting basis:

1. One year Diploma in Computer Application
2. P.G. Diploma Course in Office Management
3. Basic Course in French Language
4. Advance Course in French Language
5. Basic Course in Functional Urdu
6. Basic Course in Functional English
7. Basic Course in Craft and Designs

The Centre has been very active through its various activities comprising of five units, i.e. Adult Education,

Continuing Education, Minority Coaching, Population Education Resource Centre and Employment Information-*cum*-Advisory Bureau.

CENTRE FOR HISTORY AND CULTURE OF JAMMU AND LADAKH REGIONS

This Centre, established in 1994-95, is focusing its special attention on the neglected but highly important aspects of the history and culture of all the areas of J&K, and also to reconcile the history of Jammu and Ladakh with the history of Kashmir.

University of Jammu does not have Administrative Staff College and Evening Study Centre. A few departments like Computer Science, Library Science, and Business and Management have study centres for IGNOU and run classes in the evening.

UNIVERSITY ADMINISTRATION

Governor of J&K is the Chancellor of the University of Jammu. Universities in the State of J&K have a unique system of Pro-Chancellor who is always the Chief Minister of the State. So the Chief Minister of J&K is the Pro-Chancellor of the University of Jammu.

The University administration is hosted in two separate wings, i.e. Administrative Wing and Examination Wing. General Administration, is looked after by the Registrar and the Examination Section by the Controller of Examinations who work directly under the direction of the Vice-Chancellor. Director, College Development, looks after the affiliation of Colleges and other development aspects such as the UGC Grants, teachers' training and affiliation for new courses. Registrar is helped by Joint Registrar (Finance), and a number of Deputy Registrars and Assistant Registrars.

Under the overall direction of the Vice-Chancellor, the office of the Dean Academic Affairs (DAA) is the nerve centre for all matters concerning academic environment and activity on the campus. This office looks after student admissions and the working of various teaching departments. All research projects and research activities are coordinated through this office. Thus, DAA office gets invested with in epicentric responsibility in catering to the growth of academic in the University. All the faculties are looked after by their respective Deans.

The Department of Students' Welfare, University of Jammu, provides opportunities to all the candidates seeking admission to various Diploma/Graduate/Post-graduate Programmes in Teaching Departments of the University, particularly those who have talent in cultural and literary activities. The Department has been organizing various competitions to inculcate creativity among the students in about 30 events with the active participation from more than 80 Affiliated Colleges and 30 teaching Departments. On the basis of their performance, the meritorious students being selected in these competitions are deputed to Zonal, National and International Level Competitions. Till date, students have excelled in various competitions and have even gone abroad to visit countries like, USSR, Japan, South Korea, etc. DSW is assisted by Assistant Dean Social Welfare, Director Physical Education, and Director Yoga Centre.

Audit System

Audit system of Jammu University is quite similar to other universities of the sample. The university has got two accounts branches. Papers/bills mooted through respected departments/ centres are moved upward through these branches. Then there is a section known as Internal Audit. There is also external audit system which is done by an officer of the rank of Deputy Controller of the Local Fund Department, known as State Fund of Jammu and Kashmir. The Deputy Controller and his staff get salary from their parent Department and official accommodation in the University Campus from the University. There is also audit by the Accountant General.

Examination System

University of Jammu has annual system of examination. Paper setting is done by the external examiners, i.e. experts from other universities. However, paper marking is done by the internal examiners through a system known as table marking.

Proper secrecy is maintained by putting fictitious roll numbers. For re-evaluation of the answer-books the external examiners are also involved whenever needed. For entrance tests objective type tests of four options are given. For the annual examinations subjective type questions are set. Examination work is looked after by Controller of Examinations.

Teachers and their Association

Teachers have their own association, known as Jammu University Teachers Association (JUTA) to look after their interests. Election to this association is conducted on yearly basis. The teachers can be members of a political party. They can even contest Parliamentary or State Assembly election. However, the election to JUTA is not fought on party lines but on the basis of important issues of the university. This helps in keeping the university out of the din of the political influences.

Students and their Association

Students have their association which is known as Jammu University Students Association. They do not have direct elections for the students. It is not formed on any political basis. In fact, national level organizations of various students' bodies do not exist here. The slogans and mottos of the various students' bodies are missing on the walls of the university. However, some national students' bodies like ABVP and SFI have made written requests to the students on the walls to join their organizations. These requests have been a few and have not been exhibited on prominent places/walls.

Non-Teaching Staff and their Association

Non-teaching staff too has its own association. This also is not formed on any political basis. Employees fight election on the basis of university issues like their recruitment and promotion. Hand bills are printed and distributed but not pasted on the walls. The office bearers have a term of two years. Secretary of the Jammu University Non-Teaching Association was full of praise for the present Vice-Chancellor, Prof. Amitabh Mattoo for his being helpful to the non-teaching staff. He also informed the present researcher that all their demands have been fulfilled except the one that was "two promotions must be granted in one's entire career service".

KURUKSHETRA UNIVERSITY, KURUKSHETRA

INTRODUCTION

Kurukshetra University is located at Kurukshetra where famous Mahabharata War was fought and Lord Krishna gave message of *karma* and duty without attachment to the great warrior Arjun through the Gita. Founded in 1956, the University started as a unitary teaching and residential University to promote Indology. However, within five year of its inception, this developed into a multi-faculty University. Since then it has taken quantum leaps and has emerged as a centre of study and research in all the major academic disciplines. With its sprawling campus, sylvan setting and salubrious natural landscape, the University provides adequate atmosphere for academic pursuits and personality development. National Assessment and Accreditation Council (NAAC), Bangalore has bestowed four-star status to this University.

The University has a beautiful and sprawling campus spreading over 400 acres of land with a centrally air-conditioned Auditorium with a seating capacity of 2,500 and a 70 mm projector, a Senate Hall, a well developed Sports Complex, Teachers' Club, Club for Administrative Staff, 16 Hostels for boys and girls, School, Health Centre, Yoga Centre, Business Complex, about 700 staff quarters, Internet, Computer Centre, Museum, USIC Workshop, MSS Centre, Students' Centre, Guest House, Faculty House, Community Centre, Open Air Theatre, etc. The campus, with its lawns, hedges and flower-beds in and around the buildings and hostels, is maintained by Horticulture and Landscaping Department of the University. Kurukshetra University has a Lands and Farming Department which has been trying to make the best use of vacant land on the campus by growing various crops mainly wheat and paddy. Two submersible pumps have been installed on the campus to fulfil the requirements of irrigation. The university has provided about 58 acres of the campus land to Community Forest Project for plantation of different spices of plants and commercial trees to enhance its income and also to improve ecological balance.

The University has a faculty of about 400 teachers to cater to the needs of over 5000 students and researchers. As many as 97 colleges with an enrolment of 1,10,000 students are affiliated to the University. Two of the erstwhile Post-Graduate Regional Centres of this University have already grown into full-fledged Universities. KU attracts a large number of students from every part of the country. Many foreign students are also residing in the well furnished University hostels.

ACADEMIC DISCIPLINES

KU has ten faculties comprising over forty Post-graduate Teaching Departments offering instructions for Masters, M.Phil., and Ph.D. Courses. Faculty of Arts and Languages has following seven departments: Department of English, Hindi, Journalism, Library and Information Science, Modern European Languages, Punjabi, and Urdu and Persian. Faculty of Commerce and Management has following three departments: Department of Commerce, Management, and Tourism. Faculty of Education comprises of two departments: Department of Education, and Physical Education. Faculty of Indic Studies has following six departments: Ancient Indian History, Culture and Archaeology, Fine Arts, Institute of Sanskrit and Indological Studies, Music and Dance, Philosophy, and Sanskrit, Pali and Prakrit. Faculty of Law has two departments, first Department of Law and second is National Institute of Law. Faculty of Science is the largest faculty constituting fifteen departments. These are: Department of Bio-Chemistry, Bio-Technology, Botany, Chemistry, Computer Science and Applications, Earth Science, Geography, Home Science, Mathematics, Microbiology, Physics, Statistics and Operational Research, University Science & Operational Centre, and Zoology. Faculty of Social Science has following seven Departments: Economics, History, Psychology, Political Science, Public Administration, Social Work, and Sociology. The other three faculties are: Faculty of Ayurvedic Medicine, Faculty of Medical and Dental Science, and Faculty of Engineering & Technology.

The University has a well-known Institute of Sanskrit and Indological Studies which offers facilities in advanced research in Indic Studies. The Department of Ancient Indian History, Culture and Archaeology have been doing a commendable job in the field of excavation of sites and reconstruction of history. The Seismological Observatory in the Department of Mathematics is the only of its kind in the region for collection of data on earthquakes and subterranean disturbances. The University is also running professional courses like LLB (Hons.) 5-years Integrated Course, MHM/MTM, B.Tech. (Instrumentation) MIB/MMT/MFC/MBE. The University has been continuously introducing new courses of study to keep pace with changing needs of the time. The University has also revised the Post-graduate Courses in accordance with the UGC Model Curriculum.

UNIVERSITY COLLEGE

University College is one of the constituent colleges on the campus. The College has well-qualified teaching staff, richly maintained library, spacious playgrounds and well equipped laboratories. The students have free access to books in the University Library. There are two hostels—one for boys and another for girls—specially earmarked for the students admitted to the College. The College has three faculties—Arts, Commerce, and Science for the undergraduate students.

UNIVERSITY COLLEGE OF EDUCATION

KU has a University College of Education on its Campus. This College is headed by a Principal and has fifteen faculty members. The College offers a B.Ed. (one year) Course.

DIRECTORATE OF CORRESPONDENCE COURSES (DCC)

KU established the DCC in 1976. The Directorate at present runs 62, 1-year/2-year/3-year courses (with 97 classes), which also include job-oriented professional courses in the area of Computer, IT, Commerce, Finance, Marketing, Law, Tourism,

Hotel Management, Journalism and Communication, Library and Information Science, etc. Many of the courses also allow lateral entry for the benefit of the students. KU has broad based its distance education system by tying up with Haryana State Electronics Development Corporation Ltd. (HARTEÓN), and Zee Interactive Learning System Ltd. (Education Arm of Zee TV.) to impart distance education in the area of Computer Science, IT and Management.

As a part of the major reforms undertaken by the Directorate for making improvement in the working, 'single window service' has been introduced for the advantages of the candidates seeking admission to the distance education courses. Earlier the candidates seeking admission had to stroll between the University Press, the Directorate and the bank and it used to take about two days to complete the admission formalities. Now with the opening of an Extension Bank Counter of Oriental Bank of Commerce, counter for the sale of Commerce, counter for the sale of Prospects in the premises of the Directorate, the process takes only an hour. Computerised Inquiry, Reception-*cum*-Counselling Bureau, Course-wise Service Counters for receiving admission forms from the students also add to the convenience of the students. The Directorate has a separate section of Students' Support Services with a teacher as its Coordinator. Students finding any difficulty in pursuing courses with this Directorate may get in touch with concerned official or the Coordinator.

The study material has been developed to suit the learning needs of the students of different courses. The study material is self-explanatory, comprehensive, rich and detailed. In addition to the study material designed by the Directorate, in some selected professional courses books published by eminent authors are also supplied to the students. The objective is that the students should be able to consult some desired reference books for quality learning without any difficulty and perform better in the University Examination. Old question-papers of the examinations conducted by the University are also supplied to the students to help them in the preparation of their examinations. This material has been found to be useful for the rural students and also for the students from distant areas.

The instruction through study material is further supplemented by short term condensed Personal Contact Programmes, both for theoretical and practical contents of the courses, one to three week duration depending upon the requirements of each course. These programmes include regular effective classroom teaching/practical wherever applicable, face to face discussions, promoting thereby an interaction between the teacher and the taught. 75% attendance for M.Phil. courses and 50% for other courses during the Personal Contact Programmes is compulsory to become eligible to appear in the University examinations. The students of professional courses are also provided with guidelines for preparing the Project/ Training Reports or dissertations. Full tuition fee concession is allowed to the students of Scheduled Caste/Tribe. Financial assistance is also allowed to a limited number of poor, needy and deserving students.

With an annual enrolment of 35,000 students, the Directorate of Correspondence Courses of the University offers distance education in 54 subjects, some major ones being Computer Science, Information Technology, Management, Law, Journalism, Library and Information Science, Tourism and Marketing. The Professional Courses launched by the Directorate include P.G. Diploma in Insurance Business Management, P.G. Diploma in Human Resource Management, P.G. Diploma in Business Management, P.G. Diploma in Financial Management, Master of Computer Applications, Master of Business Administration and M.A. Communications (Lateral Entry Course). From the session 2003-04, the Directorate of Correspondence Courses has introduced eight new courses which include M.A. Education, P.G. Diploma in Rural Development, P.G. Diploma in Advertising and Computer Graphics, M.Sc. Information Technology, Advance PGDCA, B.A. (Hons.) in Mass Communications, B.Sc. and Diploma in Computer Hardware and Network Engineering.

BHARAT RATNA BABA SAHEB DR. BHIM RAO AMBEDKAR STUDIES

KU set-up the Centre for Dr. Bhim Rao Ambedkar Studies in June 1992 to mark the centenary celebrations of Baba Saheb.

The main objectives of the Centre are: To study Dr. B.R. Ambedkar's works scientifically and objectively, to understand Ambedkar's relevance in the present times, to study problems of untouchability, social injustice, etc. in the light of his ideas, to collect and publish his writings and speeches, to hold seminars, symposia, and lectures on his life, works, and ideology, and to provide a common platform to the scholars working on him in India and abroad to share their research and experience.

THE WOMEN'S STUDIES RESEARCH CENTRE

This Centre is headed by a Director who is at present assisted by three Research Officers and one Research Assistant. The Centre conducts research, and organises workshops, seminars, debates and extension lectures, vocational, career and psychological counselling, cultural programmes, plays and skits, etc. on women issues and problems. The Centre has also been working as a nodal agency to guide and monitor the functioning of all women's cells (164 cells) in the colleges of Haryana. A special cell to protect the rights of women students has been created in the Women's Studies and Research Centre. Series of events have been organised to promote better interaction between the faculty, students and officials in the University. Presentations by eminent persons during these events have covered diverse topics like corporate social responsibilities, human rights, WTO and agricultural empowerment of women, globalisation, consumer justice, Moor's Law; RASP (reading, assignment, seminar, and participation).[2]

INFRASTRUCTURE AND ALLIED ACADEMIC ACTIVITIES

The University Library

The library has a plinth area of 49,230 sq. ft. having a facility of 370 seats in six reading areas at different floors of the library and 100 seats in the rear reading hall. It is manned by nine well qualified professionals, one Programmer, thirty-four Semi-professionals, and thirty-nine staff. The library has got 2,90,670 documents including 5,074 manuscripts. It subscribes to 100 journals (Indian and foreign) and 100 on-line journals free of cost made available on Internet. Total number of Library Members (under different categories) i.e. 8772 is as follows: Teachers 608, Research Scholars 950, Students 6055, Employees 1144 and special members 15. The library facilities are provided throughout the year (except on six national/gazetted holidays). The library is open on all working days from 9 am to 9 pm. On Saturdays/Sundays/holidays it is open from 9 am to 5 pm. As for Rear Reading Hall, it is open from 9 am to 12 pm. The reprographic services are provided to academic community on subsidized rates. The ERNET Services Centre of the library has been hooked to the Information Superhighway (INTERNET) since 1996. The VSAT connectivity to ERNET has been provided by the Department of Electronics, Government of India (presently ERNET India Society). The library is progressing towards the complete computerization by way of adopting and adapting the information technology. Initially infrastructure for the computerization and automation of the library has been developed with the financial assistance of the UGC and in collaboration with the INFLIBNET, Ahmedabad. The ERNET section has recently extended the number of its computer nodes from 25 to 120.[3]

Hostels

There are sixteen hostels, eight for boys and eight for girls in the campus of the Kurukshetra University. One more Girls Hostel is under construction and is soon expected to be functional. The University hostels provide accommodation to the students of University Teaching Departments and two constituent colleges, Ph.D. research scholars and M.Phil students. In addition to these categories, accommodation is also available to casual students who come for short courses, i.e., IAS coaching classes and students attending Personal Contact Programmes (PCP) of the Directorate of Correspondence Courses. The players of various sports teams and cultural activities are also provided hostel facility, if available. Blind students who seek admission to the University hostels are provided rent free accommodation. The total number of residents in the University hostels is more than 2900.

All the Boys Hostels are situated in the vicinity of the main Shopping Complex, Post Office and State Bank of India at the University Campus. The Girls Hostels are ideally located in another sector of the campus. From the security point of view the entire Girls Hostel complex is surrounded by a high boundary wall having one entry gate. The entry of guests is regulated and is allowed only during visiting hours prescribed for the purpose. There exists one guest room attached to the canteen for the use of the bonafide guest of the residents. This guest room is well furnished. Two STD booths, photocopying facility, one tailoring shop and one Dhobi shop function for the convenience of girl students. Mess arrangements in all the hostels are made on cooperative/contract basis. Some of the facilities which have been provided to the residents are: LPG system of cooking in the kitchens, big size pressure cookers, geysers for hot water in winter season, fans and power plugs in each room of the hostels, etc. The facility of News Papers/ Magazines of national/international importance in all the hostels and the facility of Cable TV connection have also been provided. Hard beds have been provided to all the students in all the hostels.

Intra and inter-hostel cultural and indoor games competitions are also arranged in boys and girls hostels.

Beautiful well maintained grassy lawns with flower beds exist in all the hostels. To provide hygienic food, the refined oil, milk, rice, etc. of standard brands are used for cooking in all the messes. One ambulance has been purchased for the exclusive use of the students residing in the hostels. The ambulance remains parked near the security gate/main gate of the Girls Hostels Complex and two drivers are available on the ambulance during day and night.

Health Centre

The Health Centre of the University looks after the medical needs of the staff, their families and students of different colleges and departments in the campus. Medicines are also given in the Health Centre. The average daily out-door patient is 149 including dental patients and patients attended during the off hours of the University. Ambulance facility is available to shift the patients to other hospitals. The University Health

Centre has E.C.G., X-Ray, Ultra-Sonic, CPM Unit, Static Cycle, Traction Unit, Diathermy Machine, and Laboratory Tests facilities.

ACADEMIC STAFF COLLEGE (ASC)

ASC was established in 1987. This ASC has so far organised 40 orientation courses and 117 Refresher Courses besides 2 Induction Training Programmes for the teachers working in Engineering Colleges, thus covering 5855 teachers not only from the State of Haryana but also from other states of the country.

MAHATMA GANDHI ALL INDIA SERVICES COACHING INSTITUTE

This Institute was established in 1982 with the objective of providing coaching to SC/ST preparing them for various Civil Services Examinations. Apart from the Civil Services Examinations, coaching is also provided for MBA Entrance Test, and Haryana Civil Services (Executive Branch) Examination. Ministry of Social Justice and Empowerment, Government of India, New Delhi has been providing financial assistance since 1997-98. Coaching is being provided to the SC/ST candidates free of cost. Besides, free coaching a monthly stipend is also paid to the candidates belonging to these categories. From the year 2001-02, the Government has extended this benefit to the candidates belonging to OBC/Minority categories. On the recommendations of the Social Welfare Department, Government of Haryana, this Institute has agreed to admit 10-15 general category students against a very nominal fee along with 40 reserved category students so that the level of interaction and competitiveness increases. Accommodation to both male and female candidates coming from far off places is also provided for the preparation for competitive examinations. The Institute has a well equipped library in which books on all relevant subjects are available for use by the students and resource persons. The library has at present 2336 books and subscribes to 16 magazines/periodicals, and 4 daily news papers. Coaching is provided to the candidates in a fully equipped lecture room.

DR. RADHA KRISHNAN FOUNDATION FUND

In KU Dr. Radha Krishanan Foundation Fund (Dr. RFF) was established in the year 1994 for raising donation/ mobilisation of resources, etc. for the overall development of the University under Financial Resource Mobilisation (FRM) Scheme of the UGC. Only the interest incurred on the fund amount is utilised as per guidance approved by the Executive Council of the University. The decisions for the allocation of money are taken by the Standing Committee of the Dr. RFF. The interest money is utilised for giving financial assistance and various scholarships to the students of affiliated/maintained Colleges of the University and teaching Departments of the University.

Computer Centre

KU has a well-developed Computer Centre with a good number and variety of equipment to cater to the various requirements of the faculty members, administration and research scholars. Computer Centre has a number of Pentiums. In addition, Dot-matrix-printers, Laser printers, colour ink-jet printers and colour scanners are also available. The Computer Centre also has licensed software such as FORTRAN, PASCAL, COBOL, 'C', MS-DOS, LOTUS, dBASE, and NOVELL Netware. The Computer Centre has also developed and is maintaining System-Stat, a collection of statistical programmes for various statistical routines. All these services are provided free of cost to the bonafide researchers of the University for academic work.

Main aim of the Computer Centre is to computerise various functions of the different branches of the University administration. Almost all the aspects of accounts like reconciliation, budget preparation, classification, etc. have been computerised. In addition, all the work relating to salary, like preparation of bills, deductions, provident fund, etc. have also been computerised. Large component of work relating to Pension Scheme has also been computerised. A subsidiary small computer cell has been set-up in Accounts Branch for data-entry purposes.

STUDENTS' ACTIVITIES

National Cadet Corps (NCC)

Functioning of NCC is looked after by a Commanding Officer and an Officer-in-Charge. They organize annual training camps for NCC cadets and conduct certificate 'B' and certificate 'C' examinations for the cadets.

Sports and Games

KU Sports Council organises Inter Collegiate Tournaments for men and women in total 57 disciplines every session. About five hundred teams of different colleges participate in these Inter-Collegiate Tournaments. Coaching camps of the University teams ranging from 10 to 21 day duration are also organised prior to their participation in Inter-Collegiate Tournaments. University teams also participated in North Zone/North-East Zone/All Inter-University Championships in different games and sports and have won positions in it.

Youth and Cultural Affairs

Department of Youth and Cultural Affairs of KU organises/sponsors various programmes for the students.

Scheduled Caste Cell

Established with the financial assistance from the UGC in 1984, the main objectives of the Cell are to look after the work relating to the coordination, evaluation and monitoring of the implementation of the programme/works relating to the Scheduled Castes and the Scheduled Tribes students/employees of the University and the colleges maintained by it and to ensure that the guidelines issued by the Government of India/ UGC/State Government in favour of the Scheduled Castes and the Scheduled Tribes candidates are implemented effectively.

The Cell has also been working as a nodal agency for supply of various types of statistical information in respect of students, teachers and other employees of the Scheduled Castes and the Scheduled Tribes categories in the University for onward transmission to the Government of India/UGC/State

Government from time to time åfter collecting the same from various University Teaching Departments/Colleges/Branches.

UNIVERSITY EMPLOYMENT INFORMATION AND GUIDANCE BUREAU

The Bureau has been providing vocational guidance to the youths to enable them to understand the world of work, to know about occupations and to think of their own resources in terms of their match worthiness with jobs and to set vocations as goals and pursue it by proper selection of proper course of study. Although aim is to provide vocational guidance, the services rendered to students represent a blend of a help in career planning, educational planning, and guidance. Often personal guidance results in strengthening self-confidence and motivation in them.

There are other important activities of this Bureau such as providing information about competitive examinations conducted by Union/State Public Service Commission, Staff Selection Commission, Banking Service Recruitment Boards, etc. There is also a Foreign Studies Section with catalogues and bulletin of all leading universities in the United Kingdom, USA, Canada, Australia and other countries. Fortnightly Bulletin carrying career profiles, vacancy notifications, competitive examinations, appointments abroad, scholarships/fellowships offered by Indian/foreign universities are published regularly. An analytical report on "Admission Trends" is also published for guiding the admission seekers to the University. Students visiting the Bureau are also being motivated to take up self-employment ventures. Career talks are also given in the colleges affiliated with the University.

University Press

The University Press which was started in the year 1965 with the financial assistance from the UGC has bee executing the entire printing work of the University since then. The Press has well-equipped composing, letter press printing, offset printing, screen printing, and binding sections with two offset printing machines and other supporting machines as well as one folding machine capable of all types of quality letter-press and offset printing and binding work. Apart from various time bound jobs of Examination and other branches/departments of the University, the Press also prints the annual publications viz., Digest of Indological Studies, KU Law Journal, Sambhavana, Jeevani, University Calendars, Annual Report, Student Magazines, Prospectus, Syllabuses, Text-Books, Lessons of Correspondence Courses, etc. General books published by the University are also printed in the University Press.

Publication Bureau

The University has started its own Publication Bureau in 1975 with a view to publish low priced text-books for undergraduate classes. The Publication Bureau was later on merged with the University Press and Printing and Publications Department was formed in 1978 under the Manager, Printing and Publications. As many as 51 text-books in English, Hindi, Punjabi and Sanskrit have been published so far and some of them have also been printed at the University Press. Apart from the text-books, the Publication Bureau caters to the needs of students/Registered Book-Sellers by arranging sale of priced publications like admission forms, prospectuses, DCC prospectuses, examination forms, syllabi, ordinance, hostel rules, etc. The University has also published 56 learned books of teachers in the subjects like Sanskrit, Indology, History, Mathematics and Education.

COMMUNITY OUTREACH

KU has following organization to have contacts with the community:

National Service Scheme (NSS)

KU NSS was established in 1969 with the objective of providing students with an opportunity to develop their overall personality by participating in variety of social/community service programmes. This programme, organised by various units of educational institutions, aims at infusing amongst the students a spirit of group-living to create a sense of dignity of labour by developing a first hand knowledge of the life and living conditions of the people, thus helping them to develop a healthy personality and channel their energies into constructive activities.

NSS units took active part in the celebrations like Republic Day, Independence Day, Sadbhavana Day, National Integration Day, National Integration Week, NSS Day and World AIDS Day.

Administration

Top hierarchy of the University consists of the following officers: Chancellor who is always the Governor of the State, Vice-Chancellor, Pro-Vice-Chancellor, Registrar, Controller of Examination, thirteen Deans, viz., Dean of Academic Affairs, Students' Welfare, Colleges, and ten Deans of different teaching Faculties. Other officers of the University are Finance Officer, Proctor, Chief Warden, Controller of Examinations, Planning and Development Officer, Librarian, Executive Engineer, and Medical Officer. Accounts of the University are pre-audited by the Government Local Audit Department officer of the rank of Joint/Deputy Controller Finance. University is run by various bodies like University Court, Executive Council, Academic Council, Finance Committee, Board of Studies, the Faculties, the Academic Planning Board, the Selection Committee; the Establishment Committee, etc.

Teachers and their Associations

Teachers have their association, known as Kurukshetra University Teachers' Association (KUTA). This association looks after the interests of the teachers. Elections to this body, conducted every year, are not fought on party basis. Individual teachers may have their political leanings but as members of KUTA, they talk mainly of university issues and not of any political issue.

Non-Teaching Employees and their Association

Like the teachers, non-teaching employees too have their association to look after their interests. This association is known as Kurukshetra University Non-Teaching Employees' Association (KUNTEA). Elections of the non-teaching employees too have no political connections. President of the association has a well furnished office with telephone facility.

Students and their Associations

There has been no students' election since 1997. The University has provided sufficiently good facilities to the students in the hostels, departments, University Library, canteens, campus, etc. They, however, have their organizations like Indian National Students Organisation (INSO), National Students Union of India (NSUI), Independent Students' Welfare Association (ISWA), Students' Federation of India (SFI), Jaagrook Chhatra Morcha (JCM), etc. which at times voice the grievances of the students. Prolonged agitations are unknown to the campus. During many of his visits to the campus, the researcher could only once come across a students' demonstration by about 30 to 35 students, that too for a short duration of half an hour for some local issue.

Audit System

Kurukshetra University has well defined audit system. Accountant General does the audit for the central grants. Local Audit does it for the State grants. Local Audit Department has been provided sufficient facilities and accommodation in the university. LAD is headed by an officer of the rank of Joint Director. JD is assisted by two Senior Auditors and 8 Auditors. Accommodation and salaries of all the officials of LAD are charged from the University in the shape of audit fee. Accounts of the University are maintained by the Accounts Branch. There seems to be no overt conflict between the staff of the University and the LAD.

Examination System

Kurukshetra University has annual system of examination. Paper setting is done by the external examiners, i.e. experts from other universities. However, paper marking is done by the internal examiners through a system known as table marking. Proper secrecy is maintained by putting fictitious roll numbers. For re-evaluation of the answer-books the external examiners are also involved whenever needed. For entrance tests objective type tests of four options are given. For the annual examinations subjective type questions are set. Examination work is looked after by Controller of Examinations. Examination work has been fully computerized. All the results are declared regularly and are available on the internet.

PANJAB UNIVERSITY, CHANDIGARH

INTRODUCTION

The roots of the present Panjab University which was established by Ordinance-VIII of 1947 after the Partition of the country, with the present campus at Chandigarh dating back to 1958, lie in Lahore. This University is the oldest university of the North-western India and the fourth University to be established after Bombay, Madras and Calcutta in the Indian sub-continent. A bill for the establishment of the Panjab University was passed by the Legislative Council in October 1882, and the Panjab University came into existence on October 14, 1882, by a Notification issued by the Lieutenant-Governor of Panjab, in pursuance of the provisions of the Act of Incorporation. The Panjab University Act No. XIX of 1882 was published in the Gazette of India, dated December 7, 1882. Mr. Baden-Powell was appointed the first honorary Vice-Chancellor and Dr. Leitner the Registrar of the new University. . . . The first meeting of the Senate of the Panjab University was held at Barnes Court, Simla on October 14, 1882. Sir Charles Aitcheson, the Lieutenant-Governor, who was appointed the Chancellor of the new University, inaugurated the session.[4]

The Panjab University Chandigrah, the most important university north of Delhi, may be called a mother university because of the role played by it in the north-western part of India. The universities at Shimla, Kurukshetra, and Amritsar which are being covered in the present study in fact are the off spring of the Panjab University, Chandigarh, since these were the Regional Centres of this university prior to their development into full-fledged universities. With the reorganization of the State of Punjab, the Panjab University was declared as an Inter-State body corporate under the provisions of the Punjab Reorganisation Act, 1966. It still continues to serve the entire region north of Delhi drawing students from the States of Punjab, Haryana, Himachal Pradesh, Jammu and Kashmir and, of course, also from the Union Territory of Chandigarh.

This seat of learning at Chandigarh is the continuum of the Panjab University, Lahore, which was incorporated in 1882. It is now governed by the Panjab University Act, 1947 as amended from time to time. After the partition, its headquarters were shifted to Solan. Teaching departments were started at Amritsar, Jalandhar, Hoshiarpur, Ludhiana and Delhi. It moved to its present 360-acre Campus in Chandigarh during 1956. To meet the need to expand its activities over 130 acre of land in Sector 25 was purchased in 1964. Planned initially by Pierre Jeanneret, under the overall guidance of Le-Corbusier himself, it occupies an imaginatively designed campus with teaching departments, students' hostels, play-grounds and residential quarters all in one campus but deposed in such a manner that the functioning and the privacy of each segment of the University remains undisturbed.

The Panjab University has won the most coveted Jimmy & Rosalyn Carter Partnership Award for Campus-Community Collaboration (JRCPA). The awards for the three exceptional campus-community programmes for India were announced by the former First Lady of the US, Mrs. Rosalyn Carter at a glittering 'Award Ceremony' on October 27, 2006 at Taj Palace Hotel, New Delhi. The Panjab University, Chandigarh bagged the second position for Adult Literacy Programme, followed by Aligarh Muslim University for Polio Eradication Programme. Prof. R.C. Sobti, the Vice-Chancellor, Panjab University received the award comprising US $3,000 and JRCPF Certification. The award winning 'Adult Literacy Programme' has been the work of the Panjab University's Centre for Adult, Continuing Education and Extension, undertaken with the determination to tackle the most difficult problem of the neighbouring community namely the Janata Colony.

ACADEMIC DISCIPLINES

Total number of teaching Departments in the Panjab University is 55 and the total number of affiliated colleges is 115 spread over the Union Territory and four districts of the Punjab State. There are 11 Faculties—Arts, Business and Commerce, Dairying, Animal Husbandry and Agriculture, Design & Fine Arts, Education, Engineering & Technology, Languages, Law, Medical Sciences, Pharmaceutical Sciences and Science. Faculties and equipment are available for doctoral degrees.

There are 11 Science Departments—Anthropology, Bio-Chemistry, Bio-Physics, Botany, Chemistry, Geology, Mathematics, Microbiology, Physics, Statistics and Zoology. The University Grants Commission has recognized the Departments of Mathematics and Geology as Centres of Advanced Study while the Departments of Botany, Chemistry, Physics and Zoology are on the Special Assistance list of the University Grants Commission.

There are 13 Departments of Social Sciences and Humanities—Ancient Indian History, Culture & Archaeology, Economics, Fine Arts, Geography, Gandhian Studies, History, Indian Theatre, Political Science, Public Administration, Psychology, Philosophy, Sociology and also a Population Research Centre. There are 8 Departments of Professional Courses—Chemical Engineering and Technology, Commerce and Business Management, Education, Mass Communication, Laws, Library Science, Pharmaceutical Sciences and Physical Education. There are 10 Departments of Languages—English, Hindi, Punjabi, Sanskrit, French, German, Russian, Central Asian Studies, South Indian Languages and Urdu. Besides there are Chairs—Sheikh Baba Farid Chair of Medieval Indian Literature, Bhai Vir Singh Studies in Modern Literature, Dayanand Chair for Vedic Studies, and Guru Ravi Dass Chair of Sant Sahitya Studies. Panjab University has a Regional Centre at Muktsar, a Regional Centre and an extension library at Ludhiana and VVBIS & IS (Vishweshavaranand Vishva Bandhu Institute of Sanskrit and Indological Studies) at Hoshiarpur.

The University is essentially a residential campus. Mainly students hail from the neighbouring states of Haryana, Himachal, Jammu & Kashmir besides Punjab and Chandigarh. The presence of a good number of students from the rest of the country provides a national character to the University. The campus acquires an international colour because many students from the SAARC countries, the Middle East, Africa and South and South-East Asia also seek admission to various courses.

The Gandhi Bhawan on the university campus attracts scholars as well as tourists from all over the world for its wonderful architectural form, its library and auditorium. The Panjab University has four museums and the department of Indian Theatre has its own theatre lab, which is unique in the country. The university has a Botanical Garden and a Garden of Medicinal plants on the campus.

The teaching faculty consists of nearly 800 specialists and scholars of national repute and international eminence. They represent all parts of India and have regular interaction with institutions of higher learning the world over.

Sports

Department of Sports functions under the overall supervision of the Director of Sports.

NATIONAL CENTRE FOR HUMAN GENOME STUDIES AND RESEARCH

Centre came into existence in the year 2002. Thirty students are presently enrolled for Masters in Science (Human Genomics), fifteen students in M.Sc. first and fifteen in M.Sc. second year.

UNIVERSITY INSTITUTE OF ENGINEERING AND TECHNOLOGY

This Institute conducts B.E. classes in software engineering, telecommunication and IT, microelectronics, and bio-technology. It is headed by a Director of the rank of a Professor and has a number of faculty members.

CENTRE FOR DEFENCE AND NATIONAL SECURITY STUDIES

This Centre conducts MA classes in Defence and National Security Studies. It is headed by a Coordinator of the rank of a Professor and has a number of faculty members.

UNIVERSITY INSTITUTE OF PHARMACEUTICAL SCIENCES

This Institute conducts classes in B. Pharma and M. Pharma. Students also study up to the Ph.D. degree in this Institute. The Chairperson of the Institute is of the rank of Professor. There are many other faculty members of the ranks of Professors, Readers and Lecturers in the Institute.

THE SOPHISTICATED INSTRUMENTATION CENTRE

This is one of the most modern instrumentation centres in the country and houses Regional Sophisticated Centre, University Science Instrumentation Centre and Centre Instrumentation Laboratory. The instruments in the Centre are for analytical, spectroscopic and structural studies of the researchers in academic institutions and the Industry. These instruments facilitate quality control. The Centre provides consultancy services to nearly 300 organizations to promote interaction between the Industry and Research Institutions.

RESEARCH PROMOTION COMMITTEE

The Research Promotion Committee coordinates interdisciplinary interaction among faculty members, researchers and students and overseas financing, planning and organizing of seminars.

POPULATION RESEARCH CENTRE

The PRC was established in 1980 on the initiative of Prof. V.S. D'Souza, Chairman of the Department of Sociology, Panjab University who became the first Honorary Director of the centre. He very ably brought the PRC on the front scene with a team of five persons; one Assistant Director and four Research Assistants/Investigators.

ENERGY RESEARCH CENTRE

This centre was established in 1983 at Panjab University to

promote R&D and Extension activities in the emerging field of Renewable Energy. It has emerged as a major focal point of R&D and extension on energy and environment at national and international level. This Centre was the only R&D centre in the country which was designated as Nodal Agency for the implementation of different programmes of MNES. As a result of extension activities undertaken by the Centre, Chandigarh has emerged as a city with highest per capita alternate energy consumption on Asia and Pacific. As per survey conducted by NCAER, 5 million cook stoves designed by the centre are in operation in the country. Under these programmes, large number of self-employed workers and potters have been trained thus creating job avenues in rural area apart from saving huge quantity of wood. Laboratories of the Centre are equipped with the state-of-the-art equipment. Centre has been designated as a regional test centre for testing solar thermal equipment by MNES. Bureau of Indian Standard has approved the centre for testing wood burning stoves. Centre has provided consultancy to a large number of countries in Asia-Pacific region such as Maldives, Bangla Desh, Srilanka, Myanmar, Kiribati and Tuvalu, in the area of renewable energy sources, energy management and environmental protection. Centre has also helped the states of Haryana, Panjab and Himachal Pradesh in solving problems associated with energy planning and management and environmental protection.

CENTRE FOR ENVIRONMENT AND VOCATIONAL STUDIES

In view of the enormous demand of environment specialists as educators, researchers, industrial consultants, urban planners and architects for the government and non-government organizations, the Centre for Vocational Studies was upgraded to the Centre for Environment and Vocational Studies (CEVS) in 2001. Within a year of the inception of the CEVS, PU started a two-year M.Sc. degree course in Environmental Science with effect from the admissions of 2002-03.

The Centre of IAS and Other Competitive Examinations

Panjab University runs an exclusive centre for IAS and other Competitive Examinations to help aspirants compete in various national and state level examinations. The Centre has been approved by the UT's Social Welfare Department for providing assistance to economically weaker sections/reserved sections of the society. Over the years, the Centre has expanded its coverage in terms of providing coaching by including Competitive examination like IAS, UGC (NET)/CSIR, Judicial Services, etc.

Department of Correspondence Studies

This Department (earlier called Directorate of Correspondence Courses till 1989-90) was established in 1971 with the objective to take higher education to the doorsteps of those men and women who have to discontinue their formal education due to peculiar circumstances or live in geographically remote areas or discontinue their education because of lack of aptitude and motivation but later on become motivated or do not find a seat on merit or do not wish to join a College or a University although they have the necessary qualifications to pursue higher education or look upon education as a life long activity and may either like to refresh their knowledge in their own discipline or to acquire knowledge in a new area at any state of their life. Its multi-faculty comprises of 71 teachers.

The study programmes consist of Bachelor of Arts, Bachelor of Commerce, Bachelor of Library & Information Science, Post-graduate Diplomas in Health, Family Welfare and Population Education, Mass Communication, Computer Applications, Masters of Arts in English, Hindi, Punjabi, Economics, History, Political Science, Public Administration, Sociology, B.Ed., M.Ed. and some certificate courses. The Course of study, the syllabi, duration and mode of examinations are the same as prescribed for regular students of university teaching Departments/Colleges affiliated to the Panjab University. The capsule teaching programme constitutes printed lecture scripts, personal contact programmes (wherein presence is not compulsory), radio talks, audio and audio-visual lessons.

It has a richly stocked library with more than 77,000 books—text, reference and general on its shelves. In addition, 62 journals, magazines and newspapers are subscribed to. Local students can read in the library and also borrow books. For those residing outside Chandigarh, the library maintains postal service. Besides, there is a chain of 4 Study Centres at Ambala, Delhi, Jalandhar and Madras.

The Educational Media Centre (EMC) of the Department of Correspondence Studies is producing Educational Audio and Video programmes and is keeping an Audio Visual Library for the students. It has produced 325 audio lessons and 9 video programmes. Most of its video programmes have been telecast on Doordarshan in the UGC-countrywide classroom programme.

DEPARTMENT OF EVENING STUDIES

Department of Evening Studies caters to the postgraduate and undergraduate studies on the campus for the employed persons who cannot attend the day classes on the campus. It has about 1,500 students on its roll.

THE UGC-FUNDED CENTRES OF EXCELLENCE

The departments covered under various UGC and DST programmes include:

SAP : Anthropology, Botany, University Business School, Education, Geography, Geology, Political Science (Geo-Politics), University Institute of Pharmaceutical Sciences, Philosophy, Statistics, Sociology and Zoology.

COSIST : Chemistry, Geology, Mathematics, University Institute of Pharmaceutical Sciences, Physics, Zoology.

CAS : Chemistry, Geology, Mathematics, Physics.

FIST : Bio-chemistry, Bio-technology, Bio-physics, Botany, Chemistry, Geology, Mathematics, Microbiology, Physics, University Centre of Instrumentation and Microelectronics and Statistics.

Recently the University has been selected by the UGC as the "University with Potential for Excellence in Bio-Medical Sciences," Initial Grant of Rs. 5 crore has been released by the UGC under the scheme.

ICSSR NORTH-WEST REGIONAL CENTRE

This Centre aims at the promotion of social science research in the region comprising Punjab, Haryana, Himachal Pradesh, Jammu and Kashmir and the Union Territory of Chandigarh. It functions in collaboration with the University and has an Advisory Committee with members drawn from the governments and universities of the region.

INFRASTRUCTURE AND ALLIED ACADEMIC ACTIVITIES

The University Library

The Central Library of Panjab University has a holding of over 6.5 lac books and 623 periodicals, some of which are rare collections of the 19th century. There are also 1500 rare manuscripts in classical and regional languages. This Library, known after Professor A.C. Joshi, possesses facilities like photocopiers, overhead projectors, E-mail, Internet, Multimedia, and GISTNIC, CD-ROM databases, Fax and inter-connected computer terminals. The specialized library of the ICSSR is also located in the Central Library. In addition, the Library is linked to and supported by fifty Department libraries geared largely to meeting the requirements of students.

It is one of the largest libraries on the Indian sub-continent. Its five story building is centrally air-conditioned and has spacious reading halls and compact stack areas. The University Library has been recognised as one of the six national centres for data-information-distribution in the UGC's INFLIBNET programme. Besides, the National Board of Higher Education in Mathematics provides special support for the library of Mathematics Department.

The Library is fully computerized with an integrated system connected to the Campus network. There are internet and e-mail facilities in the Library. The reference collection of the Library is augmented with acquisition of CD-ROM databases and access to on-line databases on internet. On-line Public Access Catalogue can be accessed through the Campus network. There is a Cyber-café at the entrance of the Library. Photocopying facility at approved rates is available in the Library. This Library has also been designated by the INFLIBNET/UGC as the Document Delivery Centre for the North-West region. Under this arrangement, copies of articles/papers appearing in periodical publications received in this Library will be supplied on demand, through e-mail/fax/post, to libraries in the region.

The two main Reading Halls of the Library are open from 9.00 a.m to 9.00 p.m. The Textbook Section on the Ground Floor opens from 8.00 a.m. to 10.00 p.m. The Outer Reading Hall meant for studying personal books remains open round the clock. These services are open throughout the week for 362 days in a year, barring three national holidays.

The Library has open access system. Readers can browse books freely in the stacks and can select reading material of their choice. The arrangement of books on the shelves is in a numerical sequence based on Dewey Decimal Classification system which is followed world wide.

Hostels

There are six boys hostels and five girls hostel on the campus. Accommodation to about 1600 boy-students and to about 1200 girl-students is available in these hostels. The University appoints a (Teacher) Warden for each hostel who looks after day to day functioning of the hostel. The Dean Student Welfare has been entrusted with the overall responsibility of directing and functioning of the hostels and maintaining discipline.

The residents are encouraged to run co-operative messes and the Dean of Student Welfare ensures all possible facilities in this direction. This is planned with a view to create healthy competition with the contract messes. There is a special arrangement for indoor games and provision for reading material, i.e. newspaper, periodicals, etc. in the common rooms of the University Hostels. Facilities for outdoor games like badminton, volleyball and basketball have been provided. Recreation gadgets, Television and Stereo system are also available in each Hostel. Modern facilities have been provided in the hostel messes and canteens, fans, deep-freezers, geysers, water-coolers, desert-coolers, etc. have been provided in the hostels. Besides, cooking gas connections have been installed in all the hostels. New cooking instruments have been provided. To ensure good food for the residents, food is prepared under the supervision of a dietician.

PANJAB UNIVERSITY HEALTH CENTRE

The University has a well established Health Centre to take care of health needs of its students, teachers, staff and their dependants. Chief Medical Officer is the head of this centre. It has three full time Medical Officers, one Dental Surgeon, one Ayurvedic Doctor, seven part-time doctors with specializations in different fields. Para-Medical Staff of the Centre consists of seven pharmacist, one nurse, three ANS, three lab technicians, two dressers, two ward-boys, and one X-ray technician. Office staff includes one superintendent, one clerk, one steno, and three drivers.

Facilities available at the Centre include a modest clinical laboratory for routine tests, a family welfare unit (run by Red Cross) for antenatal check-up, malaria detection and treatment unit (run by NMEP) which carries out examination of blood slides for malaria, ECG services and X-ray services, physiotherapy, ultrasonic and diathermy treatment. Ambulance is available 24 hours on nominal charges. A doctor is available on call at his/her residence for emergency cases outside working hours and on holidays.

On an average, 350-400 patients visit the Health Centre daily. Medicines are supplied free of cost to the Faculty members, and staff (including retired persons and their dependants). Those not available or out of stock, but admissible are reimbursed by the University. Hospital charges and those incurred on treatment in Government Ayurvedic and Homeopathic dispensaries by the Faculty, Staff including retired persons and their dependents are also reimbursed at Punjab Government rates. Students and Research Scholars on the Campus are also extended these medical facilities.

ACADEMIC STAFF COLLEGE (ASC)

ASC of the Panjab University, established in October 1987, is one of the fifty such colleges set-up by the University Grants Commission as to provide in-service training to college and university lecturers. According to the UGC proposal, this College offers general orientation courses and refresher courses to the in-service teachers.

Alumni Relations

The Panjab University Alumni Association, with the Vice-Chancellor as its President and the Dean Alumni Relations as its Secretary, was formally inaugurated on September 30, 1972. The Association looks after the general interests of the alumni of the University. The membership of the Alumni association is open to degree holders from the pre-Independence Panjab University at Lahore, and from the present Panjab University and members of the teaching faculty of the Panjab University and the colleges affiliated to it even though they do not hold degree from the Panjab University.

COLLEGE DEVELOPMENT COUNCIL

It has 30 members with the Vice-Chancellor as its Chairman. Members include Principals, University Professors, College Lecturers, Registrar Panjab University and Directors of Public Instructions (Colleges) of Punjab and Union Territory, Chandigarh.

RESEARCH BULLETIN AND JOURNAL

The University publishes research bulletins and journals of very high standard known as, Research Bulletin (Arts), Research Bulletin (Science), and Social Sciences Research Journal.

Students' Welfare

Students' welfare is looked after by the Dean Students' Welfare. DSW caters to the ever-growing aspirations of the Campus Students—be it hostel residents' issues concerning accommodation, diet, physical fitness, recreational/cultural/ social activities/talent shows/dramatic and literary events. DSW is also engaged in guiding and helping the Panjab University Campus Students' Council in development of skills for effective future leadership roles and excelling in every sphere of life, managing the students' discipline, covering of innovative ideas to channelise their energies properly, etc.

UNESCO CENTRE

This Centre gives information about the aims and objectives of various organs of the United Nations. It celebrates days like World Peace Day and United Nations Day.

Computer Centre

The University has a well equipped Computer Centre to cater to the computational needs of the students and teachers. Computational facilities are provided on reasonable charges to users in the Centre.

Scholarships

Scholarships are awarded to students on the basis of merit in extra-curricular activities. Financial aid is given to the needy students out of Students' Aid Fund. Part time jobs are available. A special feature of the scholarship scheme is the creation of a fund to which students contribute one rupee every month. The total is matched by similar contribution by the University. Tuition fee concession is granted to the deserving up to ten percent of the total number of students in the class.

UNIVERSITY INFORMATION AND ADVISORY BUREAU

The Bureau provides guidance and counseling to the students of teaching departments, affiliated colleges and alumni of the University desirous of joining other universities in India or proceeding abroad for higher education. It keeps material pertaining to courses of study and research facilities in most countries of the world especially English speaking countries. The Bureau also receives and disseminates information relating to higher education and research in universities and institutes of higher learning and financial aid schemes offered in India or abroad. Applicants seeking admission to universities/institutes of higher learning abroad are helped in preparing their curriculum vitae/bio-data, etc. and in filling up their admission forms. Bulletins of Information along with application forms for TOFEL, GRE, GMAT, Scholastic Aptitude Test and Achievement Tests are obtained and supplied to students already in correspondence with foreign universities. Applications from faculty members for exchange visits, fellowship offered by foreign countries through University Grants Commission or through the Ministry of Human Resource Department (Department of Education), are collected and forwarded for processing.

UNIVERSITY EMPLOYMENT INFORMATION AND GUIDANCE BUREAU

The Bureau helps the students in finding jobs according to their qualifications and experience. It also guides the students about the latest employment avenues. It also assists the students in making right choice of their courses and careers.

Campus Reporter

This is a house journal published annually for circulation amongst the campus students and the faculty members on the Campus. It aims at providing a forum for expression to the students and is published with their active cooperation. Besides giving wide coverage to the activities of the students and the personal contributions various competitions such as short story writing, essay writing and poetry, cartoon and painting competitions are organized for the journal. The winners are awarded prizes and their entries are published. The journal has sections in English, Hindi, Punjabi, Sanskrit, Urdu, Science, Pahari, Fine Arts and some foreign languages. Campus Reporter is published by students under the editorship of the Dean Students Welfare.

Student Centre

Student Centre acts as a rendezvous for the youth and is housed in an attractive cylindrical building. It has a large indoor game section on the first floor in which facilities for a number of games like carom, chess and table tennis are available. A stereo-set with adequate provision of Indian and Western discs and a coloured TV set are added attractions of this section. There is a spacious reading room on the second floor in which students can browse over a variety of newspapers and periodicals in a cozy atmosphere. GD-I: Best of all GD Channels, GD-2: Interactive Distance Education and GD-3: Technical Education under the auspicious of Indira Gandhi National Open University (IGNOU), New Delhi have been provided in the library of the Student Centre which broadcast Gyan Darshan programmes. This venture has been catalysed by the Ministry of Human Resource Development, Prasar Bharati and IGNOU for the benefit of the student community. This is one of the new additions to the Student Centre. The top floor of the Student Centre building houses a modern cafeteria, where light beverages and snacks are available at concession.

COMMUNITY OUTREACH

Panjab University has following organizations to have contacts with the community:

REGIONAL RESOURCE CENTRE FOR ADULT AND CONTINUING EDUCATION

The Centre for Adult, Continuing Education, Panjab University, Chandigarh, was established in 1976. The Centre was sanctioned the programme, "Eradication of Illiteracy" under point no. 16 of the 20 Point Programme in 1983-84. The Centre has accepted the philosophy of Continuing Education as a part of its total programme and tried its best to involve university and college teachers, students, NGOs, Government officials and other welfare agencies in continuing education, extension education and field outreach work, in its endeavour to develop capabilities of the community for the overall development of the nation and helping people to improve their quality of life. The Centre caters to the needs of those people who have been deprived of benefits of formal system of education. It conducts need-based flexible programmes, which shall facilitate linking of higher education with developmental process. The Centre tries to reach to the larger sections of adults through university system to equalize the learning opportunities and to address market demands both in rural and urban areas. The Centre holds courses which are skill-based, family life education, value education or on social issues such as para-legal training for grass-root workers. The Centre endeavours to cover various geographical communities such as urban slums, city population and rural population. Presently, the Centre is organizing programmes according to the UGC guidelines

National Service Scheme (NSS)

NSS Department organized blood donation camps, tree plantation for environment protection, pulse polio drive, seminars, conferences, and extension lectures on AIDS awareness and other health-related problems.

Publication Bureau

Main function of the Bureau is to publish and sell textbooks and scholarly/general books. It also performs house-keeping activities like dispatch/sale of University Calendars, Syllabi, Handbook of Information of Teaching Departments, and Prospectus of Entrance Tests.

Public Relations

The Department of Public Relations, headed by an officer of the rank of Director, provides public relation support in media for the coverage of the programmes organized by various University Teaching Departments/university employees, attempts to strengthen internal communication and acts as a bridge between the University authorities and various publics. It assists in organizing Special Lectures, preparation of Annual

Report, providing information regarding telephone numbers and residential addresses. The Department has been undertaking formal and informal public relations programmes, including counseling, interaction with different public to know their problems and in identifying areas which need immediate attention of the authorities in addition to providing news clips. It brings out a quarterly news magazine, namely, 'The PU News' which is an official publication aimed at protecting the corporate image of the University.

Administration

The supreme authority of the University is vested in the Senate which consists of Chancellor, Vice-Chancellor, Ex-officio Fellows, and Ordinary Fellows. The Senate elects a Syndicate which has also some ex-officio members. The Syndicate is the chief decision-making body subject to the over-seeing Senate. Academic Council looks after academic matters. There is a Board of Studies in every discipline to review syllabi, to recommend appointment of examiners, and to suggest new courses. The Board of Control looks after admissions and maintenance of discipline in each department. The Vice-Chancellor is the chief executive. He is the Chairman of the Syndicate, Senate and the Academic Council. He is assisted by Deans, Registrar, and the Controller of Examinations. Dean University Instruction coordinates and supervises admission of students made by the Board of Control to the various University Departments, and deals with all other academic matters of the University Departments and Regional Centres. The Registrar is the in-charge of the University administration acting under the immediate control of the Vice-Chancellor and represents the University in all legal proceedings. Dean of Students' Welfare makes arrangements for the residence of students, supervises discipline of the students, supervises co-curricular and cultural activities of the students in the University campus, looks after the physical welfare and N.C.C. activities of the students, and devises ways and means for promoting the well-being of the University students. There is also an institution known as Finance Board to aid and advise on financial matters. There are Dean of Foreign Students, Dean of Alumni Relations, Director Academic Staff College, Director Publication Bureau, Director

Public Relations, etc. to help the Vice-Chancellor. For carrying out academic activities in addition to already mentioned Academic Council and Board of Studies, there are other bodies like Faculties, Research Degree Committees, and Joint Research Board.

Teachers and their Association

Teachers have their association, known as Panjab University Teachers' Association (PUTA). This association looks after the interests of the teachers. Elections to this body, conducted every year, are not fought on party basis. Individual teachers may have their political leanings but their behaviour in the University is seldom influenced by political considerations.

Non-Teaching Employees and their Association

Like the teachers, non-teaching employees too have their association to look after their interests. Elections of the non-teaching employees too have no political connections.

Students and their Association

Duly elected Panjab University Campus Students' Council (P.U.C.S.C.) is constituted every year for having liaison with the students of the Campus. This Council organizes various cultural functions and also helps to promote sports activities on the Campus.

Audit System

Panjab University has its own well laid system of auditing the accounts. The university has got two accounts branches. Papers/bills mooted through respected departments/centres are moved upward through these branches. There is no section known as Internal Audit which is found in other universities of the sample.[5] There is 100% pre-audit for all the bills. This is done by an officer of the rank of Deputy Controller of the Local Fund Department of the Government of Punjab. The Deputy Controller and his staff get salary from their parent Department and official accommodation in the University campus from the University. Accountant General also does post-audit of the bills wherever the State Grant from Punjab Government is involved.

Special Audit is also done in case of need only whenever some complaint about the misutilisation of funds is received.

Examination System

Panjab University has annual system of examination. Paper setting is done by the external examiners, i.e. experts from other universities. However, paper marking is done by the internal examiners through a system known as table marking. Proper secrecy is maintained by putting fictitious roll numbers. For re-evaluation of the answer-books the external examiners are also involved whenever needed. For entrance tests objective type tests of four options are given. For the annual examinations subjective type questions are set. Examination work is looked after by Controller of Examinations.

To sum up, the profile of the five universities of the sample of the north-western India has been discussed above to throw a light on the infrastructure, curricular and co-curricular activities of the universities. It will help us in understanding the strength and weakness of the universities which would be crucial in comprehending the challenges and suggesting ways and means to meet those challenges.

Notes and References

1. *The Tribune,* August 30, 2005, p. 19.
2. *Ibid.,* p. 15.
3. *The Tribune,* 9.8.2005, p. 15.
4. Sethi, R.R. and Mehta, J.L. *The History of The Panjab University, Chandigarh, 1947-67,* Chandigarh, Panjab University Publication Bureau, 1968, p. 9.
5. Please See: Still the respondents have given their reactions to the working of the Internal Audit. In fact, after inquiry from some of the respondents, it was found that the observations by the two accounts branches have been referred as those by the internal audit. So whenever we discuss internal audit with reference to the Panjab University, that would certainly mean the working of the accounts branches of the University.

CHAPTER

4

Working of the Universities

In the third chapter we have discussed the general profile of the universities of the sample. In this chapter and also in the succeeding chapters, information collected through various questionnaires has been tabulated, analysed and interpreted. The present researcher discussed the challenges to university administration with special reference to the HPU with its Chancellor, Mr. V.S. Kokje. It may be mentioned that despite many requests none of the VCs in the total sample cared to answer the questionnaire prepared by the present researcher. So the researcher had to be contended with the questionnaires filled in by the Registrars. The Registrars of all the universities, however, could find time to discuss the affairs of their respective universities with the researcher. Interviews with the Registrars have been very much helpful in understanding the challenges and giving suggestions to meet those challenges. As for questionnaires, it has been observed that in many cases the respondents have not come out with the correct answers, instead they have replied what should have been the ideal answer. However, the same question when worded differently has been answered differently and truth concealed earlier has been revealed later on. This way the present researcher has been able to extract the true picture of the whole administrative scene in the universities of the sample. Present researcher has tried to discuss this paradox of false and true as and when it occurs in the answers to the questionnaires. The responses to the questionnaires by the teachers, students, non-teaching employees, HODs, Deans, Directors, and other officers have been tabulated, analysed, and interpreted below in the present chapter. However, the responses by the librarians, chief wardens and wardens of the hostels have not been tabulated mainly because of their small numbers. Information supplied by them has been mentioned while discussing the profiles and infrastructure of the universities and drawing conclusions and making suggestions in the study. Similarly, information collected through Observation Sheet has been used for discussing the profiles and infrastructure of the universities, drawing conclusions and making suggestions in the study.

I. TEACHERS' RESPONSES

Following are the teachers' responses:

TABLE 4.1.1
Finding Teaching Interesting

Name of University	*Yes*	*No*	*Can't Say*	*Total*
GNDU, Amritsar	87.00		13.00	100.00
HPU, Shimla	96.40		3.60	100.00
JU, Jammu	100.00			100.00
KU, Kurukshetra	83.30	16.70		100.00
PU, Chandigarh	100.00			100.00
Total	90.40	5.30	4.30	100.00

Chi-square value = 17.142[a], P = 0.029, Significant at .05 level.

This clearly shows that the teachers in the sample find teaching interesting.

TABLE 4.1.2
Finding Teaching Profession Respectable

Name of University	*Yes*	*No*	*Can't Say*	*Total*
GNDU, Amritsar	87.00	13.00		100.00
HPU, Shimla	100.00			100.00
JU, Jammu	100.00			100.00
KU, Kurukshetra	93. 30	6.70		100.00
PU, Chandigarh	100.00			100.00
Total	94.70	5.30		100.00

Chi-square value = 5.136[a], P = 0.274, Significant at .05 level.

This clearly shows that the teachers in the sample find teaching profession respectable.

TABLE 4.1.3
Teachers Giving Monthly Tests

Name of University	*Yes*	*No*	*Can't Say*	*Total*
GNDU, Amritsar	43.50	52.20	4.30	100.00
HPU, Shimla	28.60	60.70	10.70	100.00
JU, Jammu	20.00	60.00	20.00	100.00
KU, Kurukshetra	50.00	50.00		100.00
PU, Chandigarh	75.00	12.50	12.50	100.00
Total	42.60	51.00	6.40	100.00

Chi-square value = 11.998[a], P = 0.151, Statistically not significant.

This shows that the situation in all the Universities is quite similar and the differences are not statistically significant. Only 42.60 percent teachers in the sample are giving monthly tests to the students. PU is at highest with 75% whereas JU is lowest with 20% only.

TABLE 4.1.4
Teachers Giving Assignments

Name of University	*Yes*	*No*	*Can't Say*	*Total*
GNDU, Amritsar	87.00	13.00		100.00
HPU, Shimla	75.00	17.90	7.10	100.00
JU, Jammu	40.00	60.00		100.00
KU, Kurukshetra	73.30	16.70	10.00	100.00
PU, Chandigarh	100.00			100.00
Total	77.70	17.00	5.30	100.00

Chi-square value = 12.122[a], P = 0.146, Statistically not significant.

This shows that the situation in all the Universities is quite similar and the differences are not statistically significant. 77.70% teachers in the sample are giving assignments to the students. PU is at highest with 100% whereas JU is lowest with 40.00% only.

TABLE 4.1.5
Teachers Adopting Lecture Method

Name of University	*Yes*	*No*	*Can't Say*	*Total*
GNDU, Amritsar	95.70	4.30		100.00
HPU, Shimla	96.40		3.60	100.00
JU, Jammu	100.00			100.00
KU, Kurukshetra	80.00	10.00	10.00	100.00
PU, Chandigarh	87.50		12.50	100.00
Total	90.40	4.30	5.30	100.00

Chi-square value = 8.333[a], P = 0.402, Statistically not significant.

This shows that the situation in all the Universities is quite similar and the differences are not statistically significant. Teachers mostly depend on the lecture method as is clear from the fact that 90.40% of the teachers in the sample say that they adopt lecture method.

TABLE 4.1.6
Teachers Adopting Discussion Method

Name of University	*Yes*	*No*	*Can't Say*	*Total*
GNDU, Amritsar	91.30	4.30	4.30	100.00
HPU, Shimla	89.30	3.60	7.10	100.00
JU, Jammu	100.00			100.00
KU, Kurukshetra	83.30	10.00	6.70	100.00
PU, Chandigarh	100.00			100.00
Total	89.40	5.30	5.30	100.00

Chi-square value = 3.435[a], P = 0.904, Statistically not significant.

This shows that the situation in all the Universities of the sample is quite similar and the differences are not statistically significant. A good number of the teachers (89.40%) adopt discussion method of teaching.

TABLE 4.1.7
Teachers Adopting Seminar Method

Name of University	*Yes*	*No*	*Can't Say*	*Total*
GNDU, Amritsar	78.30	17.40	4.30	100.00
HPU, Shimla	78.60	10.70	10.70	100.00
JU, Jammu	80.00	20.00		100.00
KU, Kurukshetra	63.3	23.30	13.30	100.00
PU, Chandigarh	100.00			100.00
Total	75.50	16.00	8.50	100.00

Chi-square value = 6.712[a], P = 0.568, Statistically not significant.

This shows that the situation in all the Universities is quite similar and the differences are not statistically significant. A good number of the teachers (75.50%) adopt seminar method of teaching.

Table 4.1.8
Teachers Adopting Project Method

Name of University	*Yes*	*No*	*Can't Say*	*Total*
GNDU, Amritsar	60.90	21.70	17.40	100.00
HPU, Shimla	64.30	21.40	14.30	100.00
JU, Jammu	20.00	60.00	20.00	100.00
KU, Kurukshetra	33.30	36.70	30.00	100.00
PU, Chandigarh	50.00	12.50	37.50	100.00
Total	50.00	27.70	22.30	100.00

Chi-square value = 11.061[a], P = 0.198, Statistically not significant.

This shows that the situation in all the Universities is quite similar and the differences are not statistically significant. 50% of the teachers in the sample adopt project method of teaching. HPU is highest with 64.30%, whereas JU is the lowest with only 20%.

Table 4.1.9
Teachers Adopting Tutorial Method

Name of University	*Yes*	*No*	*Can't Say*	*Total*
GNDU, Amritsar	30.40	56.50	13.00	100.00
HPU, Shimla	35.70	42.90	21.40	100.00
JU, Jammu	40.00	60.00		100.00
KU, Kurukshetra	73.30	10.00	16.70	100.00
PU, Chandigarh	37.50	12.50	50.00	100.00
Total	46.80	34.00	19.10	100.00

Chi-square value = 23.542[a], P = 0.003, Significant at .05 level.

This shows that the majority of the teachers in the sample adopt tutorial method of teaching. Only 46.80% of the teachers in the sample adopt tutorial method in teaching.

TABLE 4.1.10
Teachers Using Over-Head Projector (OHP)

Name of University	*Yes*	*No*	*Can't Say*	*Total*
GNDU, Amritsar	34.80	56.50	8.70	100.00
HPU, Shimla	25.00	71.40	4.60	100.00
JU, Jammu		100.00		100.00
KU, Kurukshetra	33.30	63.30	3.30	100.00
PU, Chandigarh	37.50	37.50	25.00	100.00
Total	29.80	63.80	6.40	100.00

Chi-square value = 10.164[a], P = 0.254, Statistically not significant.

This shows that the situation in all the Universities is quite similar and the differences are not statistically significant. Only 29.80% teachers in the sample use OHP as an aid in teaching the students. PU is at highest with 37.50% whereas JU is lowest with zero%.

TABLE 4.1.11
Teachers Using Video-Films

Name of University	*Yes*	*No*	*Can't Say*	*Total*
GNDU, Amritsar	8.70	78.30	13.00	100.00
HPU, Shimla	21.40	64.30	14.30	100.00
JU, Jammu	40.00	60.00		100.00
KU, Kurukshetra	26.70	66.60	6.70	100.00
PU, Chandigarh	12.50	75.00	12.50	100.00
Total	20.20	69.10	10.60	100.00

Chi-square value = 5.329[a], P = 0.722, Statistically not significant.

This shows that the situation in all the Universities is quite similar and the differences are not statistically significant. Only 20.20% teachers in the sample use video-films as an aid in teaching the students. Surprisingly, JU is the highest with 40% and GNDU is the lowest with 8.70% only.

Table 4.1.12
Students Discussing their Academic Problems with Teachers

Name of University	*Yes*	*No*	*Can't Say*	*Total*
GNDU, Amritsar	91.30	8.70		100.00
HPU, Shimla	92.80	3.60	3.60	100.00
JU, Jammu	100.00			100.00
KU, Kurukshetra	80.00	16.70	3.30	100.00
PU, Chandigarh	100.00			100.00
Total	89.40	8.50	2.10	100.00

Chi-square value = 6.007[a], P = 0.646, Statistically not significant.

This shows that the situation in all the Universities is quite similar and the differences are not statistically significant. As reported by the teachers, a good number of students (89.40%) in the sample discuss their academic problems with the teachers.

Table 4.1.13
Teachers Discussing their Academic Problems with their Colleagues

Name of University	*Yes*	*No*	*Can't Say*	*Total*
GNDU, Amritsar	82.60	8.70	8.70	100.00
HPU, Shimla	71.40	7.10	21.40	100.00
JU, Jammu	100.00			100.00
KU, Kurukshetra	56.70	23.30	20.00	100.00
PU, Chandigarh	75.00		25.00	100.00
Total	71.30	11.70	17.00	100.00

Chi-square value = 10.135[a], P = 0.256, Statistically not significant.

This shows that the situation in all the Universities is quite similar and the differences are not statistically significant. A good number of the teachers (71.30%) in the sample discuss their academic problems with their colleagues.

TABLE 4.1.14

Teachers Preferring Marking by Outside Examiners

Name of University	*Yes*	*No*	*Can't Say*	*Total*
GNDU, Amritsar	87.00	13.00		100.00
HPU, Shimla	64.30	35.70		100.00
JU, Jammu	80.00	20.00		100.00
KU, Kurukshetra	63.30	30.00	6.70	100.00
PU, Chandigarh	75.00	25.00		100.00
Total	71.30	26.60	2.10	100.00

Chi-square value = 8.270[a], P = 0.408, Statistically not significant.

This shows that the situation in all the Universities is quite similar and the differences are not statistically significant. A good number of the teachers (71.30%) in the sample prefer marking by outside teachers. This clearly shows lack of faith in the fairness of their colleagues.

TABLE 4.1.15

Teachers for the Minimum Attendance of Classes by the Students

Name of University	*Yes*	*No*	*Can't Say*	*Total*
GNDU, Amritsar	82.60	13.00	4.30	100.00
HPU, Shimla	92.90		7.10	100.00
JU, Jammu	80.00	20.00		100.00
KU, Kurukshetra	70.00	30.00		100.00
PU, Chandigarh	100.00			100.00
Total	83.00	13.80	3.20	100.00

Chi-square value = 14.861[a], P = 0.062, Statistically not significant.

This clearly shows that the majority of teachers (83%) want that there should be some minimum attendance of classes by the students. This situation in all the Universities of the sample is quite similar and the differences are not statistically significant.

Table 4.1.16
Teachers Favouring Elections to Students' Central Association (SCA)

Name of University	*Yes*	*No*	*Can't Say*	*Total*
GNDU, Amritsar	60.90	34.80	4.30	100.00
HPU, Shimla	60.70	35.70	3.60	100.00
JU, Jammu	80.00	20.00		100.00
KU, Kurukshetra	40.00	46.70	13.30	100.00
PU, Chandigarh	100.00			100.00
Total	58.50	35.10	6.40	100.00

Chi-square value = 12.426[a], P = 0.133, Statistically not significant.

This shows that the situation in all the Universities is quite similar and the differences are not statistically significant. 58.50% of the teachers in the sample favour elections to SCA. Here PU is the highest with 100% and KU the lowest with 40%.

Table 4.1.17
Teachers Filling Self-Appraisal Report Regularly Every Year

Name of University	*Yes*	*No*	*Can't Say*	*Total*
GNDU, Amritsar	34.80	60.90	4.30	100.00
HPU, Shimla	85.70	14.30		100.00
JU, Jammu	100.00			100.00
KU, Kurukshetra	73.30	16.70	10.00	100.00
PU, Chandigarh	62.50	37.50		100.00
Total	68.10	27.70	4.30	100.00

Chi-square value = 5. 136[a], P = 0.274, Significant at .05 level.

The above Table indicates that only 68.10% of the teachers fill their self-appraisal reports regularly. JU has the highest percentage, i.e. 100% whereas GNDU has the lowest with 34.80%.

TABLE 4.1.18
Teachers Favouring Rotation in Headship

Name of University	*Yes*	*No*	*Can't Say*	*Total*
GNDU, Amritsar	87.00	4.30	8.70	100.00
HPU, Shimla	82.10	14.30	3.60	100.00
JU, Jammu	80.00	20.00		100.00
KU, Kurukshetra	80.00	16.70	3.30	100.00
PU, Chandigarh	100.00			100.00
Total	84.00	11.70	4.30	100.00

Chi-square value = 5.140[a], P = 0.746, Statistically not significant.

The above Table indicates that a good number of teachers (84%) favour rotation in headship. This Table also shows that the situation in all the Universities in the sample is quite similar and the differences are not statistically significant. This shows that University teachers have strong democratic orientation and do not want to be ruled for ever by a single person.

TABLE 4.1.19
Teachers Finding Difficulties in Getting Administrative Work Done

Name of University	*Yes*	*No*	*Can't Say*	*Total*
GNDU, Amritsar	43.50	47.80	8.70	100.00
HPU, Shimla	75.00	21.40	3.60	100.00
JU, Jammu	40.00	60.00		100.00
KU, Kurukshetra	56.70	40.00	3.30	100.00
PU, Chandigarh	62.50	37.50		100.00
Total	58.50	37.20	4.30	100.00

Chi-square value = 7. 560[a], P = 0 .478.

The above Table indicates that 58.50% teachers in the total sample find difficulties in getting the administrative work done in the Universities. The worst position with 75% is in the Himachal Pradesh University followed by Panjab University with 62.5%. This clearly shows that administration in the Universities is inefficient and obstructive.

TABLE 4.1.20
Teachers Finding Difficulties in Getting the Clearance of Bills by LAD

Name of University	*Yes*	*No*	*Can't Say*	*Total*
GNDU, Amritsar	60.90	21.70	17.40	100.00
HPU, Shimla	78.60	7.10	14.30	100.00
JU, Jammu	60.00	40.00		100.00
KU, Kurukshetra	43.30	36.70	20.00	100.00
PU, Chandigarh	25.00	62.50	12.50	100.00
Total	57.40	26.60	16.00	100.00

Chi-square value = 15.525[a], P = .050, Significant at .05 level.

The above Table indicates that 57.40% teachers in the total sample find difficulties in getting their bills cleared by the Local Audit Department working in the Universities. The worst position with 78.60% is again in the Himachal Pradesh University followed by Guru Nanak Dev University with 60.90%. It is really a sad commentary that LAD which has been engaged for making sure that the moneys are properly spent and utilized plays an obstructive role making it difficult for the teachers to conduct seminars and to spend money on research projects.

TABLE 4.1.21
Teachers Finding the System of Internal Audit Effective

Name of University	*Yes*	*No*	*Can't Say*	*Total*
GNDU, Amritsar	43.50	47.80	8.70	100.00
HPU, Shimla	32.10	64.30	3.60	100.00
JU, Jammu	40.00	40.00	20.00	100.00
KU, Kurukshetra	36.70	36.70	26.60	100.00
PU, Chandigarh	62.50	25.00	12.50	100.00
Total	39.40	46.80	13.80	100.00

Chi-square value = 15.525[a], P = .050, Significance level = .05.

The working of the Internal Audit is also equally bad. The above Table indicates that only 39.40% teachers in the total sample find the system of internal audit effective. The worst position is in the HPU where 64.30% teachers do not find it effective.

TABLE 4.1.22

Teachers Easily Getting the Reading Material of their Academic Interests in the Library

Name of University	*Yes*	*No*	*Can't Say*	*Total*
GNDU, Amritsar	69.60	21.70	8.70	100.00
HPU, Shimla	39.30	53.60	7.10	100.00
JU, Jammu	80.00	20.00		100.00
KU, Kurukshetra	50.00	50.00		100.00
PU, Chandigarh	87.50		12.50	100.00
Total	56.40	38.30	5.30	100.00

Chi-square value = 15.477[a], P = .051, Significance level = .05

The above Table indicates that only 56.40% teachers in the total sample easily get the reading material of their interest in the university library. PU has the highest (87.50%) whereas the HPU the lowest (39.30%) in the respect. The differences are statistically significant at .05 level.

TABLE 4.1.23

Teachers Finding Difficulties in Getting Research Grants Released

Name of University	*Yes*	*No*	*Can't Say*	*Total*
GNDU, Amritsar	34.80	56.50	8.70	100.00
HPU, Shimla	60.70	35.70	3.60	100.00
JU, Jammu	40.00	60.00		100.00
KU, Kurukshetra	53.30	23.30	23.30	100.00
PU, Chandigarh	62.50	25.00	12.50	100.00
Total	51.10	37.20	11.70	100.00

Chi-square value = 12.767[a], P = 0.120, Statistically not significant.

This shows that the situation in all the Universities is quite similar and the differences are not statistically significant. A good number (51.10 %) of the teachers in the total sample find difficulties in getting research grants released.

TABLE 4.1.24
Teachers Finding Difficultes in Getting the Accounts of National/International Seminars Settled

Name of University	*Yes*	*No*	*Can't Say*	*Total*
GNDU, Amritsar	17.40	56.50	26.10	100.00
HPU, Shimla	67.90	32.10		100.00
JU, Jammu	40.00	60.00		100.00
KU, Kurukshetra	20.00	60.00	20.00	100.00
PU, Chandigarh	50.00	37.00	12.50	100.00
Total	37.20	48.90	13.80	100.00

Chi-square value = 23.110[a], P = .003, Significance level = .05.

Above Table indicates that 37.20% of the teachers in the total sample find difficulties in the accounts of national/ international seminars settled. Differences are statistically significant at .05 level. Position in the HPU is the worst with 67.90% and the best in GNDU with 17.40%. This certainly discourages teachers from organizing the seminars.

TABLE 4.1.25
Cases of Sexual Harassment of Female Students by Male Students

Name of University	*Yes*	*No*	*Can't Say*	*Total*
GNDU, Amritsar	21.70	73.90	4.30	100.00
HPU, Shimla	7.10	89.30	3.60	100.00
JU, Jammu		100.00		100.00
KU, Kurukshetra	6.70	73.30	20.00	100.00
PU, Chandigarh		87.50	12.50	100.00
Total	9.60	80.90	9.60	100.0

Chi-square value = 11.767[a], P = 0.162, Statistically not significant.

The above Table indicates that only a few cases of 9.60% of sexual harassment of female students by male students have been found in the Universities of the sample. Position in the JU and the PU is the best with the zero % cases whereas it is worst with 21.70% in the GNDU.

TABLE 4.1.26
Cases of Sexual Harassment of Female Students by Male Teachers

Name of University	*Yes*	*No*	*Can't Say*	*Total*
GNDU, Amritsar	34.80	60.90	4.30	100.00
HPU, Shimla		92.90	7.10	100.00
JU, Jammu	20.00	80.00		100.00
KU, Kurukshetra	10.00	80.00	10.00	100.00
PU, Chandigarh	25.00	50.00	25.00	100.00
Total	14.90	76.60	8.50	100.00

Chi-square value = 17.488[a], P = .025, Significance level = .05.

The above Table indicates that only a few cases of 14.90% of sexual harassment of female students by male teachers have been found in the Universities of the sample. Position in the HPU is the best with the zero % cases whereas it is worst with 34.80% in the GNDU.

TABLE 4.1.27
Cases of Sexual Harassment of Female Teachers by Male Teachers

Name of University	*Yes*	*No*	*Can't Say*	*Total*
GNDU, Amritsar	34.80	56.50	8.70	100.00
HPU, Shimla		89.30	10.70	100.00
JU, Jammu	40.00	60.00		100.00
KU, Kurukshetra	6.70	80.70	13.30	100.00
PU, Chandigarh	25.00	75.00		100.00
Total	14.90	75.50	9.60	100.00

Chi-square value = 18.092[a], P = .021, Significance level = .05.

The above Table indicates that only a few cases of 14.90% of sexual harassment of female teachers by male teachers have been found in the Universities of the sample. Position in the HPU is the best with the zero% cases whereas it is worst with 34.80% in the GNDU.

TABLE 4.1.28
Teachers Thinking Their University Enjoying Autonomy in Appointment of Teachers

Name of University	*Yes*	*No*	*Can't Say*	*Total*
GNDU, Amritsar	56.50	21.70	21.70	100.00
HPU, Shimla	21.40	60.70	17.90	100.00
JU, Jammu	60.00	20.00	20.00	100.00
KU, Kurukshetra	46.60	36.70	16.70	100.00
PU, Chandigarh	75.00		25.00	100.00
Total	44.70	36.20	19.10	100.00

Chi-square value = 15.636[a], P = .048, Significance level = .05.

Above Table indicates that only 44.70% of the teachers in the total sample think that their universities enjoy autonomy in the appointment of the teachers. Differences are statistically significant at .05 level. Position in the HPU is the worst with 21.40% and the best in PU with 75%.

TABLE 4.1.29
Teachers Thinking Their University Enjoying Autonomy in Promotion of Teachers

Name of University	*Yes*	*No*	*Can't Say*	*Total*
GNDU, Amritsar	65.20	13.00	21.70	100.00
HPU, Shimla	35.70	53.60	10.70	100.00
JU, Jammu	80.00	20.00		100.00
KU, Kurukshetra	43.30	36.70	20.00	100.00
PU, Chandigarh	75.00	12.50	12.50	100.00
Total	51.00	33.00	16.00	100.00

Chi-square value = 14.160[a], P = 0.078, Statistically not significant.

This shows that the situation in all the Universities is quite similar and the differences are not statistically significant. 51% of the teachers think that their universities enjoy autonomy in the promotion of teachers. Position in the HPU is the worst with 35.70% and the best in JU with 80%.

TABLE 4.1.30
Teachers Thinking Their University Enjoying Autonomy in Appointment of Deans/Directors

Name of University	*Yes*	*No*	*Can't Say*	*Total*
GNDU, Amritsar	56.50	8.70	34.80	100.00
HPU, Shimla	42.90	46.40	10.70	100.00
JU, Jammu	80.00	20.00		100.00
KU, Kurukshetra	50.00	40.00	10.00	100.00
PU, Chandigarh	75.00	12.50	12.50	100.00
Total	53.20	30.90	16.00	100.0

Chi-square value = 16.914[a], P = .031, Significance level = .05.

Above Table indicates that only 53.20% of the teachers in the total sample think that their universities enjoy autonomy in the appointment of the deans/directors. Differences are statistically significant at .05 level. Position in the HPU is the worst with 42.90% and the best in JU with 80%.

TABLE 4.1.31
Teachers Thinking of Getting Promotion on the Basis of Merit

Name of University	*Yes*	*No*	*Can't Say*	*Total*
GNDU, Amritsar	60.90	26.10	13.00	100.00
HPU, Shimla	53.60	42.90	3.60	100.00
JU, Jammu	80.00	20.00		100.00
KU, Kurukshetra	40.00	43.30	16.70	100.00
PU, Chandigarh	75.00		25.00	100.00
Total	54.30	34.00	11.70	100.00

Chi-square value = 11.440[a], P = 0.178, Statistically not significant.

This shows that the situation in all the Universities is quite similar and the differences are not statistically significant. 54.30% of the teachers think that they will get promotion on the basis of their merit. Position in the KU is the worst with 40% and the best in JU with 80%.

TABLE 4.1.32

Teachers Thinking University Education to be Limited to a Few

Name of University	*Yes*	*No*	*Can't Say*	*Total*
GNDU, Amritsar	21.70	73.90	4.30	100.00
HPU, Shimla	25.00	60.70	14.30	100.00
JU, Jammu	60.00	40.00		100.00
KU, Kurukshetra	23.30	63.30	13.30	100.00
PU, Chandigarh	25.00	62.50	12.50	100.00
Total	25.50	63.80	10.60	100.00

Chi-square value = 5.343[a], P = 0.720, Statistically not significant.

This shows that the situation in all the Universities is quite similar and the differences are not statistically significant. Majority of the teachers (63.80%) in the sample are of the view that university education should not be limited to a few only.

TABLE 4.1.33

Teachers Thinking University Education for Getting Job Only

Name of University	*Yes*	*No*	*Can't Say*	*Total*
GNDU, Amritsar	8.70	82.60	8.70	100.00
HPU, Shimla	14.30	82.10	3.60	100.00
JU, Jammu		100.00		100.00
KU, Kurukshetra	26.70	73.30		100.00
PU, Chandigarh		87.50	12.50	100.00
Total	14.90	80.90	4.30	100.00

Chi-square value = 9.687[a], P = 0.228, Statistically not significant.

This shows that the situation in all the Universities is quite similar and the differences are not statistically significant. Majority of the teachers (80.90%) in the sample are of the view that university education should not be given for getting job only.

TABLE 4.1.34
Teachers Thinking University Education for Self-Development Only

Name of University	*Yes*	*No*	*Can't Say*	*Total*
GNDU, Amritsar	13.00	73.90	13.00	100.00
HPU, Shimla	14.30	67.80	17.90	100.00
JU, Jammu	60.00	40.00		100.00
KU, Kurukshetra	33.30	56.70	10.00	100.00
PU, Chandigarh	12.50	75.00	12.50	100.00
Total	22.30	64.90	12.80	100.00

Chi-square value = 9.478[a], P = 0.304, Statistically not significant.

This shows that the situation in all the Universities is quite similar and the differences are not statistically significant. Majority of the teachers (64.90%) in the sample are of the view that university education should not be given self-development only.

TABLE 4.1.35
Teachers Thinking University Education Both for Job and Self-Development

Name of University	*Yes*	*No*	*Can't Say*	*Total*
GNDU, Amritsar	91.30	8.70		100.00
HPU, Shimla	78.60	21.40		100.00
JU, Jammu	80.00	20.00		100.00
KU, Kurukshetra	80.00	13.30	6.70	100.00
PU, Chandigarh	87.50		12.50	100.00
Total	83.00	13.80	3.20	100.00

Chi-square value = 8.266[a], P = 0.408, Statistically not significant.

This shows that the situation in all the Universities is quite similar and the differences are not statistically significant. Majority of the teachers (83%) in the sample strike a balance and are of the view that university education should be both for job as well as for self-development.

TABLE 4.1.36

Teachers Considering Quality of Education of Their University Comparable to that of Advanced Countries

Name of University	*Yes*	*No*	*Can't Say*	*Total*
GNDU, Amritsar	69.60	21.70	8.70	100.00
HPU, Shimla	17.90	71.40	10.70	100.00
JU, Jammu	60.00	40.00		100.00
KU, Kurukshetra	66.60	26.70	6.70	100.00
PU, Chandigarh	62.50	37.50		100.00
Total	52.10	40.40	7.40	100.00

Chi-square value = 20.600[a], P = .008, Significance level = .01.

Above Table indicates that only 52.10% of the teachers in the total sample think that the quality of education imparted in their universities is comparable to that of advanced countries. Differences are statistically significant at .01 level. Position in the HPU is the worst with 17.90% and the best in GNDU with 69.60%.

TABLE 4.1.37

Teachers Who Made Efforts in Bringing Quality of Education of Their University Comparable to that of Advanced Countries

Name of University	*Yes*	*No*	*Can't Say*	*Total*
GNDU, Amritsar	82.60	8.70	8.70	100.00
HPU, Shimla	57.10	28.60	14.30	100.00
JU, Jammu	100.00			100.00
KU, Kurukshetra	70.00	23.30	6.70	100.00
PU, Chandigarh	100.00			100.00
Total	73.40	18.10	8.50	100.00

Chi-square value = 10.530[a], P = 0.230, Statistically not significant.

This shows that the situation in all the Universities is quite similar and the differences are not statistically significant. However, 73.40% of the teachers in the total sample think that they are making efforts to bring the quality of education imparted in their universities comparable to that of advanced countries. Position in the HPU is the worst with 57.10% and the best in JU and PU with 100%.

TABLE 4.1.38

Teachers Considering University Administration Sympathetic to their Demands

Name of University	*Yes*	*No*	*Can't Say*	*Total*
GNDU, Amritsar	65.20	21.70	13.00	100.00
HPU, Shimla	25.00	71.40	3.60	100.00
JU, Jammu	80.00	20.00		100.00
KU, Kurukshetra	56.70	33.30	10.00	100.00
PU, Chandigarh	75.00	12.50	12.50	100.00
Total	52.10	39.40	8.50	100.00

Chi-square value = 20.600[a], P = .008, Significance level = .01.

Above Table indicates that only 52.10% of the teachers in the total sample think that the administration in their universities is sympathetic to their demands. Differences are statistically significant at .01 level. Position in the HPU is the worst with 25% and the best in JU with 80%.

TABLE 4.1.39

Teachers Considering University Administration Quick in Redressing their Grievances

Name of University	*Yes*	*No*	*Can't Say*	*Total*
GNDU, Amritsar	56.50	30.40	13.00	100.00
HPU, Shimla	28.60	64.30	7.10	100.00
JU, Jammu	20.00	80.00		100.00
KU, Kurukshetra	36.70	53.00	10.00	100.00
PU, Chandigarh	37.50	50.00	12.50	100.00
Total	38.30	52.10	9.60	100.00

Chi-square value = 19.328[a], P = 0.081, Statistically not significant.

This shows that the situation in all the Universities is quite similar and the differences are not statistically significant. Above Table indicates that only 38.30% of the teachers in the total sample think that the administration in their universities is quick in redressing their grievances. Differences are statistically significant at .01 level. Position in the JU is the worst with 20% and the best in GNDU with 56.50%.

2. STUDENTS' RESPONSES

Following are the students' responses:

TABLE 4.2.1
Students Finding Classroom Teaching Interesting

Name of University	*Yes*	*No*	*Can't Say*	*Total*
GNDU, Amritsar	69.80	26.50	3.70	100.00
HPU, Shimla	59.00	41.00		100.00
JU, Jammu	84.60	15.40		100.00
KU, Kurukshetra	73.50	21.40	5.10	100.00
PU, Chandigarh	69.80	28.00	2.20	100.00
Total	69.80	28.10	2.20	100.00

Chi-square value = 29.773[a], P = .000, Significance level = .01.

Above Table indicates that 69.80% of the students in the total sample find classroom teaching interesting. Differences are statistically significant at .01 level. Position in the HPU is the worst with 59% and the best in JU with 84.60%.

TABLE 4.2.2
Students Finding Syllabus Useful

Name of University	*Yes*	*No*	*Can't Say*	*Total*
GNDU, Amritsar	67.60	24.30	8.10	100.00
HPU, Shimla	62.50	36.10	1.40	100.00
JU, Jammu	82.10	17.90		100.00
KU, Kurukshetra	70.40	25.50	4.10	100.00
PU, Chandigarh	77.40	21.50	1.10	100.00
Total	70.50	26.20	3.30	100.00

Chi-square value = 27.274[a], P = .001, Significance level = .01.

Above Table indicates that 70.50% of the students in the total sample find classroom syllabus useful. Differences are statistically significant at .01 level. Position in the HPU is the worst with 62.50% and the best in JU with 82.10%.

TABLE 4.2.3
Students Finding Syllabus Interesting

Name of University	*Yes*	*No*	*Can't Say*	*Total*
GNDU, Amritsar	59.50	34.60	5.90	100.00
HPU, Shimla	60.40	35.40	4.20	100.00
JU, Jammu	76.90	23.10		100.00
KU, Kurukshetra	64.20	32.70	3.10	100.00
PU, Chandigarh	80.60	18.30	1.10	100.00
Total	66.70	30.10	3.30	100.00

Chi-square value = 21.091[a], P = .007, Significance level = .01.

Above Table indicates that 66.70% of the students in the total sample find syllabus interesting. Differences are statistically significant at .01 level. Position in the GNDU is the worst with 59.50% and the best in PU with 80.60%.

TABLE 4.2.4
Teachers Conducting Monthly Tests

Name of University	*Yes*	*No*	*Can't Say*	*Total*
GNDU, Amritsar	46.30	52.20	1.50	100.00
HPU, Shimla	13.20	81.90	4.90	100.00
JU, Jammu	28.20	66.70	5.10	100.00
KU, Kurukshetra	26.50	70.40	3.10	100.00
PU, Chandigarh	58.10	38.70	3.20	100.00
Total	33.50	63.00	3.50	100.00

Chi-square value = 66.704[a], P = .000, Significance level = .01.

Above Table indicates that only a small number of the students (33.50%) in the total sample say that their teachers conduct monthly tests. Differences are statistically significant at .01 level. Position in the HPU is the worst with only 13.20% and the best in PU with 58.10%.

TABLE 4.2.5
Teachers Giving Assignments

Name of University	*Yes*	*No*	*Can't Say*	*Total*
GNDU, Amritsar	71.30	25.00	3.70	100.00
HPU, Shimla	41.00	51.40	7.60	100.00
JU, Jammu	51.30	35.90	12.80	100.00
KU, Kurukshetra	50.00	44.90	5.10	100.00
PU, Chandigarh	72.00	24.70	3.20	100.00
Total	56.80	37.00	6.20	100.00

Chi-square value = 44.156[a], P = .000, Significance level = .01.

Above Table indicates that 56.80% of the students in the total sample say that their teachers give assignments to them. Differences are statistically significant at .01 level. Position in the HPU is the worst with only 41.00% and the best in PU with 72%.

TABLE 4.2.6
Teachers Using Lecture Method

Name of University	*Yes*	*No*	*Can't Say*	*Total*
GNDU, Amritsar	91.20	5.90	2.90	100.00
HPU, Shimla	90.20	5.60	4.20	100.00
JU, Jammu	92.30	7.70		100.00
KU, Kurukshetra	87.80	5.10	7.10	100.00
PU, Chandigarh	96.80	3.20		100.00
Total	91.40	5.50	3.10	100.00

Chi-square value = 13.114[a], P = 0.108, Statistically not significant.

Above table indicates that 91.40% of the students in the sample say that their teachers use lecture methods of teaching.

This situation in all the Universities is quite similar and the differences are not statistically significant.

TABLE 4.2.7
Teachers Using Discussion Method

Name of University	*Yes*	*No*	*Can't Say*	*Total*
GNDU, Amritsar	55.10	39.10	5.80	100.00
HPU, Shimla	59.00	26.40	14.60	100.00
JU, Jammu	48.70	48.70	2.60	100.00
KU, Kurukshetra	49.00	40.80	10.20	100.00
PU, Chandigarh	75.30	21.50	3.20	100.00
Total	57.60	34.40	8.00	100.00

Chi-square value = 36.052[a], P = .000, Significance level = .01.

Above Table indicates that 57.60% of the students in the total sample say that their teachers use discussion method of teaching them. Differences are statistically significant at .01 level. Position in the JU is the worst with only 48.70% and the best in PU with 75.30%.

TABLE 4.2.8
Teachers Using Seminar Method

Name of University	*Yes*	*No*	*Can't Say*	*Total*
GNDU, Amritsar	72.80	23.50	3.70	100.00
HPU, Shimla	30.60	52.70	16.70	100.00
JU, Jammu	43.60	51.30	5.10	100.00
KU, Kurukshetra	61.20	28.60	10.20	100.00
PU, Chandigarh	71.00	23.60	5.40	100.00
Total	55.20	36.20	8.70	100.00

Chi-square value = 74.740[a], P = .000, Significance level = .01.

Above Table indicates that 55.20% of the students in the total sample say that their teachers use seminar method of teaching them. Differences are statistically significant at .01

level. Position in the HPU is the worst with only 30.60% and the best in GNDU with 72.80%.

TABLE 4.2.9
Teachers Using Project Method

Name of University	*Yes*	*No*	*Can't Say*	*Total*
GNDU, Amritsar	34.60	58.80	6.60	100.00
HPU, Shimla	22.20	58.30	19.40	100.00
JU, Jammu	28.20	56.40	15.40	100.00
KU, Kurukshetra	22.40	60.20	17.30	100.00
PU, Chandigarh	61.30	32.30	6.50	100.00
Total	32.80	54.10	13.10	100.00

Chi-square value = 55.332[a], P = .000, Significance level = .01.

Above Table indicates that only 32.80% of the students in the total sample say that their teachers use project method of teaching them. Differences are statistically significant at .01 level. Position in the HPU is the worst with only 22.20% followed by KU with 22.40% and the best in PU with 61.30%.

TABLE 4.2.10
Teachers Using Tutorial Method

Name of University	*Yes*	*No*	*Can't Say*	*Total*
GNDU, Amritsar	8.10	75.70	16.20	100.00
HPU, Shimla	13.20	68.70	18.10	100.00
JU, Jammu	15.40	76.90	7.70	100.00
KU, Kurukshetra	36.50	51.30	10.20	100.00
PU, Chandigarh	46.20	44.10	9.70	100.00
Total	22.00	64.70	13.30	100.00

Chi-square value = 72.654[a], P = .000, Significance level = .01.

Above Table indicates that only a very small number of (22%) the students in the total sample say that their teachers use tutorial method of teaching them. Differences are statistically significant at .01 level. Position in the GNDU is the worst with only 8.10% and the best in PU with 46.20%.

TABLE 4.2.11
Teachers Using Over-Head Projector (OHP)

Name of University	*Yes*	*No*	*Can't Say*	*Total*
GNDU, Amritsar	27.90	67.60	4.40	100.00
HPU, Shimla	16.70	76.40	6.90	100.00
JU, Jammu	17.90	71.80	10.30	100.00
KU, Kurukshetra	22.40	73.50	4.10	100.00
PU, Chandigarh	46.20	52.70	1.10	100.00
Total	25.70	69.00	5.30	100.00

Chi-square value = 34.457[a], P = .000, Significance level = .01.

Above Table indicates that only a small number (25.70%) of the students in the total sample say that their teachers use OHP as teaching aid in teaching them. Differences are statistically significant at .01 level. Position in the HPU is the worst with only 16.70% followed by JU with 17.90% and the best in PU with 46.20%.

TABLE 4.2.12
Teachers Using Video-Films

Name of University	*Yes*	*No*	*Can't Say*	*Total*
GNDU, Amritsar	10.30	87.50	2.20	100.00
HPU, Shimla	9.70	86.10	4.20	100.00
JU, Jammu	23.10	74.40	2.50	100.00
KU, Kurukshetra	13.30	83.60	3.10	100.00
PU, Chandigarh	20.40	77.40	2.20	100.00
Total	14.20	82.90	2.90	100.00

Chi-square value = 13.212[a], P = 0.105, Statistically not significant.

Above Table indicates that the situation in all the Universities is quite similar and the differences are not statistically significant. Only a small number (14.20%) of the students in the total sample say that their teachers use video-films as teaching aid in teaching them. Position in the HPU is the worst with only 9.70% followed by GNDU with 10.30% and the best in JU with 23.10%.

TABLE 4.2.13
Students Discussing their Academic Problems with their Teachers

Name of University	*Yes*	*No*	*Can't Say*	*Total*
GNDU, Amritsar	39.00	49.30	11.70	100.00
HPU, Shimla	61.10	31.30	7.60	100.00
JU, Jammu	56.40	33.30	10.30	100.00
KU, Kurukshetra	48.00	41.80	10.20	100.00
PU, Chandigarh	62.40	34.40	3.20	100.00
Total	52.80	38.40	8.70	100.00

Chi-square value = 21.648[a], P = .006, Significance level = .01.

Above Table indicates that 52.80% of the students in the total sample say that they discuss their academic problems with their teachers. Differences are statistically significant at .01 level. Position in the GNDU is the worst with only 39% and the best in PU with 62.40% followed by HPU with 61.10%.

TABLE 4.2.14
Students who want Marking by Outside Teachers

Name of University	*Yes*	*No*	*Can't Say*	*Total*
GNDU, Amritsar	48.50	41.20	10.30	100.00
HPU, Shimla	74.30	22.20	3.50	100.00
JU, Jammu	48.70	48.70	2.60	100.00
KU, Kurukshetra	61.20	36.70	2.00	100.00
PU, Chandigarh	60.20	38.70	1.10	100.00
Total	59.60	36.10	4.40	100.00

Chi-square value = 37.209[a], P = .000, Significance level = .01.

Above Table indicates that 59.60% of the students in the total sample want marking of their answer books by outside teachers. Differences are statistically significant at .01 level. This clearly shows lack of faith in the fairness of their teachers. Position in the HPU is the worst with only 22.20% of the students expressing faith in their teachers.

TABLE 4.2.15

Should there be Minimum Attendance of Classes

Name of University	*Yes*	*No*	*Can't Say*	*Total*
GNDU, Amritsar	64.70	27.20	8.10	100.00
HPU, Shimla	63.20	34.70	2.10	100.00
JU, Jammu	53.80	35.90	10.30	100.00
KU, Kurukshetra	73.50	24.50	2.00	100.00
PU, Chandigarh	73.10	26.90		100.00
Total	65.80	29.90	4.40	100.00

Chi-square value = 24.621[a], P = .002, Significance level = .01.

Above Table indicates that 65.80% of the students in the total sample say that there should be a minimum attendance of classes by the students. Differences are statistically significant at .01 level. It is encouraging to note that majority of the students are in favour of minimum attendance of classes.

TABLE 4.2.16

Students Appearing in Other Examinations

Name of University	*Yes*	*No*	*Can't Say*	*Total*
GNDU, Amritsar	55.10	37.50	7.40	100.00
HPU, Shimla	79.90	17.30	2.80	100.00
JU, Jammu	69.20	25.60	5.10	100.00
KU, Kurukshetra	59.20	38.80	2.00	100.00
PU, Chandigarh	79.60	19.30	1.10	100.00
Total	68.50	27.70	3.80	100.00

Chi-square value = 34.082[a], P = .000, Significance level = .01.

Above Table indicates that a large majority (68.50%) of the

students in the total sample say that they were appearing for some other examinations also. Differences are statistically significant at .01 level. This clearly shows that majority of students remain busy in preparing for other examinations which give them better job prospects and naturally are not in a position to pay proper attention to their university classes.

TABLE 4.2.17
Students Finding Difficulties in Getting Administrative Work Done

Name of University	*Yes*	*No*	*Can't Say*	*Total*
GNDU, Amritsar	57.40	36.00	6.60	100.00
HPU, Shimla	66.00	31.90	2.10	100.00
JU, Jammu	66.70	33.30		100.00
KU, Kurukshetra	66.30	31.60	2.00	100.00
PU, Chandigarh	78.50	20.40	1.10	100.00
Total	66.10	31.10	2.70	100.00

Chi-square value = 19.339[a], P = .013, Significance level = .01.

Above Table indicates that a large majority (66.10%) of the students in the total sample say that they find difficulties in getting the administrative work done in their respective universities. Differences are statistically significant at .01 level.

TABLE 4.2.18
Students Favouring Election to Students' Central Association

Name of University	*Yes*	*No*	*Can't Say*	*Total*
GNDU, Amritsar	61.80	29.40	8.80	100.00
HPU, Shimla	75.70	23.60	0.70	100.00
JU, Jammu	71.80	28.20		100.00
KU, Kurukshetra	41.80	55.10	3.10	100.00
PU, Chandigarh	76.30	20.40	3.20	100.00
Total	65.80	30.80	3.50	100.00

Chi-square value = 55.006[a], P = .000, Significance level = .01.

Above Table indicates that a large majority (65.80%) of the

students in the total sample favour election to SCA. Differences are statistically significant at .01 level.

TABLE 4.2.19

Students who Indulged in Cheating in the Examinations

Name of University	*Yes*	*No*	*Can't Say*	*Total*
GNDU, Amritsar	6.60	89.70	3.70	100.00
HPU, Shimla	8.30	88.90	2.80	100.00
JU, Jammu	5.10	89.70	5.10	100.00
KU, Kurukshetra	12.20	84.70	3.10	100.00
PU, Chandigarh	12.90	83.90	3.20	100.00
Total	8.90	87.60	3.50	100.00

Chi-square value = 6.265[a], P = 0.618, Statistically not significant.

From the above Table it is clear that only a small number (8.90%) of the students admit that they have indulged in cheating in the examinations. This situation in all the Universities is quite similar and the differences are not statistically significant.

TABLE 4.2.20

Students Finding Reading Material of their Interest in the Library

Name of University	*Yes*	*No*	*Can't Say*	*Total*
GNDU, Amritsar	55.90	39.00	5.10	100.00
HPU, Shimla	49.30	47.20	3.50	100.00
JU, Jammu	48.70	46.20	5.10	100.00
KU, Kurukshetra	38.80	58.10	3.10	100.00
PU, Chandigarh	73.10	24.70	2.20	100.00
Total	53.00	43.20	3.80	100.00

Chi-square value = 27.234[a], P = .001, Significance level = .01.

Above Table indicates that 53% of the students in the total sample say that they get reading material of their interest from their respective university libraries. Differences are statistically significant at .01 level. Position in the KU is the worst with only 38.80% and the best in PU with 73.10%.

TABLE 4.2.21

Students Noticing Cases of Sexual Harassment of Female Students by Male Students

Name of University	*Yes*	*No*	*Can't Say*	*Total*
GNDU, Amritsar	11.00	84.60	4.40	100.00
HPU, Shimla	20.80	75.00	4.20	100.00
JU, Jammu	12.80	76.90	10.30	100.00
KU, Kurukshetra	34.70	65.30		100.00
PU, Chandigarh	22.50	75.30	2.20	100.00
Total	20.00	76.00	4.00	100.00

Chi-square value = 33.602[a], P = .000, Significance level = .01.

The above Table indicates that 20.00% cases of sexual harassment of female students by male students have been noticed by the students in the Universities of the sample. Position in the KU is worst with 34.70% and the best with the 11% in the GNDU. Differences are statistically significant at .01 levels.

TABLE 4.2.22

Students Noticing Cases of Sexual Harassment of Female Students by Male Teachers

Name of University	*Yes*	*No*	*Can't Say*	*Total*
GNDU, Amritsar	6.60	91.20	2.20	100.00
HPU, Shimla	18.70	75.00	6.30	100.00
JU, Jammu	12.80	76.90	10.30	100.00
KU, Kurukshetra	27.60	68.30	4.10	100.00
PU, Chandigarh	23.60	75.30	1.10	100.00
Total	17.30	78.10	4.60	100.00

Chi-square value = 33.366[a], P = .000, Significance level = .01.

The above Table indicates that only 17.30% cases of sexual harassment of female students by male teachers have been noticed by the students in the Universities of the sample. Position in the KU is worst with 27.60% and the best with only 6.60% in the GNDU. Differences are statistically significant at .01 levels.

TABLE 4.2.23
Students Favouring University Education Limited to a Few

Name of University	*Yes*	*No*	*Can't Say*	*Total*
GNDU, Amritsar	24.30	66.90	8.80	100.00
HPU, Shimla	24.30	73.60	2.10	100.00
JU, Jammu	23.10	66.70	10.30	100.00
KU, Kurukshetra	33.70	63.30	3.10	100.00
PU, Chandigarh	24.70	74.20	1.10	100.00
Total	25.50	69.20	4.90	100.00

Chi-square value = 18.845[a], P = .016, Significance level = .01.

Above Table indicates that only 25.50% of the students in the total sample are of the view that university education should be limited to a few persons. Differences are statistically significant at .01 level.

TABLE 4.2.24
Students Favouring University Education for Getting Job Only

Name of University	*Yes*	*No*	*Can't Say*	*Total*
GNDU, Amritsar	21.30	75.00	3.70	100.00
HPU, Shimla	10.40	84.00	5.60	100.00
JU, Jammu	15.40	74.40	10.20	100.00
KU, Kurukshetra	17.30	78.60	4.10	100.00
PU, Chandigarh	16.10	82.80	1.10	100.00
Total	16.00	79.20	4.70	100.00

Chi-square value = 14.715[a], P = 0.618, Statistically not significant.

Above Table indicates that only 16% of the students in the total sample are of the view that university education should be only for getting job. This situation in all the Universities is quite similar and the differences are not statistically significant.

Table 4.2.25
Students Favouring Education for Self-Development Only

Name of University	*Yes*	*No*	*Can't Say*	*Total*
GNDU, Amritsar	28.70	63.20	8.10	100.00
HPU, Shimla	29.20	63.20	7.60	100.00
JU, Jammu	35.90	56.40	7.70	100.00
KU, Kurukshetra	23.50	71.40	5.10	100.00
PU, Chandigarh	24.70	68.80	6.50	100.00
Total	28.20	64.70	7.10	100.00

Chi-square value = 5.613[a], P = 0.691, Statistically not significant.

Above Table indicates that only 28.20% of the students in the total sample are of the view that university education should be for self-development only. This situation in all the Universities is quite similar and the differences are not statistically significant.

Table 4.2.26
Students Favouring Education Both for Job and Self-Development

Name of University	*Yes*	*No*	*Can't Say*	*Total*
GNDU, Amritsar	89.70	8.80	1.50	100.00
HPU, Shimla	88.20	9.00	2.80	100.00
JU, Jammu	79.40	10.30	10.30	100.00
KU, Kurukshetra	81.60	14.30	4.10	100.00
PU, Chandigarh	86.00	14.00		100.00
Total	85.80	10.90	3.50	100.00

Chi-square value = 20.052[a], P = .010, Significance level = .01.

Above Table indicates that majority (85.80%) of the students in the total sample are of the view that university education should be both for the job as well as for self-development. Differences are statistically significant at .01 level.

TABLE 4.2.27
Students Considering Quality of Education of their University Comparable to that of Advanced Countries

Name of University	*Yes*	*No*	*Can't Say*	*Total*
GNDU, Amritsar	41.20	49.30	9.50	100.00
HPU, Shimla	41.00	53.50	5.50	100.00
JU, Jammu	35.90	59.00	5.10	100.00
KU, Kurukshetra	38.80	56.10	5.10	100.00
PU, Chandigarh	45.20	51.60	3.20	100.00
Total	40.60	53.40	6.00	100.00

Chi-square value = 6.413[a], P = 0.601, Statistically not significant.

Above Table indicates that only 40.60% of the students in the total sample are of the view that the quality of education imparted in their respective universities is comparable to that of advanced counties. This situation in all the Universities is quite similar and the differences are not statistically significant.

TABLE 4.2.28
Students Finding University Administration Sympathetic to their Demands

Name of University	*Yes*	*No*	*Can't Say*	*Total*
GNDU, Amritsar	52.90	35.30	11.80	100.00
HPU, Shimla	36.10	54.90	9.00	100.00
JU, Jammu	56.40	41.00	2.60	100.00
KU, Kurukshetra	43.90	52.00	4.10	100.00
PU, Chandigarh	41.90	54.80	3.20	100.00
Total	45.50	47.50	6.90	100.00

Chi-square value = 25.514[a], P = .001, Significance level = .01.

Above Table indicates that only 45.50% of the students in the total sample find university administration sympathetic to their demands. Differences are statistically significant at .01 levels. Position in JU is the best with 56.90% and the worst in HPU with 36.10%.

TABLE 4.2.29

Students Finding University Administration Quick in Redressing their Grievance

Name of University	*Yes*	*No*	*Can't Say*	*Total*
GNDU, Amritsar	38.20	47.80	14.00	100.00
HPU, Shimla	27.80	64.60	7.60	100.00
JU, Jammu	28.20	61.50	10.30	100.00
KU, Kurukshetra	44.90	52.00	3.10	100.00
PU, Chandigarh	35.50	59.10	5.40	100.00
Total	34.80	56.80	8.40	100.00

Chi-square value = 20.432[a], P = .009, Significance level = .01.

Above Table indicates that only 34.80% of the students in the total sample find university administration quick in redressing their grievances. Differences are statistically significant at .01 levels. Position in KU is the best with 44.90% and the worst in HPU with 27.80% followed by JU with 28.20%.

3. NON-TEACHING STAFF'S RESPONSES

Following are the responses of the non-teaching staff:

TABLE 4.3.1

Non-Teaching Staff (NTS) Finding Job Interesting

Name of University	*Yes*	*No*	*Can't Say*	*Total*
GNDU, Amritsar	80.00	13.30	6.70	100.00
HPU, Shimla	78.40	16.70	4.90	100.00
JU, Jammu	66.70	33.30		100.00
KU, Kurukshetra	60.20	33.30	6.50	100.00
PU, Chandigarh	80.00	13.30	2.30	100.00
Total	75.50	20.20	4.30	100.00

Chi-square value = 19.996[a], P = .010, Significance level = .01.

Above Table indicates that majority (75.50%) of the NTS in the total sample find job interesting. Differences are statistically significant at .01 level. Position in the GNDU is the best with 80.00% and the worst in KU with 60.20%.

TABLE 4.3.2
Non-Teaching Staff Finding Job Respectable

Name of University	*Yes*	*No*	*Can't Say*	*Total*
GNDU, Amritsar	71.10	26.60	2.30	100.00
HPU, Shimla	88.20	8.80	2.90	100.00
JU, Jammu	66.70	33.30		100.00
KU, Kurukshetra	65.60	26.90	7.50	100.00
PU, Chandigarh	93.30	6.70		100.00
Total	75.50	20.70	3.70	100.00

Chi-square value = 22.632[a], P = .004, Significance level = .01.

Above Table indicates that majority (75.50%) of the NTS in the total sample find job interesting. Differences are statistically significant at .01 level. Position in the PU is the best with 93.30% and the worst in KU with 65.60%.

TABLE 4.3.3
Non-Teaching Staff Maintaining Weekly/Monthly Diaries

Name of University	*Yes*	*No*	*Can't Say*	*Total*
GNDU, Amritsar	49.20	48.40	2.30	100.00
HPU, Shimla	57.80	35.30	6.90	100.00
JU, Jammu		100.00		100.00
KU, Kurukshetra	39.80	52.70	7.50	100.00
PU, Chandigarh	46.70	53.30		100.00
Total	47.80	47.30	4.90	100.00

Chi-square value = 21.872[a], P = .005, Significance level = .01.

Above Table indicates that only 47.80% of the NTS in the total sample maintain weekly/monthly diaries. Differences are statistically significant at .01 level. Position in the GNDU is the best with 49.20% and the worst in JU with 0%.

TABLE 4.3.4
Non-Teaching Staff Making Plan for Doing Official Work

Name of University	*Yes*	*No*	*Can't Say*	*Total*
GNDU, Amritsar	60.20	37.50	2.30	100.00
HPU, Shimla	73.50	24.50	2.00	100.00
JU, Jammu	33.30	66.70		100.00
KU, Kurukshetra	69.80	23.70	6.50	100.00
PU, Chandigarh	73.30	26.70		100.00
Total	66.60	30.30	3.20	100.00

Chi-square value = 16.629[a], P = .034, Significance level = .05.

Above Table indicates that majority (66.60%) of the NTS in the total sample make plans for doing their official work. Differences are statistically significant at .05 level. Position in the HPU is the best with 73.50% followed by PU with 73.30% and the worst in JU with 33.30%.

TABLE 4.3.5
Non-Teaching Staff who Received Training for Doing Official Work

Name of University	*Yes*	*No*	*Can't Say*	*Total*
GNDU, Amritsar	34.40	61.70	3.90	100.00
HPU, Shimla	46.00	52.00	2.00	100.00
JU, Jammu		100.00		100.00
KU, Kurukshetra	39.80	54.80	5.40	100.00
PU, Chandigarh	33.30	53.30	13.30	100.00
Total	38.30	57.60	4.00	100.00

Chi-square value = 14.721[a], P = 0.065, Statistically not significant.

Above Table indicates that only 38.30% of the NTS received training for doing their official work. This situation in all the

Universities is quite similar and the differences are not statistically significant. Position in the HPU is the best with 46.00% and the worst in JU with 0%.

Table 4.3.6
Non-Teaching Staff Finding Difficulties in Dealing With Senior Officials

Name of University	*Yes*	*No*	*Can't Say*	*Total*
GNDU, Amritsar	24.20	71.10	4.70	100.00
HPU, Shimla	23.50	69.60	6.90	100.00
JU, Jammu		66.70	33.30	100.00
KU, Kurukshetra	19.40	74.20	6.40	100.00
PU, Chandigarh	13.30	80.00	6.70	100.00
Total	21.60	71.80	6.60	100.00

Chi-square value = 13.964[a], P = 0.083, Statistically not significant.

Above Table indicates that only 21.60% of the NTS find difficulties in dealing with their senior officials This situation in all the Universities is quite similar and the differences are not statistically significant. Position in the GNDU is the worst with 24.20% followed by HPU with 23.50% and the best in JU with 0%.

Table 4.3.7
Non-Teaching Staff Finding Difficulties in Dealing with Colleagues

Name of University	*Yes*	*No*	*Can't Say*	*Total*
GNDU, Amritsar	16.40	78.10	5.50	100.00
HPU, Shimla	13.70	82.40	3.90	100.00
JU, Jammu	33.30	66.70		100.00
KU, Kurukshetra	11.80	78.50	9.70	100.00
PU, Chandigarh	6.70	86.60	6.70	100.00
Total	14.40	79.50	6.10	100.00

Chi-square value = 7.519[a], P = 0.482, Statistically not significant.

Above Table indicates that only 14.40% of the NTS find difficulties in dealing with their colleagues. This situation in all the Universities is quite similar and the differences are not statistically significant. Position in the JU is the worst with 33.30% and the best in PU with 6.70%.

Table 4.3.8
Non-Teaching Staff Finding Difficulties in Dealing with Subordinates

Name of University	*Yes*	*No*	*Can't Say*	*Total*
GNDU, Amritsar	19.50	74.20	6.30	100.00
HPU, Shimla	14.70	79.40	5.90	100.00
JU, Jammu	33.30	66.70		100.00
KU, Kurukshetra	6.50	87.00	6.50	100.00
PU, Chandigarh	20.00	73.30	6.70	100.00
Total	15.00	79.00	6.10	100.00

Chi-square value = 10.534[a], P = 0.230, Statistically not significant.

Above Table indicates that only 15% of the NTS find difficulties in dealing with their subordinates. This situation in all the Universities is quite similar and the differences are not statistically significant. Position in the JU is the worst with 33.30% and the best in KU with 6.50%.

Table 4.3.9
Non-Teaching Staff Finding Difficulties in Dealing with Teachers

Name of University	*Yes*	*No*	*Can't Say*	*Total*
GNDU, Amritsar	19.50	75.80	4.70	100.00
HPU, Shimla	14.70	77.50	7.80	100.00
JU, Jammu	66.70	33.30		100.00
KU, Kurukshetra	12.90	78.50	8.60	100.00
PU, Chandigarh	13.30	80.00	6.70	100.00
Total	17.30	76.10	6.60	100.00

Chi-square value = 19.014[a], P = .015, Significance level = .01.

Above Table indicates that only 14.40% of the NTS find difficulties in dealing with the teachers. The differences are statistically significant at .01 level. Position in the JU is the worst with 66.70% and the best in KU with 12.90% followed by PU with 13.30%.

TABLE 4.3.10
Non-Teaching Staff Finding Difficulties in Dealing with Students

Name of University	*Yes*	*No*	*Can't Say*	*Total*
GNDU, Amritsar	17.20	74.20	8.60	100.00
HPU, Shimla	25.50	68.60	5.90	100.00
JU, Jammu		100.00		100.00
KU, Kurukshetra	11.80	78.50	9.70	100.00
PU, Chandigarh	6.70	80.00	13.30	100.00
Total	17.30	74.60	8.10	100.00

Chi-square value = 11.810[a], P = 0.160, Statistically not significant.

Above table indicates that only 17.30% of the NTS find difficulties in dealing with the students. This situation in all the Universities is quite similar and the differences are not statistically significant. Position in the JU is the best with 100% and the worst in HPU with 25.50%.

TABLE 4.3.11
Non-Teaching Staff Finding Difficulties in Getting Administrative Work Done

Name of University	*Yes*	*No*	*Can't Say*	*Total*
GNDU, Amritsar	31.30	58.50	10.20	100.00
HPU, Shimla	35.30	57.80	6.90	100.00
JU, Jammu	33.30	66.70		100.00
KU, Kurukshetra	25.80	64.50	9.70	100.00
PU, Chandigarh	20.00	73.30	6.70	100.00
Total	30.50	60.80	8.60	100.00

Chi-square value = 4.599[a], P = 0.799, Statistically not significant.

Above Table indicates that only 30.50% of the NTS find difficulties in getting administrative work done. This situation in all the Universities of the sample is quite similar and the differences are not statistically significant. Position in the PU is the best with 20% and the worst in HPU with 35.30%.

TABLE 4.3.12

Non-Teaching Staff Finding Difficulties in Clearance of Bills from LAD

Name of University	*Yes*	*No*	*Can't Say*	*Total*
GNDU, Amritsar	37.50	49.20	13.30	100.00
HPU, Shimla	63.70	31.40	4.90	100.00
JU, Jammu	33.30	66.70		100.00
KU, Kurukshetra	30.10	55.90	14.00	100.00
PU, Chandigarh	6.70	86.60	6.70	100.00
Total	41.80	47.80	10.40	100.00

Chi-square value = 38.706[a], P = .015, Significance level = .01.

Above Table indicates that 41.80% of the NTS find difficulties in clearance of bills from LAD. The differences are statistically significant at .01 level. Position in the HPU is the worst with 63.70% and the best in PU with 6.70% only.

TABLE 4.3.13

Non-Teaching Staff Finding their Internal Audit Effective

Name of University	*Yes*	*No*	*Can't Say*	*Total*
GNDU, Amritsar	33.60	50.00	16.40	100.00
HPU, Shimla	45.10	43.10	11.80	100.00
JU, Jammu	66.70	33.30		100.00
KU, Kurukshetra	37.60	47.30	15.10	100.00
PU, Chandigarh	53.30	46.70		100.00
Total	39.80	46.70	13.50	100.00

Chi-square value = 9.741[a], P = 0.284, Statistically not significant.

Above Table indicates that 39.80% of the NTS find their internal audit staff effective. This situation in all the Universities of the sample is quite similar and the differences are not statistically significant. Position in the JU is the best with 66.70% and the worst in GNDU with 33.60%.

TABLE 4.3.14

Non-Teaching Staff Noticing Cases of Sexual Harassment of Female Employees by Male Employees

Name of University	*Yes*	*No*	*Can't Say*	*Total*
GNDU, Amritsar	22.70	68.00	9.30	100.00
HPU, Shimla	8.80	8.40	8.80	100.00
JU, Jammu	33.30	66.70		100.00
KU, Kurukshetra	21.50	63.40	15.10	100.00
PU, Chandigarh	13.30	86.70		100.00
Total	18.20	71.80	10.10	100.00

Chi-square value = 16.396[a], P = .037, Significance level = .05.

Above Table indicates that 18.20% of the NTS notice cases of sexual harassment of female employees by the male employees. The differences are statistically significant at .05 level. Position in the HPU is the best with 8.80% and the worst in JU with 33.30%.

TABLE 4.3.15

Non-Teaching Staff Thinking their University Enjoy Autonomy in Appointing Employees

Name of University	*Yes*	*No*	*Can't Say*	*Total*
GNDU, Amritsar	63.30	28.90	7.80	100.00
HPU, Shimla	38.20	53.90	7.80	100.00
JU, Jammu	66.70	33.30		100.00
KU, Kurukshetra	37.60	47.30	15.10	100.00
PU, Chandigarh	66.70	20.00	13.30	100.00
Total	49.30	40.90	9.80	100.00

Chi-square value = 27.643[a], P = .001, Significance level = .01.

Above Table indicates that 49.30% of the NTS think that their respective universities enjoy autonomy in the appointment of the employees. The differences are statistically significant at .01 level. Position in the KU is the worst with 37.60% followed by HPU with 38.20% and the best both in PU and JU with 66.70%.

TABLE 4.3.16

Non-Teaching Staff Thinking their University Enjoy Autonomy in Promoting Employees

Name of University	*Yes*	*No*	*Can't Say*	*Total*
GNDU, Amritsar	57.00	35.90	7.00	100.00
HPU, Shimla	54.90	38.20	6.90	100.00
JU, Jammu	66.70	33.30		100.00
KU, Kurukshetra	45.20	38.70	16.10	100.00
PU, Chandigarh	80.00	13.30	6.70	100.00
Total	54.50	36.30	9.20	100.00

Chi-square value = 13.166[a], P = 0.106, Statistically not significant.

Above Table indicates that 54.50% of the NTS think that their respective universities enjoy autonomy in the promoting their employees. This situation in all the Universities of the sample is quite similar and the differences are not statistically significant. Position in the KU is the worst with 45.20% and the best in PU with 80%.

TABLE 4.3.17

Non-Teaching Staff Thinking their University Enjoy Autonomy in Appointing Deans/Directors

Name of University	*Yes*	*No*	*Can't Say*	*Total*
GNDU, Amritsar	53.90	33.60	12.50	100.00
HPU, Shimla	51.00	35.30	13.70	100.00
JU, Jammu	33.30	66.70		100.00
KU, Kurukshetra	57.00	26.90	16.10	100.00
PU, Chandigarh	93.30	6.70		100.00
Total	55.00	32.00	13.00	100.00

Chi-square value = 16.661[a], P = .034, Significance level = .05.

Above Table indicates that 55% of the NTS think that their respective universities enjoy autonomy in the appointment of the deans/directors. The differences are statistically significant at .05 level. Position in the JU is the worst with 33.30% and the best in PU 93.30%.

TABLE 4.3.18
Non-Teaching Staff Thinking of Getting Promotion Whenever Due

Name of University	*Yes*	*No*	*Can't Say*	*Total*
GNDU, Amritsar	57.80	34.40	7.80	100.00
HPU, Shimla	59.90	36.30	3.80	100.00
JU, Jammu	66.70	33.30		100.00
KU, Kurukshetra	64.50	21.50	14.00	100.00
PU, Chandigarh	80.00	13.30	6.70	100.00
Total	61.40	30.50	8.10	100.00

Chi-square value = 13.992[a], P = 0.082, Statistically not significant.

Above Table indicates that 61.40% of the NTS think that they would get promotion when ever that was due to them. This situation in all the Universities of the sample is quite similar and the differences are not statistically significant. Position in the GNDU is the worst with 57.80% and the best in PU with 80%.

TABLE 4.3.19
Non-Teaching Staff Favouring University Education Limited to a Few

Name of University	*Yes*	*No*	*Can't Say*	*Total*
GNDU, Amritsar	25.00	68.00	7.00	100.00
HPU, Shimla	16.70	81.30	2.00	100.00
JU, Jammu	33.30	66.70		100.00
KU, Kurukshetra	17.20	71.00	11.80	100.00
PU, Chandigarh	33.30	60.00	6.70	100.00
Total	21.00	72.30	6.60	100.00

Chi-square value = 13.898[a], P = 0.084, Statistically not significant.

Above Table indicates that only 21% of the NTS favour university education to be limited to a few persons. This situation in all the Universities of the sample is quite similar and the differences are not statistically significant.

TABLE 4.3.20
Non-Teaching Staff Favouring University Education for Getting Job Only

Name of University	*Yes*	*No*	*Can't Say*	*Total*
GNDU, Amritsar	28.90	63.30	7.80	100.00
HPU, Shimla	12.70	80.40	6.90	100.00
JU, Jammu	33.30	66.70		100.00
KU, Kurukshetra	24.70	64.50	10.80	100.00
PU, Chandigarh	26.70	73.30		100.00
Total	23.10	69.20	7.80	100.00

Chi-square value = 13.084[a], P = 0.109, Statistically not significant.

Above Table indicates that 23.10% of the NTS favour university education for getting job only. This situation in all the Universities of the sample is quite similar and the differences are not statistically significant.

TABLE 4.3.21
Non-Teaching Staff Favouring University Education for Self-Development Only

Name of University	*Yes*	*No*	*Can't Say*	*Total*
GNDU, Amritsar	22.70	68.00	9.30	100.00
HPU, Shimla	27.50	69.60	2.90	100.00
JU, Jammu	33.30	66.70		100.00
KU, Kurukshetra	22.60	65.60	11.80	100.00
PU, Chandigarh	40.00	60.00		100.00
Total	25.10	67.40	7.50	100.00

Chi-square value = 10.140[a], P = 0.255, Statistically not significant.

Above Table indicates that 23.10% of the NTS favour university education for self-development only. This situation in all the Universities of the sample is quite similar and the differences are not statistically significant.

TABLE 4.3.22
Non-Teaching Staff Favouring University Education both for Job and Self-Development

Name of University	*Yes*	*No*	*Can't Say*	*Total*
GNDU, Amritsar	78.10	20.30	1.60	100.00
HPU, Shimla	92.20	6.80	1.00	100.00
JU, Jammu	66.70	33.30		100.00
KU, Kurukshetra	80.60	17.20	2.20	100.00
PU, Chandigarh	80.00	13.30	6.70	100.00
Total	82.70	15.60	1.70	100.00

Chi-square value = 13.337[a], P = 0.101, Statistically not significant.

Above Table indicates that 23.10% of the NTS favour university education for self-development only. This situation in all the Universities of the sample is quite similar and the differences are not statistically significant.

TABLE 4.3.23
Non-Teaching Staff Considering Administration Sympathetic to their Demands

Name of University	*Yes*	*No*	*Can't Say*	*Total*
GNDU, Amritsar	60.20	35.20	4.60	100.00
HPU, Shimla	37.30	54.90	7.80	100.00
JU, Jammu	66.70	33.30		100.00
KU, Kurukshetra	39.80	47.30	12.90	100.00
PU, Chandigarh	66.70	13.30	20.00	100.00
Total	48.40	43.20	8.40	100.00

Chi-square value = 25.739[a], P = .001, Significance level = .01.

Above Table indicates that 48.40% of the NTS think that administration in their respective universities is sympathetic to their demands. The differences are statistically significant at .01

level. Position in the HPU is the worst with 37.30% and the best both in PU and JU with 66.70%.

TABLE 4.3.24
Non-Teaching Staff Considering University Administration Quick in Redressing their Grievances

Name of University	*Yes*	*No*	*Can't Say*	*Total*
GNDU, Amritsar	48.40	45.30	6.30	100.00
HPU, Shimla	30.40	58.80	10.80	100.00
JU, Jammu	66.70	33.30		100.00
KU, Kurukshetra	47.30	30.10	22.60	100.00
PU, Chandigarh	66.70	20.00	13.30	100.00
Total	44.10	43.80	12.10	100.00

Chi-square value = 32.663[a], P = .000, Significance level = .01.

Above Table indicates that 44.10% of the NTS in the sample think that administration in their respective universities is quick in redressing their demands. The differences are statistically significant at .01 level. Position in the HPU is the worst with 30.40% and the best both in PU and JU with 66.70%.

4. DEANS/OTHER OFFICERS/DIRECTORS/ HOD'S RESPONSES

Following are the responses of the Deans/Other Officers/ Directors/HOD's:

TABLE 4.4.1
Officers Enjoying Administrative Work

Name of University	*Yes*	*No*	*Can't Say*	*Total*
GNDU, Amritsar	80.00	10.00	10.00	100.00
HPU, Shimla	70.00	20.00	10.00	100.00
JU, Jammu	100.00			100.00
KU, Kurukshetra	100.00			100.00
PU, Chandigarh	75.00		25.00	100.00
Total	82.40	8.80	8.80	100.00

Chi-square value = 10.726[a], P = 0.218, Statistically not significant.

Above Table indicates that majority of the officers (82.40%) in the sample enjoy their administrative work in their respective universities. This situation in all the Universities is quite similar and the differences are not statistically significant.

TABLE 4.4.2

Officers Finding Dealing with Students' Leaders Frustrating

Name of University	*Yes*	*No*	*Can't Say*	*Total*
GNDU, Amritsar			100.00	100.00
HPU, Shimla	40.00	30.00	30.00	100.00
JU, Jammu		100.00		100.00
KU, Kurukshetra		28.60	71.40	100.00
PU, Chandigarh		25.00	75.00	100.00
Total	11.80	26.50	61.80	100.00

Chi-square value = 49.019[a], P = .000, Significance level = .01.

Above Table clearly indicates that it is only HPU where a good number of officers (40%) find dealing with students leaders frustrating. Situation in all the universities is better and the best in JU where none of the officers reported any frustration in dealing with the students.

TABLE 4.4.3

Officers Finding Dealing with Students' Leaders Challenging

Name of University	*Yes*	*No*	*Can't Say*	*Total*
GNDU, Amritsar	20.00		80.00	100.00
HPU, Shimla	70.00		30.00	100.00
JU, Jammu		100.00		100.00
KU, Kurukshetra	71.40	14.30	14.30	100.00
PU, Chandigarh	25.00		75.00	100.00
Total	44.10	11.80	44.10	100.00

Chi-square value = 70.720[a], P = .000, Significance level = .01.

Above Table clearly indicates 44.10% of the officers in the total sample find dealing with students' leaders challenging.

The differences are significant at .01 level. Officers in JU do not find dealing with students' leaders challenging. It is the most challenging in KU with 71.40% followed by HPU with 70%.

TABLE 4.4.4
Officers Finding Dealing with Students' Leaders Enjoyable

Name of University	*Yes*	*No*	*Can't Say*	*Total*
GNDU, Amritsar	10.00		90.00	100.00
HPU, Shimla	40.00	20.00	40.00	100.00
JU, Jammu	100.00			100.00
KU, Kurukshetra	42.90		57.10	100.00
PU, Chandigarh	50.00	25.00	25.00	100.00
Total	38.20	8.80	52.90	100.00

Chi-square value = 29.498[a], P = .000, Significance level = .01.

Above Table clearly indicates that 38.20% of the officers in the total sample find dealing with students' leaders enjoyable. The differences are significant at .01 level. Position in JU is the best where all the officers find dealing with students' leaders enjoyable. It is worst in GNDU where only 10% of the officers find dealing with students' leaders enjoyable.

TABLE 4.4.5
Officers Finding Dealing with Students' Leaders Rewarding

Name of University	*Yes*	*No*	*Can't Say*	*Total*
GNDU, Amritsar	10.00		90.00	100.00
HPU, Shimla	10.00	40.00	50.00	100.00
JU, Jammu			100.00	100.00
KU, Kurukshetra	14.30	14.30	71.40	100.00
PU, Chandigarh	25.00	25.00	50.00	100.00
Total	11.80	17.60	70.60	100.00

Chi-square value = 16.150[a], P = .040, Significance level = .05

Above Table clearly indicates only a small number (11.80%) of the officers in the total sample find dealing with students' leaders rewarding. The differences are significant at .05 level.

TABLE 4.4.6

Officers Finding Dealing with Teachers' Leaders Frustrating

Name of University	*Yes*	*No*	*Can't Say*	*Total*
GNDU, Amritsar		30.00	70.00	100.00
HPU, Shimla	40.00	30.00	30.00	100.00
JU, Jammu		100.00		100.00
KU, Kurukshetra	14.30	28.60	57.10	100.00
PU, Chandigarh		25.00	75.00	100.00
Total	14.70	35.30	50.00	100.00

Chi-square value = 28.900[a], P = .000, Significance level = .01.

Above Table clearly indicates that in HPU, a good number of officers, i.e., 40% and in KU 14.30% find dealing with teachers' leaders frustrating. Situation in the rest of the universities is better and the best in JU where none of the officers reported any frustration in dealing with the teachers' leaders. The differences are significant at .01 level.

TABLE 4.4.7

Officers Finding Dealing with Teachers' Leaders Challenging

Name of University	*Yes*	*No*	*Can't Say*	*Total*
GNDU, Amritsar	30.00	30.00	40.00	100.00
HPU, Shimla	30.00	20.00	50.00	100.00
JU, Jammu		100.00		100.00
KU, Kurukshetra	57.10	14.30	28.60	100.00
PU, Chandigarh	50.00		50.00	100.00
Total	35.30	26.50	38.20	100.00

Chi-square value = 24.053[a], P = .002, Significance level = .01.

Above Table clearly indicates 35.30% officers in the total sample find dealing with teachers' leaders challenging. It is the most challenging in KU with 57.10%. The differences are significant at .01 levels.

TABLE 4.4.8
Officers Finding Dealing with Teachers' Leaders Enjoyable

Name of University	*Yes*	*No*	*Can't Say*	*Total*
GNDU, Amritsar	60.00		40.00	100.00
HPU, Shimla	40.00	20.00	40.00	100.00
JU, Jammu	100.00			100.00
KU, Kurukshetra	28.60		71.40	100.00
PU, Chandigarh	50.00		50.00	100.00
Total	50.00	5.90	44.10	100.00

Chi-square value = 19.916[a], P = .011, Significance level = .01.

Above Table clearly indicates that 50% officers in the total sample find dealing with teachers' leaders enjoyable. It is the most enjoyable in JU where all the officers have reported that they find dealing with teachers leaders enjoyable. In KU, only' 28.60% of the officers have reported that they find dealing with teachers' leaders enjoyable. The differences are significant at .01 level.

TABLE 4.4.9
Officers Finding Dealing with Teachers' Leaders Rewarding

Name of University	*Yes*	*No*	*Can't Say*	*Total*
GNDU, Amritsar	20.00	10.00	70.00	100.00
HPU, Shimla		30.00	70.00	100.00
JU, Jammu		100.00		100.00
KU, Kurukshetra	28.60	14.30	57.10	100.00
PU, Chandigarh	50.00		50.00	100.00
Total	17.60	23.50	58.80	100.00

Chi-square value = 34.049[a], P = .000, Significance level = .01.

Above Table clearly indicates that only a small number (17.60%) of officers in the total sample find dealing with teachers' leaders rewarding. Position is the best in PU with 50% and worst in HPU with 0%. The differences are significant at .01 level.

TABLE 4.4.10
Officers Finding Dealing with Employees' Leaders Frustrating

Name of University	*Yes*	*No*	*Can't Say*	*Total*
GNDU, Amritsar		30.00	70.00	100.00
HPU, Shimla	30.00	30.00	40.00	100.00
JU, Jammu		100.00		100.00
KU, Kurukshetra		28.60	71.40	100.00
PU, Chandigarh			100.00	100.00
Total	8.80	32.40	58.80	100.00

Chi-square value = 33.448[a], P = .000, Significance level = .01.

Above Table clearly indicates that it is only HPU where a good number of officers (30%) find dealing with employees leaders frustrating. Situation in all the universities is better.

TABLE 4.4.11
Officers Finding Dealing with Employees' Leaders Challenging

Name of University	*Yes*	*No*	*Can't Say*	*Total*
GNDU, Amritsar	30.00	30.00	40.00	100.00
HPU, Shimla	30.00	20.00	50.00	100.00
JU, Jammu	100.00			100.00
KU, Kurukshetra	42.90	14.20	42.90	100.00
PU, Chandigarh	50.00		50.00	100.00
Total	41.20	17.60	41.20	100.00

Chi-square value = 13.785[a], P = 0.088, statistically not significant.

Above Table clearly indicates that 41.20% officers in the total sample find dealing with employees' leaders challenging. It is the most challenging in JU with 100%. This situation in all the Universities is quite similar and the differences are not statistically significant.

TABLE 4.4.12
Officers Finding Dealing with Employees' Leaders Enjoyable

Name of University	*Yes*	*No*	*Can't Say*	*Total*
GNDU, Amritsar	60.00		40.00	100.00
HPU, Shimla	40.00	20.00	40.00	100.00
JU, Jammu	100.00			100.00
KU, Kurukshetra	42.90		57.10	100.00
PU, Chandigarh	50.00	25.00	25.00	100.00
Total	52.90	8.80	38.20	100.00

Chi-square value = 16.348[a], P = .038, Significance level = .05.

Above Table clearly indicates that 52.90% officers in the total sample find dealing with employees' leaders enjoyable. It is the most enjoyable in JU with 100% and the least in HPU with 40%. The differences are significant at .05 level.

TABLE 4.4.13
Officers Finding Dealing with Employees' Leaders Rewarding

Name of University	*Yes*	*No*	*Can't Say*	*Total*
GNDU, Amritsar	20.00	10.00	70.00	100.00
HPU, Shimla		40.00	60.00	100.00
JU, Jammu	100.00			100.00
KU, Kurukshetra	42.90	14.20	42.90	100.00
PU, Chandigarh		25.00	75.00	100.00
Total	23.50	20.60	55.90	100.00

Chi-square value = 35.234[a], P = .000, Significance level = .01.

Above Table clearly indicates that 23.50% officers in the total sample find dealing with employees' leaders rewarding. It is the most rewarding in JU with 100% and the least in HPU and PU with 0%. The differences are significant at .01 level.

TABLE 4.4.14

Officers Facing Political Pressure in their Administrative Work

Name of University	*Yes*	*No*	*Can't Say*	*Total*
GNDU, Amritsar	10.00	80.00	10.00	100.00
HPU, Shimla	30.00	40.00	30.00	100.00
JU, Jammu		100.00		100.00
KU, Kurukshetra		71.40	28.60	100.00
PU, Chandigarh	50.00	50.00		100.00
Total	17.60	64.70	17.60	100.00

Chi-square value = 20.606[a], P = .008, Significance level = .01.

Above Table clearly indicates that 17.60% officers in the total sample have reported that they faced political pressure in doing their administrative work. This situation is worst in PU with 50%. In JU and KU none of the officers reported that they faced political pressure in doing their administrative work. The differences are significant at .01 level.

TABLE 4.4.15

Officers Facing Pressure of Employees' Unions in their Administrative Work

Name of University	*Yes*	*No*	*Can't Say*	*Total*
GNDU, Amritsar		90.00	10.00	100.00
HPU, Shimla		40.00	60.00	100.00
JU, Jammu		100.00		100.00
KU, Kurukshetra		57.10	42.90	100.00
PU, Chandigarh		75.00	25.00	100.00
Total		67.60	32.40	100.00

Chi-square value = 15.324[a], P = .004, Significance level = .01.

It is interesting as well as heartening to note that none of the officers in any of the universities in the sample has reported that he/she faced pressure from employees' unions in doing his/her administrative work.

TABLE 4.4.16
Officers Facing Pressure of Teachers' Unions in their Administrative Work

Name of University	*Yes*	*No*	*Can't Say*	*Total*
GNDU, Amritsar		80.00	20.00	100.00
HPU, Shimla	10.00	30.00	60.00	100.00
JU, Jammu		100.00		100.00
KU, Kurukshetra	14.30	57.10	28.60	100.00
PU, Chandigarh	25.00	50.00	25.00	100.00
Total	8.80	58.80	32.40	100.00

Chi-square value = 19.168[a], P = .014, Significance level = .01.

Above Table clearly indicates that only a small number (8.80%) of the officers in the total sample have reported that they faced pressure of teachers' unions in doing their administrative work. This situation is worst in PU with 25%. In JU and GNDU none of the officers reported that he/she faced pressure of teachers' unions in doing his/her administrative work. The differences are significant at .01 level.

TABLE 4.4.17
Officers Facing Pressure of Students' Unions in their Administrative Work

Name of University	*Yes*	*No*	*Can't Say*	*Total*
GNDU, Amritsar		90.00	10.00	100.00
HPU, Shimla	44.40	11.20	44.40	100.00
JU, Jammu		100.00		100.00
KU, Kurukshetra	14.30	57.10	28.60	100.00
PU, Chandigarh	25.00	50.00	25.00	100.00
Total	18.20	57.60	24.20	100.00

Chi-square value = 30.503[a], P = .000, Significance level = .01.

Above Table clearly indicates that only a small number (18.20%) of the officers in the total sample have reported that they faced pressure of students' unions in doing their administrative work. This situation is worst in HPU with 44.40%. In JU and GNDU none of the officers reported that he/ she faced pressure of students' unions in doing his/.her administrative work. The differences are significant at .01 level.

TABLE 4.4.18

Officers Considering Quality of Education

Name of University	*Yes*	*No*	*Can't Say*	*Total*
GNDU, Amritsar	70.00	20.00	10.00	100.00
HPU, Shimla	40.00	60.00		100.00
JU, Jammu		100.00		100.00
KU, Kurukshetra	57.10	28.60	14.30	100.00
PU, Chandigarh	75.00	25.00		100.00
Total	52.90	41.20	5.90	100.00

Chi-square value = 19.937[a], P = .011, Significance level = .01.

Above Table clearly indicates that 52.90% of the officers in the total sample have reported that they considered the quality of education imparted in their respective universities comparable to that of the advanced countries. This situation is worst in JU with 0% and the best in PU with 75%. The differences are significant at .01 level.

TABLE 4.4.19

Efforts to Improve the Quality of Education

Name of University	*Yes*	*No*	*Can't Say*	*Total*
GNDU, Amritsar	90.00		10.00	100.00
HPU, Shimla	60.00	40.00		100.00
JU, Jammu	100.00			100.00
KU, Kurukshetra	71.40	14.30	14.30	100.00
PU, Chandigarh	75.00	25.00		100.00
Total	76.50	17.60	5.90	100.00

Chi-square value = 16.514[a], P = .036, Significance level = .05.

Above Table clearly indicates that majority (76.50%) of the officers in the total sample have reported that they made efforts to improve the quality of education imparted in their respective universities to make that comparable to that of the advanced countries. This situation is the best in JU with 100% and the worst in HPU with 60%. The differences are significant at .05 level.

TABLE 4.4.20

Officers Considering University Administration Sympathetic to them

Name of University	*Yes*	*No*	*Can't Say*	*Total*
GNDU, Amritsar	90.00		10.00	100.00
HPU, Shimla	40.00	60.00		100.00
JU, Jammu	100.00			100.00
KU, Kurukshetra	71.40		28.60	100.00
PU, Chandigarh	75.00		25.00	100.00
Total	70.60	17.60	11.80	100.00

Chi-square value = 40.942[a], P = .000, Significance level = .01.

Above Table clearly indicates that majority (70.60%) of the officers in the total sample have reported that they considered university administration sympathetic to their demands. This situation is the best in JU with 100% and the worst in HPU with 40%. The differences are significant at .01 level.

TABLE 4.4.21

Officers Considering University Administration Quick in Redressing their Grievances

Name of University	*Yes*	*No*	*Can't Say*	*Total*
GNDU, Amritsar	80.00	10.00	10.00	100.00
HPU, Shimla	20.00	70.00	10.00	100.00
JU, Jammu	100.00			100.00
KU, Kurukshetra	71.40	28.60		100.00
PU, Chandigarh	50.00		50.00	100.00
Total	58.80	29.40	11.80	100.00

Chi-square value = 39.149[a], P = .000, Significance level = .01.

Above Table clearly indicates that majority (58.80%) of the officers in the total sample have reported that they considered university administration quick in redressing their grievances. This situation is the best in JU with 100% and the worst in HPU with 20%. The differences are significant at .01 level.

TABLE 4.4.22

Officers Finding Difficulties in Getting their Work Done

Name of University	*Yes*	*No*	*Can't Say*	*Total*
GNDU, Amritsar	20.00	70.00	10.00	100.00
HPU, Shimla	70.00	20.00	10.00	100.00
JU, Jammu		100.00		100.00
KU, Kurukshetra	28.60	71.40		100.00
PU, Chandigarh	25.00	75.00		100.00
Total	35.30	58.80	5.90	100.00

Chi-square value = 21.501[a], P = .006, Significance level = .01.

Above Table clearly indicates that 35.30% of the officers in the total sample have reported that they found difficulties in getting their work done in their respective universities. This situation is the best in JU with 0% and the worst in HPU with 70%. The differences are significant at .01 level.

TABLE 4.4.23

Officers Finding Difficulties in Getting the Clearance of their Bills from LAD

Name of University	*Yes*	*No*	*Can't Say*	*Total*
GNDU, Amritsar	10.00	70.00	20.00	100.00
HPU, Shimla	80.00	20.00		100.00
JU, Jammu		100.00		100.00
KU, Kurukshetra	28.60	71.40		100.00
PU, Chandigarh	25.00	75.00		100.00
Total	35.30	58.80	5.90	100.00

Chi-square value = 35.101[a], P = .000, Significance level = .01.

Above Table clearly indicates that 35.30% of the officers in the total sample have reported that they found difficulties in getting the clearance of their bills from LAD. This situation is the best in JU with 0% and the worst in HPU with 80%. The differences are significant at .01 level.

TABLE 4.4.24
Officers Finding Internal Audit Effective

Name of University	*Yes*	*No*	*Can't Say*	*Total*
GNDU, Amritsar	70.00	20.00	10.00	100.00
HPU, Shimla	40.00	40.00	20.00	100.00
JU, Jammu		100.00		100.00
KU, Kurukshetra	42.90	57.10		100.00
PU, Chandigarh	50.00	50.00		100.00
Total	47.10	44.10	8.80	100.00

Chi-square value = 18.235[a], P = .020, Significance level = .05.

Above Table clearly indicates that 47.10% of the officers in the total sample have reported that they found internal audit effective. This situation is the worst in JU with 0% and the best in GNDU with 70%. The differences are significant at .05 level.

To sum up, above discussion unambiguously reveals that answers to the most of the questions have not been found statistically significant. This clearly shows that the administrative situation and reactions of the respondents are almost similar in the universities of the sample. Some of the answers are statistically significant. These too have been discussed to find out the real position and the reasons for their differences.

CHAPTER 5

University Administration : Some Case Studies

Quantitative information collected and presented in the fourth chapter has been supplemented with qualitative information in the form of case studies in this chapter. Information about the case studies has been collected during the visits to the universities of the sample by interviewing the officials, through official records, and news papers reports. Case studies in this chapter relate to how some individuals have behaved in a particular way, how the events have taken place, and how different organizations, i.e., universities of the sample, have reacted differently under almost similar situations. This, it is believed, will help not only in understanding the academic and administrative culture of different universities but also in suggesting better and effective method of decision-making.

GURU NANAK DEV UNIVERSITY

1. Punjab Medical Entrance Test (PMET), 2005

PMET conducted by the Baba Farid University of Health

Services, Faridkot, on 5th June, 2005 was cancelled since the paper leaked. Government of Punjab then entrusted the Guru Nanak Dev University with the responsibility of conducting a fresh test, keeping in view its past credibility regarding conducting state-level tests in different disciplines. GNDU conducted the second test on 30th June, 2005. GNDU after re-conducting the PMET, asked the state government to appoint two observers from non-medical stream to be present during the evaluation of answer-sheets from the opening of packets till the declaration of results. The Vice-Chancellor, Dr. S.P. Singh, said with a view to maintain transparency, the university had decided to do videography of each packet before the start of evaluation in the presence of observers. Moreover, candidates would be allowed to see their own answer-sheets and those of other candidates by paying a prescribed fee for the purpose.

Even this test came under cloud for various discrepancies. Expressing dissatisfaction over the OMR (Optical Mark Reader), parents and candidates protested against the university authorities in the administrative block of the GNDU on 4th July, 2005. The protesters alleged that about seven questions and keys of more than 10 questions were incorrect. They demanded rechecking of the correctness of the keys provided by the university and sought re-evaluation of the answer-sheets of the PMET. The ABVP also took notice of the alleged discrepancies. Mr. Subhash Sharma, the state general secretary of the Parishad, said the organization was moving High Court in this regard. Dr. R.S. Bawa, Registrar, and coordinator of the examination, said the keys were made by the experts in the presence of government nominees appointed for the evaluation of the examination. He said that it was impossible to satisfy all students. He, however, said credit of seven questions, which were doubtful, had been given to all students.

Giving grace marks to all candidates for the seven 'doubtful' questions came under attack by parents who said it affected the ranking of deserving candidates who could be out of the race due to it. They said the university should evaluate remaining questions barring such 'doubtful' questions. They alleged that students were not allowed to note down the serial number of questions whose answers were wrong.

A tiff reportedly took place between the Vice- Chancellor, Dr. S.P. Singh, and eight experts appointed by the University for evaluating the answer-sheets of the PMET. The experts expressed their resentment to Dr. S.P. Singh for filing the alleged 'fake' affidavit. They blamed the university authorities for making them "scapegoats" in the ongoing controversy regarding the re-evaluation of the answer-sheets. They charged the University of shielding the actual culprits, who were the paper setters for the examination. Meanwhile, the Guru Nanak Dev University Teachers' Association (GNDUTA) was up in arms against the university authorities regarding the filling of the alleged fake affidavit containing declarations on behalf of the experts.

The Punjab and Haryana High Court on 22nd July, 2005 asked the Central Board of Secondary Education (CBSE) to constitute a high-powered Committee of experts to re-evaluate the 21 controversial questions that were part of the PMET 2005 examination conducted by GNDU. The Bench of Mr. Justice J.S. Khehar and Mr. Justice S.N. Aggarwal also directed the Director, CBSE to ensure that the Committee consisting of two experts each from the four subjects of the PMET, submitted its report on or before July 27, 2005.

However, the Bench expressed satisfaction over the manner in which the examination was re-conducted by the GNDU. It noted that the university not only had the courage to allow students to examine their own answer-sheets after the declaration of results but had allowed them to check the answer-sheets of other students also. "This speaks volumes about the transparency in the entire process", the Bench observed.[1]

A group of 34 selected candidates also moved the High Court, opposing any move to quash the result. They stated that they had already been selected through a thorough process and they could not be made to suffer for follies that were not theirs.

On the August 8, 2005, the Bench of Mr. Justice J.S. Khehar and Mr. Justice S.N. Aggarwal of the Punjab and Haryana High Court directed the Vice-Chancellor of GNDU to get all the answer-sheets re-evaluated on or before August 17 on the basis of answer-keys corrected by an independent agency. At this the petitioners again moved the High Court seeking review of

August 8 order. In their application, Saumil Garg and other students prayed that in view of the reports, the GNDU should be restrained from having anything further to do with the re-evaluation of answer-sheets as ordered by the Bench. They also prayed that appropriate orders be passed for conduct of an inquiry into the conduct of the second examination. The petitioners also sought action against GNDU Registrar and any other officer who may be involved in the attempt to allegedly mislead the Court by filling a "false affidavit".

On 11th August, 2005, the Supreme Court stayed the Punjab and Haryana High Court order quashing the results of Punjab PMET, 2005 conducted by GNDU. A three-judge Bench, headed by Mr. Justice Y.K. Sabharwal, granted the stay on the High Court order after petitioner's counsel Manjeet Khosla and senior advocate Mukul Rohtagi made a special mention of the filing of the Special Leave Petition against the directive issued by the High Court. While quashing the results, the High Court had directed the CBSE to reframe answers to all 200 questions following complaints of large-scale cheating in the PMET, with at least 37 students accused of using unfair means and attaining higher ranks. The matter was investigated by State Vigilance Bureau. But the 37 candidates had moved the High Court, claiming that they were being harassed on wrong premise of resorting to unfair means.

Aggrieved by the High Court order, a special leave petition (SLP) was moved by Ms Khosla on behalf of Harmandeep Singh and other students, contending that such a directive would jeopardize the chances of those successful students who had worked hard throughout the year and passed the test honestly. The Supreme Court posted further hearing on the two SLP's on August 17, 2005.

On August 17, overruling the Punjab and Haryana High Court's directive to send the entire question paper of the Punjab PMET to the CBSE for determining the correctness of "key answers" set out by GNDU, the Supreme Court ordered fresh examination of only 10 answers by the CBSE and Delhi University (DU) simultaneously. These 10 answers were the same regarding which the CBSE earlier expressed its opinion, when referred to it by the High Court. But it was stated in the apex court by the counsel for various litigating parties that the

GNDU had not sent the original questions of the 21 alleged incorrect answers to the CBSE, which found 10 out of them as wrong on the basis of the questions as re-produced in the affidavits of the students who challenged their veracity in the High Court on the basis of questions referred in the counter affidavit of the university. In view of this, a Bench of Mr. Justice Y.K. Sabharwal, Mr. Justice B.N. Srikrishna and Mr. Justice P.P. Naolekar directed that correctness of only 10 "key answers" would be determined afresh by the CBSE as well as DU and the GNDU was asked to supply to these instructions the entire set of the question paper along with the key answers set out by its experts. The CBSE and DU were directed to submit their reports by August 20 while fixing the next hearing on August 23 when the outcome of the fresh examination would be known and further direction would be issued by the court accordingly. "The experts of the CBSE and DU shall give their opinion on the basis of the questions prepared by the GNDU. If the answers to these 10 questions are not found correct, they will say what are the correct answers," the Bench said.

On August 24, the Supreme Court imposed a cost of Rs. 1 lakh on the GNDU for its "apathetic and casual" approach in preparing the PMET paper with a number of wrong questions and incorrect "key answers". The apex court also directed the varsity to prepare fresh merit list by including correct answers to eight questions suggested unanimously by DU and CBSE in their reports submitted to it. It also recommended actions against persons responsible for the whole mess. In respect of seven other questions, which the GNDU had itself admitted to be incorrect initially and gave 28 marks in lieu of those to every student across the board irrespective of the fact whether a student had attempted those questions or not, the court said the university's approach was not right as it had given advantage to those students as well who did not attempt those seven questions at all against those who had either attempted all or some of them. The court said that marks for those seven questions would be given to the students who had attempted either all of them or some of them in that proportion and allowed two day's time to the university to declare the result to draw afresh the merit list as per the rank obtained by the students after the completion of this exercise. The court said it was the only possible remedy at this late stage of the admission process to the MBBS, BDS and other courses, which were being unduly delayed due to the "apathy" of the GNDU in preparing the questions and answers in a "casual manner". While asking the university to deposit the amount of Rs. 1 lakh with the Punjab State Legal Aid Authority, to be used exclusively for legal aid of the students by it, the court also permitted the students to seek rechecking of the answer-sheets on payment within 72 hours of the declaration of the fresh result as had been prescribed in the varsity's advertisement. The students who had earlier deposited the required fee for rechecking of the answer-sheets, need not pay any further fee, it clarified. Lambasting the university, it said, "There was total apathy and lapse on its part, which resulted in the litigation, which otherwise was avoidable."[2]

The university declared the results for the second time after re-evaluation of the previous results as per the guidelines of the apex court. Scores of parents and candidates even then expressed dissatisfaction over the results. They demanded cancellation of the entire examination as it allegedly still had certain anomalies in the question paper.

The Vigilance Bureau (VB) submitted its final report on the PMET paper leak on 15th September, 2005. The Vice-Chancellor of the Baba Farid University of Health Sciences, Dr. J.S. Gujral was not directly involved in the leak. It said that there was "supervisory failure" on the part of the VC and his personal staff was directly involved in the scam. The bureau recommended the imposition of major penalty on the VC as for administrative lapses and cases of financial mismanagement. These lapses like bungling in appointments, promotions and recruitment came to the notice of the Bureau during its investigation into the paper leak case. Separate inquiries were then instituted. The report also mentioned that there had been a trend of leaking question papers in the Baba Farid University ever since it started conducting the PMT in 2002. Meanwhile, the sources said Dr. Gujral had explained his position to the Chief Minister, Captain Amarinder Singh, during a personal meeting saying there was no proper office for the VC and the university was being run from dilapidated rented premises. It was not possible for him to maintain tight administrative control over the staff. In fact, there were no proper rooms, lockers or systems to ensure the safety of examination papers. The sources said the Chief Minister was by and large, convinced with his explanation.[3]

2. Chancellor's Advice and University Autonomy

A controversy arose over the denial of headship of the Department of Sports Medicine and Physiotherapy to Dr. J.S. Kang, Reader of the Department, because of the fact that he was a non-medical graduate and did not belong to medical or physiotherapy stream.

The stormy general house meeting of GNDUTA held on 13th January, 2005 rejected the directive of the Governor-Chancellor of the university for alleviation of Heads of Departments and authorized its executive body to chalk out the next course of action to stage a protest *dharna* in front of VC's office. A press note, jointly issued by Dr. Devinder Singh and Dr. Kuldeep Singh, president and general secretary of the Association respectively alleged that the 'coterie' of Vice-Chancellor tried to create hurdles in evolving a consensus at the meeting. They alleged that the varsity authorities tried to fizzle out the meeting by declaring January 13 as holiday. However, despite the hurdles created by the university authorities, the general meeting was attended by more than 100 members. They alleged that the authorities used all means to thwart holding of the meeting. They claimed that it was for the first time in the history of the university that the authorities individually informed the teachers about the decision of declaration of a holiday. The house unanimously rejected 'the illogical and ill-conceived' directive issued by the Governor regarding the headship of Department of Sports Medicine and Physiotherapy. The members wondered how the appointment of a person with academic background of physiotherapy had become so important in the case of the GNDU, whereas the physiotherapy department at Patiala is headed by a person with academic background in biological sciences. Ironically the Governor is Chancellor of both the universities. This was clear from the fact that the non-issue was made an issue by instigating the students. The press note alleged that the Governor, too, was misguided.[4]

In a published letter, Apropos to the article, "Chancellor's Advice *versus* University Autonomy" in Education Tribune on January 25, 2005, Mr. D.S. Kalha, Principal Secretary to the Governor, Punjab in a clarification, issued here, says that an advisory issued by the Chancellor, GNDU to the Vice-Chancellor of the university in the matter of appointment of Head of the Department of Medicine and Physiotherapy raised vital issues. These include whether the university was created to nurture and build career prospects of its students or whether the career advancement of a member of the faculty has precedence and whether "autonomy" means autonomy in the pursuit of excellence in academic affairs or does it permit compromise with academic interests. The letter pointed out that there can be no doubt that the universities are established and exist for students and that autonomy mandates a single-minded devotion and pursuit of academic excellence and pursuit of academic excellence without any interference, be it the government or any other pressure group. If that were so, would an advice given by the Chancellor in a matter concerning pursuit of academic excellence and the future of students tantamount to interference? Would the Chancellor not be failing in his duties if he did not advise the university authorities to have the matter considered in the Syndicate? This is the core issue and the debate should not be reduced to promotion of individual interests. It was also pointed out that, on facts as well it was not in the public knowledge that the Chancellor has asked the Vice-Chancellor to offer his comments on the following:

1. The promotion of Dr. Kang as Reader in the Department was recommended in a personal scale by the Selection Committee in its meeting held on December 3, 2003 and subject to the condition that "under no circumstance and/or at any later stage, he can be considered for the headship of the Department of Sports, Medicine and Physiotherapy, being a non-medical graduate. He would not be considered, at any stage, for any assignment of even officiating as head of the department or even on rotational basis." Under

what circumstances, therefore, is the appointment being considered at this stage?

2. The HOD in a letter addressed to Dr. Kang (February 5, 2003) had addressed Dr. Kang of "willfully presenting himself as a psychologist without possessing a requisite degree in the relevant subject" and had him ineligible to teach the subject of psychology. What action did the university take in this matter?
3. Dr. Kang has himself in a letter dated 13.12.2004, addressed to the VC, stated that he does not belong to the medical or physiotherapy stream and it would not be proper for him to claim headship of the department. He had requested to be shifted to the Department of Physical Education. Has this request been considered?

The letter from the office of the Chancellor further says that the appointment of Dr. Kang as HOD would result in de-recognition of the course by the Indian Physiotherapist Association and thereby jeopardize the future of the students. It is the desire of the Chancellor that the academic interest of the students was kept paramount and not compromised under any circumstance. The VC has, therefore, been adverse to initiate suitable amendments in the University Calendar regarding the appointments of HODs, Dean of Faculties and Dean of Academic Affairs, keeping in view specialized/professional nature of courses.[5]

GNDUTA in a 12-page letter to the President of India demanded that the Chancellor may be directed to withdraw his 'illegal advice' of an amendment to the University Calendar given to the VC. The Association said that the Chancellor also owed an explanation as to why he issued advice only to GNDU and not to other university where such a department existed. However, the Vice-Chancellor, following the reported 'interference', appointed the Dean faculty as the acting head of the physiotherapy department.

3. Students' Fudge Records

Fearing shortage of lectures, about 10 students of the

GNDU resorted to stealing their attendance register to temper with the records. Unfortunately, they did not prove smart enough for their seniors and consequently four of them were expelled from the hostel. After detecting the tempering, the university authorities constituted a five-member panel under the Dean of Students Welfare R.K. Bedi to probe into the matter and recommend the action against the guilty students. The 10 students belonging to the eighth semester of the B.Tech (Planning) of Guru Ram Dass School of Planning Department, involved in the act were identified. Sources said the students were running short of lectures and would not have been allowed to sit for the semester examination scheduled for the end of May. About 10 days back, they stole the attendance register from the office of the head of department to fudge records. Though they kept the register back the very next day fulfilling the conditions, the change came to the notice of the HOD. He summoned some of the students whose records have been tempered with and after questioning, he sent a written complaint to the Vice-Chancellor. In the absence of the V.C., HOD Bedi said it was well established that the students had tempered with the records and therefore they had summoned their parents. HOD was also scrutinizing some other students whose records were tempered with.[6]

HIMACHAL PRADESH UNIVERSITY

1. Examination Papers Printing Scam

Himachal Pradesh University can certainly take credit for conducting efficient, timely and honest examinations and entrance tests like PMT/PET and other admission tests (with only one exception of the CPMT, 2006 paper leak) especially in the background of paper leaks and other irregularities reported in other Universities/Institutions in the country. However, only one exceptional case of a question paper printing scam blotted its otherwise good reputation. This case study is related not only to the printing of the question papers but also to other acts of irregularities which ultimately led the dilution and erosion of autonomy of Himachal Pradesh University and humiliating exit of its Vice-Chancellor, Prof. S.D Sharma. The heading, "Examination Papers Printing Scam" has been given because this was the major factor in the ouster of the Vice-Chancellor. The whole story is presented below.

As a matter of practice, examination and paper setting work was got done by the Assistant Controller of Examinations. But the then Vice-Chancellor, Prof. S.D. Sharma assigned this job to Mr. P.N. Bhardwaj, the then Assistant Registrar (Secrecy). Annual examination papers of the undergraduate classes held in April, 2002 were of very poor printing quality and contained many mistakes. The students' unions did not take the situation lightly and started agitation against it. This agitation was spearheaded by Students Federation of India (SFI). Agitators, giving the details of the large amounts spent by the Secrecy Branch, demanded the sacking of the VC and threatened of starting legal proceedings against him. By and by other irregularities like withdrawal of secrecy funds, messing up in appointments, hiring of accommodation for International Centre for Distance Education and Open Learning (ICDEOL) without requirement, appointing consultants, etc also came to light. The students vociferously pointed out all these irregularities in their rallies and *dharnas*. Their agitation got momentum day-by-day and the normal functioning of the university got seriously paralysed.

Pointing out systemic failure in the university, the Secretary to Governor, on 14th August, 2003, wrote to the Vice-Chancellor of the university:

> It has come to the notice of His Excellency that the University is not functioning strictly in accordance with the mandate of the Himachal Pradesh University's Act and the Statutes and Ordinances made thereunder. Meetings of the Court, the Executive Council, Finance Committee and the Academic Council are not held regularly within the prescribed time frame. Regular appointments by selection to the posts of Registrar, Controller of Examinations and the Finance Officer are not being made and *ad-hoc* appointments under emergency powers of the Vice-Chancellor are invoked for making these appointments. It has also come to the notice of His Excellency that the present posts of Registrar, Controller of Examinations and the Finance Officer do not hold the prescribed eligibility

> qualifications for the posts. ...It has further been noticed by His Excellency that the emergency powers under Section 12-C (7) are being invoked by the Vice-Chancellor for routine matters which do not require any urgent action. These powers have been used for the purpose of granting promotions, pay scales, amendment of the Constitution of Students' Council and even for passing the Annual Budget. This is highly objectionable. Decisions of substantial nature, which are to be taken by the statutory bodies of the University like Executive Council and Academic Council, cannot be taken by the Vice-Chancellor by invoking emergency powers.[7]

A special meeting of the Executive Council (EC) was then convened on August 30, 2003 to discuss the issues raised by the Governor, Mr. V.S. Kokje. This meeting turned out to be unprecedented one with members asking the Vice-Chancellor to leave the board room so that the EC could take a decision on the allegations of financial irregularities and misuse of emergency powers by him. Dr. S.D. Sharma then left in protest. In the absence of the Vice-Chancellor, the meeting proceeded under the chairmanship of Mr. Sudipto Roy, Principal Secretary, Education, Government of Himachal Pradesh. The EC then recommended to the Governor that the Vice-Chancellor should be asked to proceed on leave immediately as no meaningful inquiry could be held into the affairs of the institution as long as he was at the helm of affairs. It was also resolved in the meeting that an officiating Vice-Chancellor be appointed by the Governor who would conduct an inquiry into all acts of omission and commission.

On September 2, 2003, vigilance men raided various offices of the university to seize records pertaining to the inquiries against the VC. The case under Section 13(2) of the Prevention of Corruption Act and Sections 420, 468 and 471 of the IPC was registered against the VC, Deputy Registrar and some other officials. A team led by Mr. A.P. Siddiqui, Superintendent of Police, Vigilance, seized records from the office of the Registrar and the Secrecy Branch. On the same day, the Chancellor, Mr. V.S. Kokje instituted two inquiries in exercise of the powers vested in him under Section 9 of the Himachal Pradesh

University Act. First inquiry related to financial matters and the second with the administrative matter. Financial inquiry was to be done by the Accountant General and the administrative one by Mr. Arvind Kaul, the Additional Chief Secretary to the Government of Himachal Pradesh. The financial matters included the management of university funds, including misappropriation, siphoning-off of funds, accounts and audit of secrecy fund and any mismanagement, hiring of accommodation in and out of the state for the university and any financial mismanagement in such deals, contracts for printing of question papers and financial mismanagement in entering or performing them and all aspects of financial mismanagement and irregularities relating to all the institutions established by the university. The administrative matters included the legality and validity of all appointments made in the university, violations of University Act and the statutes, ordinances and regulations made thereunder, mistakes and irregularities in printing of question papers and in general conduct of examinations and legality and validity of all administrative actions taken by various authorities of the university.[8]

Vigilance continued raids for more records on the third September also. A team of Vigilance Department questioned Dr. S.D. Sharma on the 4th September for about four hours in connection with the case registered against him. Dr. Sharma denied all charges and refused to divulge anything about secrecy matters which he maintained were highly confidential and were looked after by a Deputy Registrar. It may also be mentioned that Dr. Sharma moved an anticipatory bail in the Himachal Pradesh High Court on third September which was granted to him next day up to the 15th September.

Another ramification of the case, Mr. R.D. Panwar, an administrative officer of the State Cadre who was on deputation as Registrar at that time was not on good terms with the VC. Mr. Panwar was unilaterally repatriated by the VC. Mr. Panwar apprehending that the records might be destroyed or doctored sealed some of the records on the night of first September, 2003 and deployed security men outside his office. This preemptive action was taken by Mr. Panwar on coming to know of VC's decision to send him back to the government and appoint

Dr. Suresh Kapoor, a senior Professor in his place. The VC, using his emergency powers, appointed Professor Suresh Kapoor of the Law Department as the Registrar of the university and ordered the repatriation of Mr. Panwar. The government reacted sharply on Dr. Sharma's action. Mrs. Asha Kumari, the then Education Minister, criticized the decision and said that all required steps would be taken to set the matters right. A major confrontation between the Raj Bhavan and the state government was averted following an impromptu meeting on 2nd September between Mr. Virbhadra Singh, Chief Minister, and Mr. V.S. Kokje, Governor leading to reversal of a decision of Dr. S.D. Sharma to unilaterally send back the Registrar. Now two Registrars started working in the university, one sent back by Governor and the other appointed by the VC. This naturally affected the working of the university. Two students of the Department of Computer Sciences then filed a writ in the Himachal Pradesh High Court to end this unusual administrative situation so that students did not suffer. The High Court on 15th September directed the government to send back university Registrar, Mr. Panwar to his parent department and held him ineligible for the post of the Registrar as per the statute of the university. (He was not having M.A. degree required for the post of Registrar as per statute applicable at that time). He was also directed to hand over the records pertaining to ongoing inquiries in the university to the investing agency. A Division Bench comprising Chief Justice Vinod Kumar Gupta and Mr. Justice R.L. Khurana said a meeting of the EC should be held that week and a regular appointment of Registrar should be made. As a stop gap arrangement, the Court appointed Prof. Suresh Kapoor as Registrar. Prof. Kapoor was restrained from taking policy decisions or those relating financial matters.[9] Following the decision of the High Court, Prof. Suresh Kapoor joined as Registrar and the government called Mr. Panwar back to the Himachal Pradesh Government Secretariat, thus ending the 16 day duration of two Registrars working simultaneously in the University.

Another action taken by the Cabinet of Himachal Pradesh as a sequel to all what happened in the University under the vice-chancellorship of Dr. Sharma need to be mentioned here to comprehend the total dimension of the case. The Cabinet met in

Shimla on 5th September, 2003 under the chairmanship of Mr. Virbhadra Singh and decided to incorporate a new Section 9(b) in the Act to empower it to institute an inquiry into financial and administrative matters. Another proposed amendment made it obligatory to get the decisions taken by the Vice-Chancellor using emergency powers ratified within 60 days. The Vice-Chancellor was required to justify in writing the reasons for the use of emergency powers. The provisions pertaining to the appointment of Registrar and the Finance Officer were also proposed to be amended to make an IAS officer with five years of service and an HAS officer with nine years of service eligible for the post. The Finance Officer would be an officer of state Finance Department. It was also decided that the government would issue an ordinance after seeking assent of the Governor. At this Mr. P.K. Dhumal, a former Chief Minister, said that the "BJP would oppose the promulgation of an ordinance to amend the Himachal Pradesh University Act as the proposed amendments were an onslaught on the autonomy of the institution".[10]

The district committee of the CPM lambasted the BJP for supporting, what they called "tainted Vice-Chancellor" of Himachal Pradesh University and said that the move of the party smacked of the deep nexus between the top functionary of the university and the party pointing to corrupt deals involving the two. Mr. Rakesh Singha, the secretary of the district unit of the party, said the BJP was trying to save its leaders who were involved in rampant corruption in the university during the Dhumal regime. He urged the government to speed up the inquiry so that all officials and politically influential persons were held accountable for their misdeeds. The party ridiculed the Congress government for adopting dilatory tactics in probing the university affairs. A section of the leadership of pro-Congress teachers, employees and students was also a part of VC's bandwagon because of their personal benefits and they were against any action to bring the corrupt officials to book.[11]

The Governor suggested some improvements and sent the ordinance back to the government. The government again sent the ordinance to the Governor for approval after incorporating some of the suggestions made by him. The revised draft was approved by the Cabinet on 20th September by circulation.

While the government made most of the suggestions suggested by the Governor part of the ordinance, it refused to dilute the provision for "suspending" the VC. The Governor was of the view that the term like "suspension" was too harsh for the head of the institution and suggested that instead a provision be made for sending the VC on leave or withdrawal of his financial and administrative powers. However, the government saw nothing wrong in it as much as such provisions were applicable to all top civil servants. A new Section 9(b) was added to the Act under which the government would be empowered to order inquiry into the financial and administrative affairs of the university. The Cabinet sent the revised ordinance to the Governor on 21st September who approved the same the next day.

On 21st September, 2003, HPU Teachers' Cell of the State Congress urged the Chancellor to send the VC Professor Sharma on leave till the inquiry was pending against him. In a release, the convener of the Cell, Dr. Rajinder Singh Chauhan hailed the proposed ordinance on the university affairs being brought by the state government and said the proposed ordinance would not undermine the autonomy of the university. He said in the past, the BJP government had also amended the HPU Act to transfer the permanent registrar. He further added, "Autonomy means the decentralistion of power to various bodies of the university like Executive Council, Board of Studies, Staff Council, etc. In the past, the Vice-Chancellor has used emergency powers by evading all these bodies. Autonomy does not mean to save and encourage corrupt person. No person is above law and rule of law shall prevail."[12] State NSUI vice-president Arun Mehta asked the HPU VC to quit from his post by sending his resignation to the government, otherwise the students' union would be forced to launch agitation against him.[13] After the promulgation of the ordinance, the Chief Minister of Himachal Pradesh, Mr. Virbhadra Singh asked the VC to proceed on leave to pave the way for an impartial inquiry against him.

This Ordinance issued by the Governor on 22nd September 2003, ultimately led to the amendment by the State Legislative Assembly in the Himachal Pradesh University Act, 1970 and inclusion of "Section 35-A Creation of posts, etc. No post, position and assignment created by the University shall have any effect unless approved by the State Government." Government of Himachal Pradesh went still further and its Department of Education issued a Notification No. EDN-A-Ga (10)-1/2004 dated Shimla 171002, 22.5.2005 framing rules regulating payment of grant-in-aid to HPU, Shimla. First condition under the above rules was "that the university shall function smoothly to the satisfaction of the Government". Imposing so many other stringent conditions indicating exacting control the Notification ended: "The University will furnish information indicating various categories of posts which are being charged out of grant-in-aid and it shall be mandatory for the Himachal Pradesh University to seek approval of the Government to fill up any of the sanctioned vacant posts."

On November 4, 2003, Mr. Arvid Kaul, the then Chief Secretary to the Government of Himachal Pradesh submitted the report of the inquiry conducted by him into the allegations against the VC to the Governor. The report indicted the VC of various administrative and financial irregularities, and blatant misuse of emergency powers. It hold him guilty of committing serious irregularities in the appointment of teaching and non-teaching staff, hiring accommodation without requirement, and spending funds without any administrative approval. The most serious irregularities pertain to the Himalayan Studies Centre and the International Centre for Distance Education and Learning. Some of the appointments were not even approved by the executive council of the University. Two private buildings, one at Panchkula, owned by a son of Dr. Suraj Bhan, a former Governor of the state, and another at Shimla were hired without any requirement raising doubts about the motive. No procedure was followed in the appointments of Class III and Class IV staff.[14]

The second inquiry report relates to the special audit conducted by the Comptroller and Auditor General on the directions of the Governor, Mr. V.S. Kokje. This report, submitted to the Governor on 12th November, 2003, indicted the VC by directly linking him with the irregularities in the printing of question papers. The 37-page audit report, submitted to Mr. Kokje pointed out that the contract for the printing of question papers and booklets was awarded without observing procedural norms, causing a wrongful loss of Rs. 43.49 lakh to the University from January 2002 to March 2003. Dr. Sharma had personally obtained three quotations for the purpose and awarded contract on January 9, 2002, on the spot. The existing rates were not kept in view while awarding the contract and no comparison was made. No condition for ensuring the quality of paper to be used and printing was imposed. It was found that the firm had used poor quality paper for printing. Contrary to the prevailing practice of giving 50 per cent payment as advance, the entire payment was made in advance and no action was taken against it despite mistakes and other shortcomings in the printing of question papers. As many as 7,110 question papers were received short and the minimum quantity of question papers to be printed was fixed at 300, even though in many cases only 100 papers were actually printed. In all, a sum of Rs. 72,24,128 was drawn as advance for secrecy work. The entire expenditure was irregular, as under the statutes of the university, the secrecy work is assigned to the Controller of Examination and the Additional Controller of Examination. Besides, a sum of Rs. 20 lakh was diverted from the NRI fund for secrecy work. In this case, the Vice-Chancellor allotted the secrecy work to a Deputy Registrar in violation of the statutes. The officer concerned drew funds from the finance officer in cash with the approval of the Vice-Chancellor for payment to the printer. Serious irregularities have also been revealed in the appointment of teaching and non-teaching staff. As many as 59 employees of the D staff category were employed in excess of the sanctioned 326 posts. Out of these, 47 were appointed between October 2001 and November 2002 by the Vice-Chancellor using his emergency powers. ICDEOL hired accommodation at Panchkula for a study centre, which was not centrally located, ignoring the better offer of a fully furnished house in Sector 12-A in the heart of Chandigarh. No reasons were assigned for not considering the offer. Incidentally, the house in Panchkula hired by the university is owned by Mr. Devender Kumar, son of a former Governor, Dr. Suraj Bhan. The university incurred an expenditure of Rs. 1.99 lakh in furnishing the house. The centre appointed three consultants one of whom happened to be the wife of the Vice-Chancellor, without the mandatory approval of the executive council at a salary of Rs. 20,000 per month. While one of the persons appointed was from the ministerial staff of the University, in the case of other two, nothing was on record to show that their parent institution had duly relieved them. While one consultant revised just three lessons of Hindi (BA-III), the other two together wrote lessons of music (BA-III) and five lessons of history (M.Phil) during the entire period of their appointment, which cost university Rs. 7.20 lakh.[15]

All the three students' bodies- the SFI, ABVP and NSUI asked for the immediate sacking of the VC on the basis of the reports of the two inquiries. The executive council of the University which met under the chairmanship of Dr. L.R. Verma, Pro-Vice-Chancellor on 24th November, recommended the immediate removal of Dr. Sharma and initiation of criminal action against those responsible for financial irregularities of serious nature. It also took an adverse view of the fact that Dr. Sharma still indulged in such acts as was evident from the approval granted by him for releasing Rs. 30 lakh as advance for the printing of question papers. It asked the Pro-Vice-Chancellor not to release the amount and instead change the controversial printer to get the printing work done. In such a situation it felt that the continuation of Dr. Sharma as the VC would be detrimental to the functioning of the University and should be removed forthwith.

Finally, the HPU Vice-Chancellor, Prof S.D. Sharma tendered his resignation on the 9th December, 2003. He resisted the attempts to remove him for a long time but ultimately he had no option but to resign. His resignation was accepted by the Governor and Dr. Sharma joined his duties back as Professor in the Department of English in the Kurukshetra University. SFI, the main students' organization which has been spearheading the agitation against Dr. Sharma, celebrated the exit.

The exit of Dr. Sharma has not ended the case. The law of the land is taking its own usual slow course. The three accused in the printing paper scam were, Mr. P.N. Bhardwaj, the Deputy Registrar (Secrecy), Mr. L.R. Jindal, the printer, and Dr. Sharma, the former VC. Mr. Bhardwaj has been suspended. He remained in the police custody for three days. Mr. Jindal was also arrested and was released after spending 60 days in custody. Dr. Sharma has also been arrested once and grilled by the Vigilance

Department for the irregularities committed by him. He, however, continues to be a Professor in Kurukshetra University.

2. Terminating the Services of Three Teachers and a Security Officer

As mentioned in the previous case study relating to HPU, on September 2, 2003, the Chancellor, Mr. V.S. Kokje instituted two inquiries in exercise of the powers vested in him under Section 9 of the Himachal Pradesh University Act. First inquiry related to financial matters and the second to the administrative matter. Financial inquiry was to be done by the Accountant General and the administrative one by Mr. Arvind Kaul, the then Additional Chief Secretary to the Government of Himachal Pradesh. On November 4, 2003, Mr. Arvid Kaul, the then Chief Secretary to the Government of Himachal Pradesh submitted the report of the inquiry conducted by him into the allegations against the VC to the Governor. The report indicted the VC of various administrative and financial irregularities, and blatant misuse of emergency powers. It hold him guilty of committing serious irregularities in the appointment of teaching and non-teaching staff, hiring accommodation without requirement, and spending funds without any administrative approval.

On 23rd November, 2003, the BJP teachers' cell in the HPU urged the Governor to shelve the Arvind Kaul Committee report discarding it as a mere "government-tutored document" and instead order an inquiry into the appointments made during the Congress period from 1994 to 1998. The memorandum included a list of 70 "irregular" appointments, including 12 of teachers. The memorandum said the Kaul Committee report was full of "coloured" statements, suppression and "twisted" facts, reflecting bias.[16]

It may be mentioned that Prof. S.D. Sharma, the VC, indicted by both the above mentioned reports, ultimately resigned on 9th December, 2003 and Prof. L.R. Verma who was the Pro-Vice-Chancellor of HPU at that time was appointed Vice-Chancellor of HPU on 1st January, 2004. Actions on both the reports started in the usual snail speed. More than one year passed but no action was proposed or taken on Kaul Committee report. The report, however, provided a battlefield for the ruling Congress Party and the State opposition party BJP to settle their political scores. Accusing the state government of implementing its political agenda in HPU, a former minister and BJP leader, Dr. Radha Raman Shastri, said employees were being pressurized to make wrong statements regarding the Kaul Committee report. In a statement issued on 17th November, 2004 he said that the VC was pressurizing employees to make wrong statements as regards Kaul Committee report. Employees who refused to make such statements were vicitimised and 14 employees, including the president and secretary of the HPU Employees' Union, had been transferred. He further added that the VC himself ordered these transfers although the Registrar, the competent authority in the case was present in the university, on October 16. "This proves that employees were being victimized for refusing to toe the line of HPU authorities," he added.[17]

Even as the matter was challenged in the court in the form of public interest litigation, the HPU faces a piquant situation, as employees refused to file affidavits in those cases, saying they were being pressurized to make wrong statements. The sub-committee, which was constituted by the executive council to look into the matter after certain anomalies were pointed out in the Kaul Committee report, submitted its report almost a year ago, but no final decision was taken on the matter. The HPU Teachers' Association and the HP Employees' Union resented the pressure tactics and pick-and-choose policy being adopted by the university.[18]

On 18th February, 2005, EC of the HPU termed the appointment of three teachers and a security officer illegal on the recommendations of the Kaul Committee. Four employees, whose appointments have been termed illegal included Dr. Ajay Srivastav, Reader in the Department of Journalism and Mass Communication ICDEOL, Dr. Mamta Sharma, Lecturer in the Bio-Sciences Department, Dr. Kuldeep Chand Agnihotri, Director, HPU Regional Centre, Dharmshala, and Mr. I.S. Dogra, Security Officer. The Kaul Committee report initially pointed out irregularities in the appointment of about 250 employees, both from teaching and non-teaching. However, cases against majority of them were dropped and show-cause notices were issued only to 11 of them. Later, cases were dropped against seven of them, as the EC approved their appointments by terming their qualifications adequate for the job. The show-cause notices were pursued only against the four whose services were finally termed illegal.[19]

Dr. Ajay Srivastav, one of the terminated employees, wrote a letter to the Chief Minister for the correction of his academic records and lambasted the Kaul Committee for twisting the facts.[20] This proved to be of no avail to him. The terminated employees were left with no alternative but to move the H.P. Administrative Tribunal.

Some developments after the termination of the employees may be mentioned to comprehend the broader dimensions of the case. On the issue of the termination of three teachers, Himachal Pradesh University Teachers' Association (HPUTA) was in a very confused sort of position. Pro-BJP Teachers were very much annoyed with the termination and were in agitative mood. Pro-Congress and pro-left teachers, on the other hand felt unconcerned. They could neither openly criticise the Congress government nor could happily tolerate the injustice done to the teaching community whose cause they professed to plead. Dr. Vijay Kaushal, Secretary of the HPUTA, who was associated with the CPM, however, did criticise the university administration for the termination of the teachers and said that a deputation of the HPUTA would meet the Chancellor.[21] A meeting of the General House of the HPUTA was held on 4th March, 2005 but no steps were proposed during the meeting. This frustrated the pro-BJP teachers. Ultimately more than 50 pro-BJP teachers resigned from the membership of the HPUTA on 15th March, 2005 for its failure in taking effective steps for the withdrawal of termination of three teachers. Prof. D.R. Sharma said that there was a strong resentment amongst the teachers that despite the assurance given by the HPUTA in the General House meeting on March 4, no substantial steps were been taken. "It is due to political affiliations of the HPUTA and its office-bearers that the matter has not been taken seriously," he said. He regretted that despite the teachers expressing full faith in the HPUTA, no attempt was made to meet the Chancellor to bring the matter into his notice. Prof. Sharma said as a mark of protest against the inaction by the HPUTA, the teachers decided to resign from the association and decided to meet on March 22 to decide the future course of action.[22] And on March 22, 2005, the pro-BJP teachers formed their own separate association which they called, Himachal Teachers' Association (HUTA). This association flayed the functioning of the university for what they alleged violation of the University Act, statutes, and ordinances during the regime of the present VC. HUTA in the meeting held under the chairmanship of its president Prof. C.L. Gupta on 16th July, 2005 demanded immediate reinstatement of the three teachers whose services were terminated by the university authorities on political considerations.[23]

The helpless employees whose cases were pending with the H.P. Administrative Tribunal looked towards the blind Goddess of Justice to see them and give justice so that they could live honourably. This continued for about three years with the University giving rejoinder after rejoinder and the employees answering those rejoinders. However, in 2008 with the coming back to power of the BJP Government in the state and as a natural corollary to it—appointment of their own man as the Vice-Chancellor, all the terminated employees were re-instated. Moral of the story—political problems have political solutions.

3. Local Audit Department (LAD) and HP University (HPU)

As mentioned earlier, HPU has got four systems of audit. Firstly, Internal Audit, secondly, CAGI Audit, thirdly, LAD Audit, and fourthly, Special Audit. To these four systems has been added another system of audit which can be named as a different version of Internal Audit, i.e., audit by two Accounts Branches—Accounts-I and Accounts-II. Every bill has to be processed and got cleared through either of these branches depending upon the areas allotted to them. Internal Audit is done by the non-teaching employees of the Internal Audit Section of the University who have been given this task vide Government of Himachal Pradesh Notification No. Fin. (LA) (2) (15) XIV, 106-87 Vol. IV, dated 31.07.2005 after a long battle between the non-teaching employees of the University and the officials of Local Area Department (LAD). Since the inception of the University, accounts of the University have been audited by the Comptroller and Auditor General, Government of India (CAGI). Audit of the accounts has to be done by the CAGI, in as much as according to the Sections 14 and 15 of the

Comptroller and Auditor General Act, 1971, the Boards and Corporations getting more than 75% grant-in-aid from a State Government has to get their accounts audited by the CAGI. However, after the increase of the amount of grants, a system of 100% pre-audit by the Local Audit Department (LAD) of the Government was added on 1st April, 1981. So now the University has got double audit system, 100% pre-audit by the LAD and some sample or special audit by AG. Background for the addition of LAD may be explained as follows: Some posts of accounts clerks were created in the University in September, 1977 to look after the accounting work in the University. A specific syllabus was prescribed for the examination of the accounts clerks. It was assured that those who qualify the examination would be promoted to those posts. But the non-teaching employees did not agree to this. They simply wanted the promotions according to their seniority without qualifying the examination. The employees had their way and got promotions to those posts without passing the examination. However, the accounts of the University required expert handling and thus came the LAD.

LAD has its own way of auditing. It started delaying the work. At times, it would point out certain unimaginative objections. It has got a yardstick with which it would measure or deal with the University accounts and matters. It cannot distinguish between a Government Department and the University. The officials in the LAD were not trained to understand that University is not a Government Department and has to be treated differently. So the teachers, students and the non-teaching staff all started feeling the pinch. The clash between the LAD staff posted at the university and employees of the HPU started taking acrimonious turn after the second half of the year 2000 when LAD raised some objections to waiving off leave encashment amount by the Executive Council (EC) of the university. This way LAD bypassed the decisions of the EC. LAD was of the view that such provisions did not exist in the state government departments. University was required to follow the state government rules and the EC had no powers to amend the rules. At this the Registrar vide letter No. 6-21/76-HPU, (Estt.), Vol. II-147 dated 9th January, 2001 requested the LAD of the Government of Himachal Pradesh to allow leave encashment without deducting the period of leave encashment as decided by the EC. In response to the above letter the LAD, H.P. Government wrote to the Joint Controller of LAD, HPU Shimla with a copy to the Registrar vide letter No. Fin. (LA)H(2)C(15)-14-52/82Vol.15-480, Government of Himachal Pradesh, dated Shimla-9, the 18th January, 2001:

> "Since, the Executive Council, which is the highest Executive Body of the HPU, had already taken a view on this matter and waived off recoveries, there is no reason to take up the matter again with the Executive Council, as rightly suggested by the Registrar, HPU. Hence to deduct leave encashment at this stage would amount to making recoveries in far more volume than would have been had the money been recovered in 1985 itself. Moreover, it will be against the spirit of the decision of the Executive Council. Therefore, there is no case for deducting leave encashment for the period of leave salary as encashed by the employees during service in this case. Thus, the payment for leave encashment without deducting the period of leave encashment already taken during service period by an employee of HPU may be made without any further delay."

The case was settled but the internal differences, and bad feelings toward each other continued. HPU employees, both teaching and not teaching, criticised the LAD (HPU) for its obstructionist attitude of pointing out unnecessary objections, adopting delaying techniques and negative attitude and always sensing dishonesty and fraud in all the bills involving even paltry sums. The LAD, on the other hand, criticised the university employees for their impertinent behaviour by alleging that numerous self-styled leaders with their broad chests would often barge into their rooms and pressurize them for passing their bills immediately, and accepting the wrong fixations. The employees were getting many illegal allowances, increments and just enjoying themselves with the money of the university which they easily get by pressurising the VC and EC through their trade union activities. Similarly, the teachers and outside experts were also making money by adopting techniques like traveling in the ordinary buses and claiming fudged taxi charges. They would openly say that everybody in the university was after money whatever method one found. They were from the government side and were duty bound to point out any misuse of the funds.

The atmosphere of mutual distrust, hatred, allegations and counter-allegations continuing for many years suddenly bursted when the LAD deducted the secretarial allowance availed by the employees from their salary for the month of May, 2004. At this the employees got flared up. They held a rally in front of VC office and raised slogans against the LAD on the 1st of June, 2004. Mr. O.P. Sharma, the then president, Mr. Waryam Singh Bains and other leaders spoke against the LAD and asked the VC to send the LAD officials back to their parent department. Their protests continued next day also. Employees, teachers and students also constituted a joint-coordination committee to proceed further with the agitation. However, on 2nd June, they resumed work after being assured by the VC that in future they would not face any problem from the LAD. The VC also assured them that he would personally take up the matter with the LAD to ensure that in future they did not face a similar problem.[24] However, again on 21 June the employees held a rally, sat on *dharna* in front of VC office and threatened to go on strike on their demand for removing the LAD personnel from the university. On 22nd June, joint-coordination committee under the leadership of its president, Mr. Amar Nath Gupta met the Governor and apprised him of their demands and problems. The deputation included Prof. Shiv Raj Singh, the then president of the HPUTA, Mr. O.P. Sharma, the then president HPU Non-Teaching Employees' Association, and Mr. Dilay Ram, the then president HPU Class Four and Technical Employees' Association. The Governor assured the deputation that he would ask the VC and the Registrar that the LAD completed their work within a well defined period of time. The employees, thus, withdrew their *dharna* on the assurance of the Governor. Finance Department, Government of Himachal Pradesh vide Notification No. Fin. (LA) (2) (15) XIV, 106-87 Vol. IV, dated 31.07.2004 allotted some audit work to the university and withdrew some of the staff from LAD of the university. Some changes were introduced by another notification on 11.8.2004.

HPU accordingly created an internal audit section comprising of its non-teaching staff to look after the audit work assigned to the university. So, now two audit systems are currently working simultaneously in the university. Their behaviour seems more like two warring camps with no cooperation at all, always trying to outsmart each other. LAD personnel are qualified and trained in audit procedure whereas the internal audit section personnel have picked up some pieces of information through their long service in the university. This non-cooperation is naturally affecting the working of the university. Cold war between HPU and the LAD is still continuing. Some examples are cited below. Finance Officer of the HPU wrote a letter No. 1-1/IAS/HPU/2005, dated 15.10.2005 to the Additional Chief Secretary (Fin.) seeking some clarification on the notifications dated 31.7.2004 and 11.8.2004. To quote the letter, "At present certain bills either have been examined and settled/paid by the University in spite of its submission to LAD but these were not attended to by the (the LAD) and the same has been hanging fire on the one pretext or the other. Thus, the university had to clear such urgent bills under compulsion being time bound working process of the university, for which specific clarification and directions on the issues be given on priority so that work of the university may not suffer." Another example—Mr. Waryam Singh Bains, president of another association of the employees known as Himachal Pradesh University Welfare Association (HPUWA) on 28th December, 2005 wrote a seven page long letter on the subject entitled, "Pay-fixation dispute(s) and negative functioning of the Local Audit Department (LAD) in the University (HPU)." This letter addressed to the VC of the university presents a long saga of the rivalry between the HPU and LAD.

4. HPCPMT-2006

HPU conducted HPCPMT-2006 for MBBS, BDS and Ayurveda on 28th May, 2006, result to which was declared on 3rd June, 2006. Outcome of the result was a bad news for many of the brilliant students who could not find their names in the list of successful candidates. Average students and many of whom were from one locality of the Shimla city made their way not only to the list of successful candidates but even managed to get top ranks. This raised doubts in the minds of the brilliant but unsuccessful students and their parents. They formed an "Action Committee of Aggrieved Students and Parents (ACASP) on 7th June and demanded a high level probe into the HPCPMT-2006 'paper leak'." They alleged that the examination for most of the top-ranking students had turned out to be frustrating as those who had scored average in the last CBSE and other examinations had scored much higher than the former. In a memorandum to the Chief Minister, Mr. Virbhadra Singh, the ACASP alleged large-scale irregularities in the conduct of the HPCPMT-2006. The ACASP chairperson, Dr. Kuldeep Singh Tanwar, claimed that the "examination mafia have started operating in the state ensuring cent percent success in the PMT through advertisement in newspapers, telephone calls and through personal approaches to the parents of the concerned children. "The rates range from Rs. 5 to 20 lakhs and they operate in league with some corrupt officials," he alleged. Mr. Naresh Gupta, convener, ACASP, stated that HPCPMT-2006 should be cancelled and fresh examination ordered."[25] The Chief Minister, Mr. Virbhadra Singh after a patient hearing to the ACASP assured that he would get the matter investigated. It may be mentioned that the ACASP also met the HP State Congress President and Rajya Sabha Member, Mrs. Viplav Thakur and BJP State President and Rajya Sabha Member, Mr. Suresh Bhardwaj and made them abreast of the leakage of the HPCPMT-2006. Vice-Chancellor of the University, Dr. L.R. Verma denied that there had been any bungling in the PMT as the entire record had been examined in view of the allegations by some parents. ACASP demanded that the government should make public the name of the agency entrusted with the task of holding an enquiry. They took strong exception to the statements of Dr. Verma that there was no need for an enquiry. The chairperson of ACASP, Dr. Kuldeep Singh Tanwar said that the committee would hold its district level meeting on June 11 and state level meeting on June 13 to decide the future course of action. He made an appeal to various NGO's and responsible citizens to extend their cooperation on the issue. [26]

ABVP organized state-wide demonstrations in protest against the 'paper-leak' on 9th June. Their leaders alleged that though the VC had got complaint about the 'paper-leak' on 23rd May, he did not take the matter seriously. They demanded the resignation of the VC and dismissal of the CoE. Continuation of the CoE even after his retirement was also strongly criticized. SFI also threatened to launch an agitation in case an enquiry into the allegations was not conducted. Students Central Association (SCA) declared the allegations a shame on the University and demanded that culprits be punished after a judicial probe. Ex-Chief Minister, Mr. Prem Kumar Dhumal also demanded that the VC be suspended.[27] Mr. J.P. Nadda, ex-Health Minister of Himachal Pradesh demanded intervention of the Governor of the State and an independent inquiry to save the prestige of the University. SFI also announced that they would hold demonstrations in all the colleges of the Pradesh.[28]

H.P. University in view of the pressure by the students' organizations, ACASP, and leaders of BJP, the main opposition party of the State, appointed ex-Registrar and CoE, now a retired but a member of the EC of the University, Mr. A.R. Chauhan to inquire into the matter and report within three days. The one man committee started the probe on 13th June. The protesters, however, were not satisfied with the constitution of this committee. ACASP termed the inquiry a mere show off and said they would not cooperate with the committee. SFI rejected the constitution of the committee by saying that, "It was an attempt to save the culprits." H.P. University Teachers' Welfare Association in a meeting under the chairmanship of its President, Professor C.L. Gupta demanded a judicial probe into the matter connected with thousands of the students and their parents. Secretary of the Association, Professor Sunil Gupta remarked that the matter was a blot on the unblemished image of the University, inquiry by the ex-Registrar and CoE of the University would not bring the truth, and only judicial probe could reveal the truth of the whole matter.[29]

The one-man inquiry committee, headed by Mr. A.R. Chauhan submitted its report on 15th June, held that all procedures and formalities were duly followed and complete secrecy was maintained while conducting the test. The report pointed out that the media reports which forced the university to hold and inquiry was a mere propaganda based on conjectures, hearsay and rumours, spread by vested interests.

Meanwhile, the university authorities also released the final merit list of the HPCPMT on 16th. Reacting to the inquiry report and the release of the merit list, some of the unsuccessful candidates said that seeing the attitude of Mr. A.R. Chauhan, they were not hoping to get justice. "The inquiry was a mere eyewash basically to mislead the public and we never expected to get justice," said Mr. Akarshan Chauhan and Bhanu Pratap Singh, two students who failed to make it to the PMT. "They also demanded that inquiry report should be made public so that the public could know the seriousness with which it was conducted." ACASP said, "It was not at all surprised that the university had gone ahead and released the merit list of the HPCPMT." The committee said it was not against the success of any particular student but against the mafia, who had spread their tentacles outside Himachal as well, and as such it was only a thorough probe that could ensure justice.[30]

ACASP filed a PIL in the HP High Court for a thorough inquiry. In the PIL, the coordinator of the ACASP, Mr. Naresh Kumar mentioned that since the University and the State Government made no efforts to conduct a thorough inquiry into the matter they were forced to take to the recourse. The High Court appointed a three-member police investigating committee to find out the alleged leakage. The team found enough evidence to conclude the leakage was "comprehensive" and on "large-scale." The most striking evidence was that the candidates who knew the question paper had not done any rough work. They had solved the questions of Physics and Mathematics, which involved lengthy calculations, without doing any rough work. There were others who had done partial rough work. The team examined the answer sheets of the candidates who bagged the first 60 ranks and found evidence to establish that as many as 38 candidates knew the question paper. It was enough to draw the conclusion that the leak was on large scale. Further the pattern of answers also indicated that some candidates had been tutored to solve the paper. All of them had wrongly answered certain questions.[31] The three-member committee also went into the details of the bank accounts, mobile phone calls and answer-sheets of some of the candidates to whom the paper was allegedly leaked.

H.P. High Court on 26th July cancelled the HPCPMT conducted by the HPU on the basis that there was leakage of the question paper. The Court also directed the University to conduct the CPMT-2006 afresh in a week commencing on 14th August. The Court directed the University that only those candidates would be eligible to take the examination who had appeared in the cancelled examination. The date of the examination would be notified by the University latest by July 30 and the result be declared within a week of the conduct of the examination. A Division Bench, comprising Chief Justice Vinod Kumar Gupta and Mr. Justice Surjit Singh, observed that the report of the committee of police officers clearly pointed out that question paper might have been leaked. Therefore, the Registrar of the University was to register a case formally with the police station concerned. Further, regular investigation after the registration of the case be entrusted to the same committee which conducted the initial inquiry. The investigations be completed expeditiously, possibly within two months. The Court also directed the Vice-Chancellor to put forth within three months a detailed comprehensive scheme to ensure that in future the leakage of the question paper did not take place at all.[32]

The interested parties moved the Supreme Court against the decision of the HP High Court. The Supreme Court on 11th August, 2006 declined to interfere with the Himachal Pradesh High Court order cancelling the HPCPMT and ordering fresh entrance examination in the wake of the leak. A Bench of Mr. Justice K.G. Balakrishnan and Mr. Justice D.K. Jain also refused to defer the date of the fresh entrance test scheduled for August 20 by the HPU following the High Court's July 26 order. The Court, however, restrained the state police from summoning for questioning till 23rd August those students as well as their parents against whom allegations were levelled for adopting foul means in the cancelled PMT.

The paper leak had connections with many northern states. Some news paper reports in this respect deserve mention here. "PMT Leak: Report Traces Bihar Link. . . . The sources said some men involved in this racket had worked in close association with Rajesh Don from Bihar, who two years back had been involved in the CBSE medical exam paper leak, investigated by the CBI."[33] "Docs involved in HP-CPMT Leak. . . .The state police has identified an Amritsar-based doctor, who is also wanted by the Punjab Police in the leak of Punjab PMT question paper. The doctor who is learnt to have solicited students and parents personally is absconding and is now wanted by the Himachal Police as well."[34] "Breakthrough in HP CPMT Paper Leak Case. . . . Making a breakthrough in the alleged HP-CPMT question paper leak, the police arrested a youth, Manoj, from Nagchalla in Mandi (Himachal Pradesh) who has given vital information which will help in the investigation of the case. Manoj is learnt to have told the police about the identity of the person who got the question paper from the press in Lucknow where the papers had been sent for printing has named a person from Bijnaur in Uttar Pradesh who was involved in the racket in a big way along with an Amritsar-based doctor. . . . According to the police, Manoj is an alleged *dalal* who found prospective clients in the form of parents wanting to ensure admission of their children to medical colleges. . . . A majority of persons, who were behind the racket, are outsiders and people from Himachal were only involved at the very lower level, with the task of finding parents of candidates as clients. Those involved in the racket from Punjab and Uttar Pradesh used Himachali youths to act as *dalals* and look for parents who were willing to pay. In return these youths were given sums ranging from Rs. 20,000 to Rs. 25,900 per client.[35]

This paper leak scam tarnished the image of the University. It was for the first time in the history of the University that an examination was cancelled on the grounds of the leakage It was the worst scam to hit the university after the question printing scam four years ago which made the Vice-Chancellor, Dr S.D. Sharma quit his post. Some words from the editorial of *The Tribune* asking the VC to resign may be mentioned here:

> When there was a leakage of examination papers in Baba Farid University and Panjab University, newspapers and TV channels were full of the scandals. It was thought that this would have set alarm bells ringing in every university of the country. But it seems the incidents did not make the officials of Himachal Pradesh University any wiser.

> Otherwise, how could they have allowed the Combined Pre-Medical Test (CPMT) conducted by their university to be compromised in quite a similar manner? ...The enquiry report confirmed the leakage of the paper and the High Court has now taken the extreme but logical step of cancelling the examination. There could not be a bigger slur on the name of the university. After all, conducting a free and fair examination is one of its primary duties. . . . The trend can be reversed only if heads begin to roll, right up to the top. In fact, continuation of even the Vice-Chancellor has now become untenable on the touchstone of propriety.[36]

Some of the students who were involved in the paper leak did not appear in the second examination conducted by the HPU on 20th August. Wide gap between the marks of the first and the second examinations of the tainted students who appeared in the second examination convinced the shocked people of the large-scale leakage of the paper. Even the topper of the leaked paper (one of the tainted students) was nowhere in the merit list!

UNIVERSITY OF JAMMU, JAMMU

1. A University Student Attacked with Sharp Weapons

Jammu University campus is well protected by a military post at the very entrance of the University. Even then, Ajay Pal Singh, a student of the first semester of the Department of Punjabi was attacked with sharp edged weapons by some assailants on the second November, 2004. The incident occurred in the lawns of the University when Ajay Pal Singh came out from the Punjabi Department at about 12 pm. The assailants exchanged hot words with the student before attacking him with the sharp weapons. He tried to save himself from the assailants through his hands which got wounded in the process. Soon the security guards came to the lawns. But the assailants had fled by that time. The matter has been reported to the police without getting the FIR properly written by the police. The relatives of both the victim and the assailants approached the Dean Academic Affairs and requested him for the patch up.

2. J&K College Non-Teaching Employees' Association Boycott Exam Duty

Jammu University, being a state multi-faculty affiliating university, is responsible for conducting annual examinations in the affiliating colleges. Non-teaching staff in these affiliating colleges have not been given UGC pay scales due to them since 1st January 1986. They have been agitating since long. Authority to release these pay scales lies with the State Government. But the University authorities responsible for the fair conduct of the graduation-level examinations have to bear the burnt if they fail to conduct these examinations which were to start on 25th March, 2006. Agitated non-teaching staff, which included library staff and class four staff, refused to work for the ensuing examinations till they were released UGC scales with effect from 1st January 1986. On 22nd March all the affiliated colleges under the banner of J&K Non-Teaching Employees' Association observed pen-down strike and demonstrated at many places of the State. They also declared that they would continue their strike next day also. Their main demands were releasing of UGC scales with effect from 1st January, 1986, time-bound promotions, and recruitment of new staff in view of the burden increased with the starting of PG classes in the colleges of the State. This situation led to sleepless nights for the University authorities. Prof. Lokesh Verma, Controller of Examinations said that only the Government of the State could decide on the demands of the employees. The University would not be in a position to conduct the examinations without the help of the employees. In case they continue their strike, the University would take a decision about the new dates of examinations by the 24th March. The whole situation would surely keep the University authorities on their tenterhooks for no fault of theirs and the examinees worried about their studies and future career.

3. B.Ed. Students Seek Recognition

Students of private B.Ed. Colleges of the State staged a *dharna* on the campus of the university on 28th November, 2003 after realizing that the course for which they paid heavy fees was not recognized by National Council of Teachers' Education (NCTE). They raised slogans against the authorities and demanded that steps should be taken to get the course recognized by the NCTE, without which their future prospects would be bleak.

There are 41 B.Ed. colleges in the Jammu region and 32 in the Kashmir valley. Most of the students in these institutions are from Punjab, Himachal Pradesh, Haryana, Rajasthan, Uttar Pradesh, Uttaranchal and Delhi. The Vice-Chancellor Prof. Amitabh Mattoo, tried to pacify the students by saying that a team of the university officials would be dispatched to Jaipur to settle the issue with the NCTE and the Rajasthan Government which had disqualified from the government jobs the candidates who did the course in the State.

The fact came to light when a few students with a B.Ed. degree from Jammu University were denied Government jobs in Rajasthan on the plea that NCTE did not recognize the institutions in this State. The University authorities said that NCTE Act of 1994, passed by the Parliament, was not applicable to Jammu and Kashmir as the state assembly had not ratified that. Prof. Mattoo said that the problem had come up for the first time. No student had faced any problem in the past ten years, during which more than 80,000 students has received training in these institutions.[37]

KURUKSHETRA UNIVERSITY, KURUKSHETRA

1. Fake Certificate Case

During the year 2003, as many as 80 candidates had allegedly tried to get admission to the certificate and diploma courses in the Department of Physical Education of Kurukshetra University by submitting fake certificates of participation in the sports events. These students produced certificates of participation in national events of the games for which Haryana had never sent any players. Subsequently, a few of the certificates were sent to the state directorate of sports at Chandigarh for verification of authenticity. The directorate declared them as fake, following which the University registered a case in Adarsh Police Station, Kurukshetra. However, even after the registration of a criminal case in this regard, the investigation was left pending allegedly due to political pressure by the then Indian National Lok Dal (INDL) Government.

The case has been reopened after a gap of two years on the formation of the Government by Indian National Congress. Now the police has recorded the statements of many students and some officials of the University in a bid to speed up the investigation process and to book the alleged culprits.[38]

2. Irregularities in Examination Wing

Several irregularities, including issue of fake DMC's and substandard printing came to light in the examination wing of the Kurukshetra University. As a result of this exposure, the Executive Committee decided to remove controller of examination, J.S. Kadian. The Executive Committee also recommended an open inquiry by a High Court Judge.[39]

3. Contractual KU Employees Stage Dharna

Kurukshetra University employees working under self-finance scheme and on contract demonstrated and staged a *dharna* in front of the VC office on the 30th June, 2005 in protest against their alleged removal. According to them, they called upon the university Registrar, Mr. Yudhbeer Singh, previous day along with the President of Kurukshetra University Non-Teaching Employees' Association (KUNTEA), Mr. Karan Singh and urged upon the Registrar to release their pending salaries for the past three to four months and extend their contacts.

But, after giving them a patient hearing the Registrar told them that "such employees will not be paid salaries and they should seek the same from the university officers who had registered them" they alleged. They added that as they had been appointed by the last government so they were being harassed by the university administration. . . . Mr. Karan Singh said the employees were appointed against vacant posts created by the university executive council on the recommendations of the State Government. But they have not been paid salaries for the past few months, he added. Refuting the allegations levelled against the university administration, Mr. Yudhbeer Singh said the university had not issued any notice for their removal and he could not understand the reason of launching the agitation. However, he refused to comment further.[40]

4. Students' Protests Against Rise in Eve-Teasing

Members of various students' organizations demonstrated in front of the office of the Vice-Chancellor, Kurukshetra University, in protests against increasing incidents of eve-teasing on the campus on 21st September, 2004. The agitators demanded stern action against students who were involved in an eve-teasing incident near girls' hostels on the university campus on September 16, 2004.

The demonstrators raised slogans and held a *dharna*. The *dharna* was addressed by leaders of organization like Mahila Mukti Morcha, Ismailabad, Yamuna Nagar district, and the Karamchari Union. While talking to media persons, state joint secretary of Jaagrook Chhatra Morcha (JCM), Ms Arti alleged that the Indian National Students' Organisation (INSO) had hired men from Pehowa, Ladwa, Kaithal and Narwana to curb the agitation. She alleged that the "hired" men had approached and threatened students against joining the strike on 21st September. She further alleged that six girls who went to the Adarsh Police Station for registering a case for eve-teasing on September 16, were made to stay there from 5.30 pm to 9.30 pm and no official of the university administration came to their help during that period. Instead, she said, hostel warden telephoned parents of the girls to create panic. She also pointed out that the cases of eve-teasing referred to the Anti-Sexual Harassment Committee (ASHC) in the past had not been settled so far.

Their demands included forwarding of the case to the ASHC, arrest and rustication of the two culprits, check on incidents of eve-teasing on the university campus, and preventing roguish elements from entering the campus. She also demanded a referendum on deciding the visiting hours to girls' hostels and the stepping up of security for girls on the campus. She said if the university administration failed to take the action within a week's time the organization would intensify the agitation.

State vice-president of the National Students Union of India (NSUI) Mr. Sanjay, state secretary, Mr. Rohit Chowdhary, and district president, Mr. Sumit Chowdhary told media persons that some outsiders have threatened students against participating in today's agitation. Similarly, state president of the Students' Federation of India (SFI) Mr. Rajvinder Chandi and state general secretary, Mr. Jai Bhagwan urged the university authorities to take steps to curb incidents of eve-teasing. Former state president of the INSO, Mr. Krishan Sheokand, while addressing the rally, said, outsiders were politicizing the academic atmosphere of the campus.

Dr. J.S. Kadian, Registrar of the University, however, claimed that the case of eve teasing had been sent to a board for inquiry and the security on the road leading to the girls' hostels had been tightened. He said although checking of identity cards to regulate the entry to the campus was a problem, security personnel would be instructed to prevent groups of persons on private vehicles from entering without permission. On why the university officials had failed to turn up at the Adarsh police station when girls have gone to get a case registered, Dr. Kadian said the girls got the FIR lodged late in the night without informing the university authorities. On the demand of referring the case to the ASHC, Dr. Kadian said, "We have not received any such demand. However, the case would be referred to the committee only after clearance from the inquiry board and the police."[41]

PANJAB UNIVERSITY, CHANDIGARH

I. FIR against Five Students

Following a complaint by Panjab University, the police booked five students who had sought admission to certain affiliated colleges on the basis of fake certificates. At the same time, the university was planning to lodge an FIR against six more candidates who were not on rolls of any college but had also used fake degrees for securing admissions.

The university initiated action in to the case after a news item appeared in the Ludhiana *Tribune* on the use of forged stamps of the Controller of Examinations for preparing forged documents. The university then sent four teams to the Ludhiana region to investigate the issue. The team under Dr. Sodhi Ram, Controller of Examinations detected two cases of admission on the basis of fake documents, one at SCD Government College and another at Guru Nanak Girls' College. Another team under Mr. Ashok Raj Bhandari, officiating Finance and Development

Officer, detected three cases at Kamla Lohia SD College. The candidates were given one chance to appear before the university and give their version. None of the candidates turned up at the meeting.[42]

2. Senate Nomination Controversy

A controversy over the nomination to the Panjab University Senate by the Vice-President of India has been continuing for a long time. The nominations made in the month of November, 2004 came in for criticism from many quarters. Dust of the controversy was not yet settled when the HRD Ministry of Government of India shot off a missive to the university authorities for failing to notify names of nominated members. In a letter received from the ministry, the university was asked why it had not bothered to get the names of the 36 members nominated by the Vice-President notified in the official gazette of the government as was mandatory under the Panjab University Act, Regulation 35. According to the rules, while the university had to seek the approval of the Vice-President for those elected to the Senate, the names had to be notified in the case of nominated members. The university had already sought the approval of the Vice-President in the case of elected members. The letter from the ministry assumed greater significance because none of the names recommended by the HRD Ministry made it to the list of nominations released by the office of the Vice-President. It may be mentioned that the university had already fixed the date for the first meeting of the Senate for December 20. Strictly following the rules, the nominated members would not be eligible to sit in the House and be party to the decisions taken at the meetings.

Prof. K.N. Pathak, the Vice-Chancellor, when contacted replied, "We have never got the names of Senators of other appointees notified in the past 50 years though the Act says it is mandatory. The HRD Ministry has written a letter to us in this regard and the Registrar has sent a reply. However, I don't think the absence of notification would have any bearing on the meeting and the election of faculties scheduled for next month."[43]

It may also be mentioned that the nominations to the Senate made by the Vice-President were criticized by

Congressmen who claimed it had a "BJP bias" and none of the names recommended by the Punjab Government (Congress Government) and the HRD Ministry (UPA Government), the two funding agencies of the government, as also the MP (Belonging to Congress Party), had been included.[44]

3. Common Entrance Test (CET) Fiasco

The Panjab University Common Entrance Test (CET) was to be held on 20th May, 2006. But the question papers did not reach even on the morning of the 20th May. The CET, therefore, had to be postponed from 20th May to 12 June. Prof. K.K. Bajaj was asked to conduct inquiry into the fiasco and report within 72 hours.

The inquiry named three persons responsible for the non-receipt of the question papers: the printer (whose identity is kept confidential), Assistant Registrar Conduct (ARC), Mr. S.K. Sharma and Controller of Examinations, Dr. Sodhi Ram. All the three have been charged with negligence. A perusal of the report indicates that the real culprit is also the university authority's lack of long-term vision to provide a contingency plan and a total lack of any written accountability. While the printer's lapse lay in his failure to deliver the papers in time, the report says the "action of ARC S.K. Sharma in merely waiting perpetually for the receipt of question papers from the printer till it became so late and not raising a serious alarm in writing a day advance cannot be appreciated." On CoE's role, the report stated: "The lack of active monitoring and timely sharing of information by Sodhi Ram with VC and DUI for appropriate timely intervention cannot be ignored" and calls for in-depth regular inquiry and appropriate action if deemed necessary. The CoE, who was aware of the delay on May 19, informed the VC on the morning of May 20. The inquiry reported: "There had been a complete lack of responsible monitoring of the task of receipt of printed question papers from the confidential printer. The averment that the printer has dispatched the material in good time and there was an accident on the way due to bad weather/ rain and due to which even the communication was lost, does not carry conviction in this age of quick and instant connectivity." The report has also ruled out the probability of *malafide* intention or conspiracy to defame the university by any individual, as "these aspects cannot be examined in such a short notice."

Varsity never had system of written accountability in the process of question paper printing and procurement. It follows a "faith-based" examination system. The documents sought by the inquiry officer which were never maintained include:

- File notings from CoE's office assuring availability of manuscripts of CET question papers and their timely supply. "It was stated that there was no such practice and this used to be done as per the practice of traditional faith implicit in the practice in relevant branches."
- Record showing the date of dispatch of manuscripts to the printer. "No record was produced."
- Receipt/acknowledgement of the manuscript by the printer. "No correspondence related to this was provided."
- Relevant provision of timely printing and supply of question papers. "No such written document was stated by the CoE to be in existence."

Panjab University seems to function on the basis of trust and verbal instructions when it comes to confidential work like the printing of question papers. As per the inquiry report by Prof. K.K. Bajaj into the cancellation of PU CET, 2006 examination circulated to the syndicate members, PU had no documented agreement with the printer who failed to deliver the CET question papers in time.

Following is the printer's version as thrashed by the inquiry report:

> "I dispatched 118 sealed boxes of printed papers vide truck no. HR 45/5557 on May 16 at 11.45 pm . . . . On May 17 informed S.K. Sharma (ARC) that papers will reach Chandigarh by May 19 morning... at 10 am on May 19, I receive call from Sharma that material has not reached. My transporter told me that the truck could not be located. I received a call from Sharma at 3 pm that my courier told him that the truck will reach between 11-12 midnight. Immediately CoE also called and I explained the position.

May 20, 5.30 am . . . call from Sharma that the material has not yet reached. I sent another man by road to search for the truck and also stated contacting the transporter on phone . . . by 9 am, the truck could not be located. I informed the police that our truck was missing . . .
9.30 am, I was informed by transporter that perhaps there was an accident or there was some breakdown in the truck and same was informed to CoE.
May 21: I received the call from the transporter that... truck after mishap was struck up due to engine seizure and has managed to come to Merrut Bypass and was again struck there. After reaching there at 4 pm, another truck was sent to Chandigarh and the material was delivered at 9 pm."

CONCLUDING REMARKS

From the study of the above mentioned cases some of the common and special features of all the universities of the sample may be mentioned as follows:

(i) Entrance Test Paper-Leak Mafia has sets its tentacles in the universities;
(ii) Fake certificates, degrees and other related frauds have spread in the universities;
(iii) Lack of well defined procedures and contingency plans, and over dependence on 'faith-based' routine system has led to maladies like leakages, preparation of wrong answer-keys, damaging delays, etc.;
(iv) Political interference is bashlessly visible in the universities especially in HPU followed by KU;
(v) Politics has become bane of the university system. In HPU, politics has degenerated to cancerous proportions where most of the teachers, students, non-teaching staff behave not as colleagues and fellow-students but as members of warring groups;
(vi) Sporadic violence and quarrels are unnecessarily spoiling the image of GNDU which otherwise is a University with excellence in the fields of sports and academics; and

(vii) Difference between the rules and practice is quite visible.

NOTES AND REFERENCES

1. *The Tribune,* July 23, 2005, p. 1.
2. *The Tribune,* August 25, 2005, pp. 1 and 15.
3. *The Tribune,* September 15, 2005, p. 1.
4. *The Tribune,* January 14, 2005, p. 4.
5. *The Tribune,* February 1, 2005, p. 15.
6. *Hindustan Times,* May 12, 2003, p. 2.
7. *The Tribune,* August 15, 2003. p. 7.
8. *The Tribune,* September 3, 2003, p. 1.
9. *The Tribune,* September 16, 2003, p. 2.
10. *The Tribune,* September 9, 2003, p. 7.
11. *Ibid.,* p. 7.
12. *Hindustan Times,* September 22, 2003, p. 4.
13. *Ibid.,* p. 4.
14. *The Tribune,* November 5, 2003, p. 1.
15. *The Tribune,* November 13, 2003, p. 1.
16. *The Tribune,* November 24, 2003, p. 7.
17. *The Tribune,* November 18, 2004, p. 12.
18. *The Tribune,* November 23, 2004, p. 15.
19. *The Tribune,* February 19, 2005, p. 17.
20. *Amar Ujala,* March 3, 2005, p. 7.
21. *Amar Ujala,* March 7, 2005, p. 6.
22. *The Tribune,* March 16, 2005, p. 8.
23. *The Tribune,* May 17, 2005, p. 9.
24. *The Tribune,* June 3, 2004, p. 13.
25. *The Tribune,* June 9 2006, p. 15.
26. *The Tribune,* June 10, 2006, p. 9.
27. *Amar Ujala,* June 10, 2006, p. 5.
28. *Amar Ujala,* June 11, 2006, p. 5.
29. *Amar Ujala,* June 14, 2006, p. 5.
30. *The Tribune,* June 17, 2006, p. 19.
31. *The Tribune,* July 15, 2006, p. 9.
32. *The Tribune,* July 27, 2006, p. 9.
33. *The Tribune,* July 16, 2006, p. 8.
34. *The Tribune,* August 11, 2006, p. 9.
35. *The Tribune,* August 16, 2006, p. 9.
36. *The Tribune,* July 28, 2006, p. 12.
37. *The Tribune,* November 29, 2003, p. 11.
38. *The Tribune,* March 28, 2005, p. 9.
39. Dharmendra Joshi, *The Tribune,* December 26, 2005.
40. *The Tribune,* July 1, 2005, p. 7.
41. *The Tribune,* September 22, 2004, p. 7.
42. *The Tribune,* September 17, 2003, p. 3.
43. *The Tribune,* November 26, 2004, p. 3.
44. *Ibid.,* p. 3.

CHAPTER

6

Comparative Study

As pointed out in the beginning of the fourth chapter, answers to the most of the questionnaires have not been found statistically significant. That clearly showed that the administrative situation and reactions of the respondents were almost similar in the universities of the sample. However, some of the answers were statistically significant. These too have been discussed to find out the real position and the reasons for their differences. On the basis of the picture emerged after the data collected through primary sources like observation, interviews, and responses to the various questionnaires, and secondary sources like profiles of the universities, case studies, Annual Budget Reports, Annual Administrative Reports, information collected through the websites of the universities and news paper reports, a comparative position of the universities of the sample may be presented as follows:

I. INFRASTRUCTURE

Panjab University, fourth university after the universities of Calcutta, Bombay and Madras, set-up in 1882, is in fact the mother of all the universities of the North-Western region of undivided India. As for other universities, Kurukshetra University was set-up in 1956, both Guru Nanak Dev University and Jammu University were set-up in 1969, and latest to be set-up was Himachal Pradesh University in 1970. All the universities in the sample, except HPU have got well marked, walled and beautiful campus(es). HPU campus is sprawled over an area of 200 acres of lush green spurs and valleys surrounded by tall deodars, pines, rhododendrons and oaks overlooking snow-peaked majestic mountain ranges. Many private shops catering to the needs of the university students, teachers, staff and the general public are located in the campus. Campuses of the Universities have the facilities like lecture halls, auditoriums, canteens, libraries, banks, post offices, health centres, separate hostels for boys and girls, clubs, quarters for officers, teachers, non-teaching staff, etc. Beautiful and well laid campus of the Panjab University is "showing its age", buildings, roads, furniture, etc. require better upkeep and improvement. Same is the condition of the campus of Kurukshetra University. However, many of the hostels of KU are newly constructed and are well equipped with all the facilities. Campuses of GNDU and JU have also many newly constructed and well designed buildings with all the reasonably good facilities. Libraries of the GNDU and PU are fully computerized. Efforts are on in the libraries of HPU, KU and JU to make them fully computerized. Teachers in GNDU and PU have been provided with internet facilities in their rooms.

As for HPU, it has the worst infrastructure. Buildings with broken window-panes and dirty walls urgently require better upkeep. Toilets throughout the campus are the worst amongst all the Universities of the sample and are certainly even worse than proverbial municipal toilets. Many of the hostels in the campus are in the dilapidated buildings having dark and dingy rooms, dirty bathrooms and toilets with erratic water supply, very poor water heating arrangements—a necessity throughout the year, and lacking so many facilities. Students have often been complaining and agitating against the poor facilities in the hostels. Many of the hostlers have been falling sick due to diarrhea. The researcher was taken aback when he was told by the hostlers that no lunch is served to the hostlers in any of the hostels of the University!—Hungry man is always an angry man. These hostels in fact are the epicentres of all the troubles of this beleaguered university. Some of the students continue to occupy the hostel rooms for a decade or so even after they cease to be students of the University. Authorities seem to be helpless in getting these rooms vacated from these "students". Their efforts so far have not brought desired results. Sticks, iron-rods and even swords, used as weapons among the different warring students' associations, are hidden in these rooms. These weapons have been discovered many a time during police-raids on the hostels.

2. GENERAL SATISFACTION IN THE UNIVERSITIES

General satisfaction of the teachers, students and non-teaching staff of the universities in the sample collected through the questionnaires may be presented as follows:

TABLE 6.1
Finding Teaching Interesting

Name of University	*Teachers*		*Students*		*Non-Teaching*	
	Teaching Interesting	*Teaching Respectable*	*Classroom-Teaching Interesting*	*Syllabus Useful*	*Job Interesting*	*Job Respectable*
GNDU, Amritsar	87.00	87.00	69.90	67.60	84.40	84.40
HPU, Shimla	96.40	100.00	59.00	62.50	78.40	78.40
JU, Jammu	100.00	100.00	84.60	82.10	66.70	66.70
KU, Kurukshetra	83.30	93. 30	73.50	70.40	60.20	60.20
PU, Chandigarh	100.00	100.00	69.90	77.40	80.00	80.00
Total	90.40	94.70	69.80	70.50	75.50	75.50

Above table computed on the basis of the data in the fourth chapter, Working of the Universities, clearly shows a very high level of satisfaction of the university personnel. As high as 90.40% of the teachers in the sample feel teaching interesting and 94.70% of the teachers consider teaching profession respectable. A large majority of students (69.80%) finds classroom teaching interesting and 70.50% of the students consider the syllabus useful. As for non-teaching employees, 75.50% of them find their job interesting as well as respectable.

From the above level of satisfaction it can safely be assumed that, the universities included in the study have played a great role in the development of the north-western region of India. Panjab University has no doubt contributed a lot in the socio-economic and intellectual development of the region. Other State universities like GNDU, HPU, JU, and KU have been instrumental in the socio-economic development of their respective States as well as that of the neighbouring States also. India has undoubtedly emerged as a great force to reckon with in many fields in the world and for this achievement the role of the universities of the country and also of the north-western universities cannot be denied. After all these were the universities which produced doctors who controlled epidemics, cured many deadly diseases and raised the average age to 62 years, engineers who built bridges, constructed roads, scientists aiming at the moon, IT professions who made India an IT superpower, Prime-Ministers who achieved nine percent GDP growth, and gave world-class leaders in all the walks of life.

3. QUALITY OF EDUCATION

Quality of education being imparted in different universities of the sample has been discussed on the basis of teaching methodology, aids used by the teachers, students-teachers interaction with respect to the academic problems, students-teachers views with respect to minimum attendances of classes by the students, cheating in the examinations, views of the students and teachers with respect to marking of examination answer-books by outside examiners, availability of reading material in their libraries, and difficulties of the teachers in pursuing their academic activities, and perception of students, teachers and officers whether the quality of education imparted in their universities is of international standards and the efforts made for the improvement.

TABLE 6.2
Teaching Methodology (1)

Name of University	Monthly Tests		Assignments		Tutorials	
	Teachers	Students	Teachers	Students	Teachers	Students
GNDU, Amritsar	43.50	30.40	87.00	71.30	30.40	8.10
HPU, Shimla	28.60	35.70	75.00	41.00	35.70	13.20
JU, Jammu	20.00	40.00	40.60	51.30	40.00	15.40
KU, Kurukshetra	50.00	73.30	73.30	50.00	73.30	36.70
PU, Chandigarh	75.00	37.50	100.00	72.00	37.50	46.20
Total	42.60	46.80	77.70	56.80	46.80	22.00

TABLE 6.3
Teaching Methodology (2)

Name of University	Lecture Method		Discussion		Seminar	
	Teachers	Students	Teachers	Students	Teachers	Students
GNDU, Amritsar	95.70	91.20	91.30	55.10	78.30	72.80
HPU, Shimla	96.40	90.30	89.30	59.00	78.60	30.60
JU, Jammu	100.00	92.30	100.00	48.70	80.00	43.60
KU, Kurukshetra	80.00	87.80	83.30	49.00	63.3.	61.20
PU, Chandigarh	87.50	96.80	100.00	75.30	100.00	71.00
Total	90.40	91.40	89.40	57.60	75.50	55.20

A study of above tables (Tables 6.2 to 6.4) shows that teachers mostly depend upon lecture method (Teachers point out 90.40% and the students point out 91.40%). They also use other methods like discussion, seminar, project, and tutorial. They also give assignments and take monthly tests. Some of the teachers also use OHP (Teachers point out 29.80% and the students point out 25.70%) and video-films (Teachers point out 20.20% and the students point out 14.20%) as aids for teaching.

TABLE 6.4

Teaching Methodology (3)

Name of University	*Project Method*		*Over-Head Projector*		*Video-Films*	
	Teachers	*Students*	*Teachers*	*Students*	*Teachers*	*Students*
GNDU, Amritsar	60.90	34.60	34.80	27.90	8.70	10.30
HPU, Shimla	64.30	22.20	25.00	16.70	21.40	9.70
JU, Jammu	20.00	28.20	—	17.90	40.00	23.10
KU, Kurukshetra	33.30	22.40	33.30	22.40	26.70	13.30
PU, Chandigarh	50.00	61.30	37.50	46.20	12.50	20.40
Total	50.00	32.80	29.80	25.70	20.20	14.20

Overall picture may not be quite bright and rosy but it is not quite dark as well.

TABLE 6.5

Students Discussing their Academic Problems with the Teachers

Name of University	*Teachers*	*Students*
GNDU, Amritsar	91.30	39.00
HPU, Shimla	92.90	61.10
JU, Jammu	100.00	56.40
KU, Kurukshetra	80.00	48.00
PU, Chandigarh	100.00	62.40
Total	89.40	52.80

From the study of the above Table it is clear that 89.40% teachers say that students discuss their academic problems with them, whereas only 52.80% students agree that they discuss their academic problems with their teachers. This wide gap between the opinions of the teachers and students clearly points out the lack of academic interaction between the teachers and their students.

TABLE 6.6
Minimum Attendance of Classes by the Students

Name of University	*Teachers*	*Students*
GNDU, Amritsar	82.60	64.70
HPU, Shimla	92.90	63.20
JU, Jammu	80.00	53.80
KU, Kurukshetra	70.00	73.50
PU, Chandigarh	100.00	73.10
Total	83.00	65.80

From the study of the above Table it is clear that 83.00% teachers are in favour of making minimum attendance of classes by the students compulsory, whereas only 65.80% students are in favour of making minimum attendance of classes by the students compulsory. This wide gap between the opinions of the teachers and students clearly points out that many of the students are not in favour of attending the classes. This deserves mention here that this question was asked in view of the fact that all the Universities have made some percentage of classes compulsory for the students. Many of the students do not attend the prescribed percentage of classes, and when their examination forms are not forwarded to the Examination Branch they resent and agitate. It has been mentioned in one of the case studies that students of GNDU fudged the attendance register to fulfil the lecture condition. Similarly, it has been observed that students in HPU are in the habit of agitating and pressurizing the Chairpersons of their departments by adopting highly objectionable methods to forward their Examination Forms to the Examination Branch. This has been a practice despite the orders of the Shimla High Court. Contempt of the Court is not understood here!

From the study of the Table 6.7 it is clear that 71.30% teachers are in favour of marking of answer-books by the outside examiners, whereas 59.60% students are in favour of marking of answer-books by the outside examiners. This gap clearly shows that students have more faith in their teachers than the teachers have faith in themselves or in their colleagues.

TABLE 6.7
Preferring of Marking of Answer-books by Outside Examiners

Name of University	*Teachers*	*Students*
GNDU, Amritsar	87.00	48.50
HPU, Shimla	64.30	74.30
JU, Jammu	80.00	48.70
KU, Kurukshetra	63.30	61.20
PU, Chandigarh	75.00	60.20
Total	71.30	59.60

Only exception is HPU where the percentage of students in favour of marking of answer-books by outside examiners is more than that of the teachers. It is 74.30% in case of students and 64.30% in case of teachers. Whatever may be the reasons, such a high percentage of teachers (71.30%) and students (59.60%) favouring marking of answer-books my outside examiners clearly underlines the atmosphere of distrust in the fairness and impartiality of the teachers. It is also against the ideal, those who teach must evaluate.

TABLE 6.8
Cheating Cases

Name of University	*Teachers*	*Students*
GNDU, Amritsar	43.50	6.60
HPU, Shimla	50.00	8.30
JU, Jammu	80.00	5.10
KU, Kurukshetra	63.30	12.20
PU, Chandigarh	75.00	12.90
Total	56.40	8.90

From the above Table we find that majority of teachers (56.40%) have noticed cheating in the examinations by the students, whereas only 8.90% students have admitted of being indulged in cheating. Cheating as well as lying by the students is a clear message if we read between the percentages of both the teachers and the students in the above Table. This perhaps is the result of not only of our examination system but that of our education system also.

TABLE 6.9
Reading Material of their Interest in the Library

Name of University	*Teachers*	*Students*
GNDU, Amritsar	69.60	55.90
HPU, Shimla	39.30	49.30
JU, Jammu	80.00	48.70
KU, Kurukshetra	50.00	38.80
PU, Chandigarh	87.50	73.10
Total	56.40	53.00

From the above Table it is clear that only 56.40% teachers and 53% students in the total sample get reading material of their interest from their respective University libraries. From the teachers' point of view HPU is the worst with 39.30% and from the student's point of view KU is the worst with 38-80%. PU is the best both from teachers' (87.50%) and from students' (73.10) point of view.

TABLE 6.10
Teachers Facing Difficulties in Pursuing Academic Activities

Name of University	*Research Grant Release*	*Settling Seminar Accounts*
GNDU, Amritsar	34.80	17.40
HPU, Shimla	60.70	67.90
JU, Jammu	40.00	40.00
KU, Kurukshetra	53.30	20.00
PU, Chandigarh	62.50	50.00
Total	51.10	37.20

From the above Table it is clear that 51.10% Teachers in the total sample find it difficult to get the research grant released. PU with 62.50% is the worst in this respect, second worst is HPU with 60.70, whereas GNDU is the best with 34.80. Similarly, 37.20% teachers in the total sample find it difficult to settle accounts of National/International Seminars conducted by them. HPU with 67.90% is the worst in this respect and second worst is PU with 50%, whereas GNDU is the best with only 17.40%. Difficulties faced by the teachers in pursuing their academic activities certainly hamper their academic growth.

TABLE 6.11

Quality of Education Comparable to that of Advanced Countries

Name of University	*Teachers*	*Students*	*Officers*
GNDU, Amritsar	69.60	41.20	70.00
HPU, Shimla	17.90	41.00	40.00
JU, Jammu	60.00	35.90	—
KU, Kurukshetra	66.70	38.80	57.10
PU, Chandigarh	62.50	45.20	75.00
Total	52.10	40.60	52.90

Above Table clearly shows that 52.10% teachers, 40.60% students and 52.90% officers in the total sample find the quality

TABLE 6.12

Efforts made to Improve the Quality of Education to make it Comparable to that of Advanced Countries

Name of University	*Teachers*	*Officers*
GNDU, Amritsar	82.60	90.00
HPU, Shimla	57.10	60.00
JU, Jammu	100.00	100.00
KU, Kurukshetra	70.00	71.40
PU, Chandigarh	100.00	75.00
Total	73.40	76.50

of education imparted in their respective Universities comparable to that of advanced countries. Overall position of PU and GNDU is better in this respect.

Table 6.12 clearly shows that 73.40% teachers and 76.50% officers in the total sample say that they have made efforts to improve the quality of education in their respective Universities to make that comparable to the standards of advanced countries. Overall position of HPU is the worst in this respect.

4. OBJECTIVES OF UNIVERSITY EDUCATION

Under this heading questions like should university education be limited to a few, should it be only for job, or only for self-development, or for both, and election to SCA have been included.

TABLE 6.13
Preferring University Education for a Few Only

Name of University	*Teachers*	*Students*	*Non-Teaching*
GNDU, Amritsar	21.70	24.30	25.00
HPU, Shimla	25.00	24.30	16.70
JU, Jammu	60.00	23.10	33.30
KU, Kurukshetra	23.30	33.70	17.20
PU, Chandigarh	25.00	24.70	33.30
Total	25.50	25.90	21.00

Table 6.13 points out that only a small percentage of teachers (25.50%), students (25.90%) and non-teaching staff (21.00%) prefer university education to be limited to a few persons only, whereas a greater percentage is in favour providing university education to all.

Table 6.14 points out that only a small percentage of teachers (14.90%), students (16%) and non-teaching staff (23.10%) prefer university education for job only.

Table 6.15 points out that only a small percentage of teachers (14.90%), students (28.20%) and non-teaching staff (25.10%) prefer university education for self-development only.

TABLE 6.14
Preferring University Education for Job Only

Name of University	*Teachers*	*Students*	*Non-Teaching*
GNDU, Amritsar	8.70	21.30	28.90
HPU, Shimla	14.30	10.40	12.70
JU, Jammu	—	15.40	33.30
KU, Kurukshetra	26.70	17.30	24.70
PU, Chandigarh	—	16.10	26.70
Total	14.90	16.00	23.10

TABLE 6.15
Preferring University Education for Self-Development Only

Name of University	*Teachers*	*Students*	*Non-Teaching*
GNDU, Amritsar	8.70	28.70	22.70
HPU, Shimla	14.30	29.20	27.50
JU, Jammu		35.90	33.30
KU, Kurukshetra	26.70	23.50	22.60
PU, Chandigarh		24.70	40.00
Total	14.90	28.20	25.10

TABLE 6.16
Preferring University Education both for Job and Self-Development

Name of University	*Teachers*	*Students*	*Non-Teaching*
GNDU, Amritsar	91.30	89.70	78.10
HPU, Shimla	78.60	88.20	92.20
JU, Jammu	80.00	79.50	66.70
KU, Kurukshetra	80.00	81.60	80.60
PU, Chandigarh	87.50	86.00	80.00
Total	83.00	85.80	82.70

Table 6.16 clearly shows out that a large majority of teachers (83.00%), students (85.80%) and non-teaching staff (82.70%) prefer university education both for job as well as for self-development.

TABLE 6.17
Election to SCA

Name of University	*Teachers*	*Students*
GNDU, Amritsar	60.90	61.80
HPU, Shimla	60.70	75.70
JU, Jammu	80.00	71.80
KU, Kurukshetra	40.00	41.80
PU, Chandigarh	100.00	76.30
Total	58.50	65.80

From the above Table we find that 58.50% of the teachers and 65.80% of the students in the total sample are in favour of election to Students' Central Association. Thus, the percentage of students in favour of election to SCA is slightly higher. In KU only 40% of teachers and 41.80% of students are in favour of election to SCA. This small percentage may perhaps be due to the bad consequences of the students' elections.

5. ADMINISTRATIVE EFFICIENCY

Under the heading Administrative Efficiency, following topics have been included: VCs and their tenures has been included in view of close relationship between the administrative efficiency of the VCs and their tenure in the universities. Other topics are, NTS and administration, NTS finding difficulties in dealing with different persons in the universities, different persons in the universities finding difficulties in getting administrative work done, percentage of the persons finding university administration sympathetic and quick in redressing their grievances, difficulties experienced by the people in getting the clearance of their bills from LAD, and effectiveness of the Internal Audit of the universities in the sample.

TABLE 6.18
VCs and their Tenure

Name of University	*Year of Estt.*	*Years up to 2006*	*No. of VCs*	*Average years*
GNDU, Amritsar	1969	38	7	5.43
HPU, Shimla	1971	36	20	1.80
JU, Jammu	1969	38	9	4.31
KU, Kurukshetra	1956	51	25	2.00
PU, Chandigarh	1948⊕	58	10	5.80

⊕ Calculated from the year it was shifted to different cities of India from Lahore after Partition.

From the above Table it is clear that Panjab University had only ten VCs during its 58 years of existence, average years of tenure of a VC thus comes to 5.80 years, whereas HPU had 20 VCs during its 36 years of existence, average years of tenure of a VC thus comes to 1.80 years. Next to HPU comes the KU, where 25 VCs worked during its 51 years of existence, average years of tenure of a VC thus comes to 2.00 years. In HPU, only four VCs completed their full term, one VC died of heart attack because of the constant pressure of students' agitations, three VCs resigned again due to the pressure of students' agitations, one resigned due to the alleged misuse of funds. Not only VCs but Registrars were also changed equally frequently. Changing of PVCs, Deans, Hostel Chief Wardens, Wardens, and even the HODs with the change of Government has also become an established practice for more than a decade. Resigning and threatening to resign by above high officials like Deans, Hostel Chief Warden and Wardens in wake of students' agitations or some other pressures are also day-to-day stories. Same is the case with KU. In KU also, VCs and other high officers have to resign with the change of the Government. In Haryana, all the VCs except one were removed with the change of the last Government.

TABLE 6.19

Non-Teaching Staff and Administration

Name of University	*Keeping Weekly/ Monthly Diaries*	*Planning for Official Work*	*Received Training for Doing Official work*
GNDU, Amritsar	49.20	60.20	34.40
HPU, Shimla	57.80	73.50	46.10
JU, Jammu	—	33.30	—
KU, Kurukshetra	39.80	69.90	39.80
PU, Chandigarh	46.70	73.30	33.30
Total	47.80	66.60	38.30

From the above Table it is clear that only 47.80% of the employees in the total sample say that they keep weekly/ monthly diaries of their official work. 66.60% of the employees say that they make planning for doing their official work. Only 38.30% of the employees say that they have received training for doing their official work. Overall position in JU is the worst.

TABLE 6.20

Non-Teaching Staff Facing Difficulties in Dealing

Name of University	*Seniors*	*Colleagues*	*Subordinates*	*Teachers*	*Students*
GNDU, Amritsar	34.40	16.40	19.50	19.50	17.20
HPU, Shimla	46.10	13.70	14.70	14.70	25.50
JU, Jammu	—	33.30	33.30	66.70	—
KU, Kurukshetra	39.80	11.80	6.50	12.90	11.80
PU, Chandigarh	33.30	6.70	20.00	13.30	6.70
Total	38.30	14.40	15.00	17.30	17.30

From the above Table we observe the employees (38.30%) find greater difficulties in dealing with their seniors. Next in the difficulty level are teachers and students both with 17.30% each. In HPU, 46.10% of the employees find difficulties in dealing with their seniors and 25.50% of the employees find difficulties in dealing students. In JU, 66.70% of the employees find difficulties in dealing with the teachers. Above high percentage of employees pointing out their difficulties in dealing with the groups is an indication of the conflict in the groups. This conflict has also been pointed out by P.R. Dubhashi in what he called "Discordance Amongst Participants": It is often said that the students do not study, the teachers do not teach and the *karmacharis* do not work even though all of them are dependent on the university and are morally bound to promote the cause of the university. However, they do not see their role in this manner and go about setting their own goals which are contrary to the goals of the university. This is the tragedy of many universities and also other organizations in our country.[1]

TABLE 6.21
Respondents Finding Difficulties in Getting Administrative Work Done

Name of University	*Teachers*	*Officers*	*Students*	*Employees*
GNDU, Amritsar	43.50	20.00	57.40	31.30
HPU, Shimla	75.00	70.00	66.00	35.30
JU, Jammu	40.00	Nil	66.70	33.30
KU, Kurukshetra	56.70	28.60	66.30	25.80
PU, Chandigarh	62.50	25.00	78.50	20.00
Total	58.50	35.30	66.10	30.50

Above Table points out that 58.50% of teachers, 35.30% of officers, 66.10% of students, and 30.50% of the employees in the total sample find difficulties in getting their administrative work done. Employees with 30.50% are the best placed. Percentage of teachers and students finding difficulties is very high. Position in HPU is the worst where 75% teachers, 70% officers, 66% students and 35.30% employees find difficulties in getting their administrative work done. However, the position in PU is the worst in case of students where the highest percentage of the students (78.50%) in the total sample finds difficulties in getting their administrative work done.

Table 6.22
Respondents Finding Administration Sympathetic

Name of University	*Teachers*	*Officers*	*Students*	*Employees*
GNDU, Amritsar	65.20	90.00	52.90	60.20
HPU, Shimla	25.00	40.00	36.10	37.30
JU, Jammu	80.00	100.00	56.40	66.70
KU, Kurukshetra	56.70	71.40	43.90	39.80
PU, Chandigarh	75.00	75.00	41.90	66.70
Total	52.10	70.60	45.50	48.40

Table 6.22 points out that 52.10% of teachers, 70.60% of officers, 45.50% of students, and 48.40% of the employees in the total sample find the administration of their respective universities sympathetic to them. Position in JU is the best where 80% teachers, 100% officers, 56.40% students and 66.70% employees find their university administration sympathetic to them. Position in HPU is the worst where only 25% teachers, 40% officers, 36.10% students and 37.30% employees find university administration sympathetic to them. Strangely enough amongst the officers who constitute part of administration themselves, only 40% find it sympathetic to them. May be this explains the spate of resignations by officers which was noticed during 2005-06.

Table 6.23
Respondents Finding Administration Quick in Redressing their Grievances

Name of University	*Teachers*	*Officers*	*Students*	*Employees*
GNDU, Amritsar	56.50	80.00	38.20	48.40
HPU, Shimla	28.60	20.00	27.80	30.40
JU, Jammu	20.00	100.00	28.20	66.70
KU, Kurukshetra	36.70	71.40	44.90	47.30
PU, Chandigarh	37.50	50.00	35.50	66.70
Total	38.30	58.80	34.80	44.10

Table 6.23 points out that only 38.30% of teachers, 58.80% of officers, 34.80% of students, and 44.10% of the employees in the total sample find the administration of their respective universities quick in redressing their grievances. Here again position in HPU is the worst where only 28.60% teachers, 20% officers, 27.80% students and 30.40% employees find university administration quick in redressing their grievances. Strangely enough amongst the officers who constitute part of administration themselves, the lowest percentage, i.e., only 20% find university administration quick in redressing their grievances. It means the officers are feeling the pinch much more than what the teachers, students and employees are feeling. Some drastic steps are needed to ameliorate this condition. In JU, it has also been observed that the lowest percentage of teachers, i.e., 20% only in the total sample find university administration quick in redressing their grievances. This may be because of the conflict between employees and the teachers noticed earlier. The employees are also a part of university administration.

TABLE 6.24
Difficulties in Getting the Clearance of Bills from LAD*

Name of University	*Teachers*	*Officers*	*Employees*
GNDU, Amritsar	60.90	10.00	37.50
HPU, Shimla	78.60	80.00	63.70
JU, Jammu	60.00	Nil	33.30
KU, Kurukshetra	43.30	28.60	30.10
PU, Chandigarh	25.00	25.00	6.70
Total	57.40	35.30	41.80

* LAD stands for Local Audit Department.

Table 6.24 points out that 57.40% of teachers, 35.30% of officers and 41.80% of the employees in the total sample find difficulties in getting the clearance of their bills from LAD. Here again position in HPU is the worst where as many as 78.60% teachers, 80% officers and 63.70% employees find difficulties in getting the clearance of their bills from LAD. It may be mentioned here that in the chapter relating to case studies we have discussed the conflict between audit officials and the university personnel in detail. This conflict is reflected in the answers given by teachers, officers and employees here also. Table 6.24 also points out that the overall situation of the teachers is the worst with 57.40% facing difficulties in the clearance of their bills from the LAD.

TABLE 6.25
Internal Audit System is Effective

Name of University	*Teachers*	*Officers*	*Employees*
GNDU, Amritsar	43.50	70.00	33.60
HPU, Shimla	32.10	40.00	45.10
JU, Jammu	40.00	Nil	66.70
KU, Kurukshetra	36.70	42.90	37.60
PU, Chandigarh	62.50	50.00	53.30
Total	39.40	47.10	39.80

From the Table 6.25 it is clear that only 39.40% of teachers, 47.10% of officers and 39.80% of the employees in the total sample find Internal Audit System effective. Here again position in HPU is the worst where only 32.10% teachers, 40% officers and 45.10% employees find Internal Audit effective. It may be mentioned here that the HPU employees got Internal Audit after a long battle against the LAD, and still ironically only a small percentage of university personnel are finding it effective. It means the persons posted in the Internal Audit Section of the HPU are not trained and also there are some basic flaws with the audit system of the university itself. Moreover, persisting conflict due to lack of clarity at many points in the instructions issued on the division of work between the Internal Audit Section and the LAD also hampers the smooth functioning of the Internal Audit Section.

6. AUTONOMY

TABLE 6.26
Universities Enjoying Autonomy in Appointments

Name of University	*Teachers*	*Employees*
GNDU, Amritsar	56.50	63.30
HPU, Shimla	21.40	38.20
JU, Jammu	60.00	66.70
KU, Kurukshetra	46.70	37.60
PU, Chandigarh	75.00	66.70
Total	44.70	49.30

Table 6.26 points out that only 44.70% of teachers and 49.30% of employees say that their universities enjoy autonomy in the appointments. Overall position of PU is the best with the 75% of teachers and 66.70% of employees mentioning that their university enjoys autonomy in the appointments. Overall position of HPU is the worst with only 21.40% of teachers and 38.20% of employees saying that their university enjoys autonomy in the appointments. However, in KU a slightly lower percent of employees, i.e., 37.60% of employees say that their university enjoys autonomy in the appointments.

TABLE 6.27
Universities Enjoying Autonomy in Promotions

Name of University	*Teachers*	*Employees*
GNDU, Amritsar	65.20	57.00
HPU, Shimla	35.70	54.90
JU, Jammu	80.00	66.70
KU, Kurukshetra	43.30	45.29
PU, Chandigarh	75.00	80.00
Total	51.00	54.50

Table 6.27 points out that only 510% of teachers and 54.50% of employees say that their universities enjoy autonomy in the promotions. Overall position in JU and PU is the best and worst in HPU and KU.

TABLE 6.28
Universities Enjoying Autonomy in Appointing Officers

Name of University	*Teachers*	*Employees*
GNDU, Amritsar	56.50	53.90
HPU, Shimla	42.90	51.00
JU, Jammu	80.00	33.30
KU, Kurukshetra	50.00	57.00
PU, Chandigarh	75.00	93.30
Total	53.20	55.00

Table 6.28 points out that 53.20% of teachers and 55% of employees say that their universities enjoy autonomy in appointing officers in their universities. Overall position of PU is the best with the 75% of teachers and 93.30% of employees mentioning that their university enjoys autonomy in appointing officers in their universities. Overall position of HPU is not good since the lowest percent (42.90%) of teachers in the total sample and only 51% of employees say that their university enjoys autonomy in appointing the officers. However, in JU strangely enough the highest percent (80%) of teachers and lowest percent (33.30%) of employees in the total sample point out that their university enjoys autonomy in the appointments of officers. This difference of opinion may be attributed to the conflict between the teachers and the employees noticed earlier also.

Table 6.29 points out that only 54.30% of teachers and 61.40% of employees have the faith that they will get promotion on merit/whenever it is due to them. Overall position of JU and PU is the best. In KU only 40% and in HPU 53.60% have the faith that they will get promotion on merit/whenever it is due to them.

It may be pointed out that as sequel to the case of "Question Papers Printing Scam" in HPU the State Legislative

TABLE 6.29

Faith in Getting Promotion on Merit/Whenever Due

Name of University	*Teachers*	*Employees*
GNDU, Amritsar	60.90	57.80
HPU, Shimla	53.60	59.90
JU, Jammu	80.00	66.70
KU, Kurukshetra	40.00	64.50
PU, Chandigarh	75.00	80.00
Total	54.30	61.40

Assembly amended the Himachal Pradesh University Act, 1970 by including "Section 35-A Creation of posts, etc. No post, position and assignment created by the University shall have any effect unless approved by the State Government." Government of Himachal Pradesh went still further and its Department of Education issued a Notification No. EDN-A-Ga (10)-1/2004 dated Shimla 171002, 22.5.2005 framing rules regulating payment of grant-in-aid to HPU, Shimla. First condition under the above rules was "that the university shall function smoothly to the satisfaction of the Government". Imposing so many other stringent conditions indicating exacting control the Notification ended: "The University will furnish information indicating various categories of posts which are being charged out of grant-in-aid and it shall be mandatory for the Himachal Pradesh University to seek approval of the Government to fill up any of the sanctioned vacant posts." It was another serious blow to the university autonomy which was already working as a State Government Department even without the above amendment.

7. VIOLENCE

Violence in the present context includes sexual harassment, eve-teasing, ragging, using abusive language, group clashes, murder, and destruction of university property. Cases of sexual harassment can be presented as follows:

TABLE 6.30
Cases of Sexual Harassment Noticed by Teachers

Name of University	*Female Students by Male Students*	*Female Students by Male Teachers*	*Female Teachers by Male Teachers*
GNDU, Amritsar	21.70	34.80	34.80
HPU, Shimla	7.10	—	—
JU, Jammu	—	20.00	40.00
KU, Kurukshetra	6.70	10.00	6.70
PU, Chandigarh	—	25.00	25.00
Total	9.60	14.90	14.90

TABLE 6.31
Cases of Sexual Harassment Noticed by Students

Name of University	*Female Students by Male Students*	*Female Students by Male Teachers*
GNDU, Amritsar	11.00	6.60
HPU, Shimla	20.80	18.80
JU, Jammu	12.80	12.80
KU, Kurukshetra	34.70	27.60
PU, Chandigarh	22.60	23.70
Total	20.00	17.30

From a comparative study of the above two Tables it is clear that 9.60% teachers and 20% of students have noticed sexual harassment of female students by male students. In the eyes of teachers, position in GNDU is worst with 21.70% and best in JU and PU with 0%, whereas in the eyes of students it is worst in KU with 34.70% and the best in GNDU with 11%. Whatever may be the reasons for the difference in perception, harassment is there. Similarly, as for sexual harassment of female students by male teachers, in the eyes of teachers, position in GNDU is worst with 34.80% and best in HPU with 0%, whereas in the eyes of students it is worst in KU with 27.60% and the best in GNDU with 6.60%. Again we may say whatever may be the reasons for the difference in perception, harassment is there. As for sexual harassment of female teachers by male teachers, it is worst in JU with 40% and the best in HPU with 0%.

TABLE 6.32
Cases of Sexual Harassment Noticed by Non-Teaching Employees

Name of University	*Female Employees by Male Employees*
GNDU, Amritsar	22.70
HPU, Shimla	8.80
JU, Jammu	33.30
KU, Kurukshetra	21.50
PU, Chandigarh	13.30
Total	18.20

From the above Table it is clear that position of sexual harassment of female employees by male employees is worst in JU with 33.30% and the best in HPU with 8.80%.

Eve teasing as observed in KU has been discussed in detail in a case reported in the chapter on Case Studies in the present research study. News paper reports with respect to GNDU writing about frequent quarrels even among senior officers and faculty members alleging threats to life from colleagues, beating up of even Head of a Department, conviction of a coach in a case of sexual harassment, verbal abuses, charges and counter-charges, shoot out cases, SP's son allegedly forced a final year student to commit suicide, varsity don held for student's suicide, quarrel over alleged irregularities in research degree panel, publishing of a booklet entitled "Akhin Dithian, Kujh Khattian Kujh Mithian" (eyewitness account sweet and sour incidents) by Sukhwinder Singh Narula, etc. present a very poor picture of the university. In HPU, murders of two students' leaders by the rival political groups, usual violence during and after the SCA elections, breaking of window panes of VC office by students' unions, breaking of even the table glass of the VC, use of not only aggressive but at times also abusive language of unprintable variety, colloquially called non-vegetarian, in slogans and lectures by students, etc. are painful pointers to imminent educational fiasco going to engulf the other wise peaceful and fast developing state. In JU too, some stray cases of students' violence of a very small scale have been reported. In PU also, students have been observed resorting to strikes for getting their grievances the redressed, but surprisingly in a very peaceful manner.

8. CRIMINALISATION

Next to violence, criminalization too has entered some of the universities of the sample in a big way. As observed in the case studies, entrance test mafia has spread its tentacles in HPU. The police have discovered the connection of the HPCPMT paper leak with Punjab, Uttar Pradesh, Uttrakhand, Bihar, and New Delhi. Paper printing scam of the HPU in which the VC and the Deputy Registrar Secrecy are involved is still pending with the High Court. A superintendent of the Academic Branch of HPU was caught red handed by.the police while accepting a bribe of Rs. 2000 for increasing marks in a paper. In GNDU, shoot out cases and instigation to suicide have been reported. In KU, fake certificate cases and irregularities in examination wing have come to light. In PU, FIR has been lodged for fake degrees. These cases have certainly spoiled the academic atmosphere of the universities.

9. FINANCES

Universities of the sample draw their finances mainly from the grants from the respective State Governments. Only exception is the Panjab University, Chandigarh which gets grant from the Central Government as well as State Government of Punjab in the ratio of 60:40. In addition to these grants, these universities raise their own resources by way of fees, and special fees for self-financing courses from NRI's and other students studying on paid seats. These universities also get development grants from UGC for developing their infrastructure like library books, computer facility, buildings, etc. Various bodies like UGC, DST, CSIR, ICHR, ICAR, ICMR, ICSSR, and other agencies also give research grants for the various research projects known as SAP, FIST, etc. Funds from their own resources are quite insufficient and the universities have to depend almost entirely on the grants from the State Governments. With the rising costs of running the day-to-day activities, universities are not in a position to carry out their responsibilities. Demands by the universities for enhancing the grants or for starting some new useful courses as per the requirements of the competitive world are usually replied by State Governments by saying, "Raise your own resources". Any attempt to raising the resources by increasing fees or charges by the universities are promptly rebuffed by strong students' agitations supported by trade unions and interested political parties. This situation ultimately leads to commercialization of education by starting fully self-financing courses or by introducing a good number of paying seats in addition to those having normal rates of fees. This also erodes university autonomy by adjusting the tune and tone to the demands of those who are paying the piper, read pauper.

A comparative financial position of the universities of the sample is presented below:

I. GNDU, BUDGET ESTIMATES, 2006-07

	Actuals of 2004-05 Rs. in Lacs	*Estimates 2005-06 (Original) Rs. in Lacs*	*Estimates 2005-06 (Revised) Rs. in Lacs*	*Estimates 2006-07 Rs. in Lacs*
1. Opening Balance	(+)1705.31	(+) 765.14	(+) 2488.30	(+) 2297.65
2. Expenditure Committed	6035.80	7974.68	7115.81	8900.65
3. Total Requirement of Funds (2 minus 1)	4330.49	6209.54	4627.51	6608.00
4. Maintenance Grant from Punjab Government	1980.90	1781.88	1795.88	1781.88
5. Grant from D.C., Amritsar	1.00	—	—	—
6. Total Deficit (3 minus 4)	2348.59	4427.66	2831.63	4826.12
7. Revenue Receipts	4836.89	4394.69	5124.28	# 4836.91
8. Net Deficit/Surplus (6 minus 7)	(+) 2488.30	(-) 32.97	(+) 2292.65	(+) 10.79

Out of this an amount of Rs. 8.00 crores is not assured. It depends upon admission of Students against NRI/NRI Sponsored quota of seats.

From the study of the summary of the budget of GNDU for the last three financial years, it is clear that the financial position of the university is quite sound. The budget has been running in surplus for the last four financial years. Though the Punjab Government has been continuously reducing the maintenance grant, the university, however, has increased its revenue receipts from the self-financing courses. It may be added that as observed earlier, for starting self-financing courses, the university is well equipped with the required infrastructure.

2. HIMACHAL PRADESH UNIVERSITY

(Non-Plan Budget) Part I

	Abstract, 2004-05	
Grant-in-aid from H.P. State Government		15,1710,000
University Domestic Receipts		17,07,15,964
Total Receipt		32,24,85,964
Expenditure		33,48,05,659
Closing balance		1,23,19,695
	Abstract, 2005-06	
Grant-in-aid from H.P. State Government		10,17,70,000
University Domestic Receipts		19,08,60,000
Total Receipt		29,26,30,000
Expenditure		30,06,30,000
Closing balance	(-)	80,00,000
	Abstract 2006-07	
Grant-in-aid from H.P. State Government		10,17,70,000
University Domestic Receipts		20,72,60,000
Total Receipt		30,90,30,000
Expenditure		33,82,30,000
Closing Balance	(-)	2,92,00,000
	Abstract 2006-07 for Plan Budget Part-II	
Grant-in-aid from H.P. State Government		10,82,30,000
Grant-in-aid from H.P. State for Construction work		3,53,50,000
Grant-in-aid from U.G.C.		7,57,40,000
Grant in aid from Central Assistance		10,00,000

Total Receipt		22,03,20,000
Expenditure		25,40,90,000
Closing Balance	(-)	3,37,70,000
	Expected Deficit for 2006-07	
Plan		3,37,70,000
Non-plan		2,92,00,000
Total		6,29,70,000

Study of the HPU Part-I Non-Plan Budget for the last three financial years clearly reveals the financial position of the university is not sound. It has been in considerable deficit for the last three years. To add to the troubles, Himachal Pradesh Government has reduced the grant-in-aid to the non-plan budget of the beleaguered and impoverished university to a considerable extent. Efforts of the university to increase its domestic receipts added only a few chips and did not make much difference to its financial health. Combination of both plan and non-plan budget also makes addition to the deficit.

3. JAMMU UNIVERSITY
Budget at a Glance

Part I—Non-Plan

(Rs. in Lakh)

	Accounts 2004-05	*Budget Estimates 2005-06*	*Revised Estimates 2005-06 (Based on Actuals)*	*Proposed Estimates 2006-07*
Opening Balance	208.22	43.59	43.59	336.35
University Receipts	1051.44	979.96	1133.56	1158.10
State Grants	1821.08	2550.00	2550.00	2690.00
Hundi	—	—	369.18	—
Loans	135.00	—	—	—
Total	3215.74	3573.55	4096.33	4184.45
Expenditure	3172.15	3541.80	3759.98	4158.90
Closing Balance	43.59	31.75	336.35	25.55

Part II—Plan

(*Rs. in Lakh*)

	Accounts 2004-05	*Budget Estimates 2005-06*	*Revised Estimates 2005-06 (Based on Actuals)*	*Proposed Estimates 2006-07*
Opening Balance	1120.26	1838.34	1838.34	1231.80
U.G.C	1084.63	1459.37	322.15	1170.23
State Grants	125.00	240.00	240.00	265.00
Hundi	44.00	85.00	85.00	—
Loans	96.00	—	—	—
D.B.T.	7.18	15.00	9.56	10.00
Total	2477.07	3637.71	2495.05	2677.03
Expenditure	638.73	3585.54	1263.25	2432.60
Closing Balance	**1838.34**	**52.17**	**1231.80**	**244.43**

Part III—Specific

(*Rs. in Lakh*)

	Accounts 2004-05	*Budget Estimates 2005-06*	*Revised Estimates 2005-06 (Based on Actuals)*	*Proposed Estimates 2006-07*
Opening Balance	224.21	280.62	283.62	377.86
Receipt	256.81	247.30	295.38	317.94
Total	481.02	527.92	579.00	695.80
Expenditure	197.40	465.53	201.14	596.97
Closing Balance	**283.62**	**62.39**	**377.86**	**98.83**

From the glance of the budget of JU for the last three financial years, it is clear that the financial position of the university is quite sound. The budget has been in surplus for the last four financial years. State Government has been increasing the grant of the university as per its requirements. University receipts have also increased.

4. KU BUDGET AT A GLANCE

(Figures in lakhs of Rupees)

Head of Account	*Actuals 2004-05*	*Budget Estimates 2005-06*		*Budget Estimates 2006-07*
		Original	*Revised*	
(1)	*(2)*	*(3)*	*(4)*	*(5)*
I. Non-plan				
(i) Income and Expenditure towards Maintenance				
A. Income				
State Government Grant	2039.60	2243.56	2202.76	2423.00
Internal Income	2868.74	3538.90	3101.96	3177.50
Total (A) (Income)	4908.34	4782.46	5304.72	5600.50
B. Expenditure				
Salaries	3573.15	4346.13	4031.90	4811.53
Other Charges	1347.66	1619.60	1740.70	1882.92
Total (B) (Expenditure)	4920.81	5965.81	5772.60	6694.45
Deficit/Surplus under (i)	(-) 12.47	(-) 1183.35	(-) 467.88	(-) 1093.95
(ii) Self Financing Schemes (Additional Resources Generated)				
Deficit/Surplus under (ii)	(+) 4928.64	(+)4677.77	(+) 2853.09	(+)1136.64
Overall Deficit/ Surplus of (i) and (ii)	(+) 4916.17	(+)3494.42	(+) 2385.21	(+) 42.69
(iii) Debt, Deposits and Remittance Heads, etc.				
Deficit (-)/Surlpus (+)	(+) 261.58	(+) 261.38	(+) 263.45	(+) 263.25
(iv) Schemes				
Deficit (-)/Surplus (+)	(+) 282.92	(+) 259.76	(+) 102.32	(+) 87.76
II. Plan				
Income				
Opening Balance	(+) 4.62	(-) 259.56	(-) 259.56	(-) 83.56

(Contd.)

(1)	(2)	(3)	(4)	(5)
(a) State Government Grant	130.00	30.00	500.00	200.00
(b) UGC Grant	—	23.00	12.50	35.50
(c) Government of India	35.82	—	—	—
Total Income	170.44	(-) 206.56	(+) 252.94	(+) 151.94
Expenditure	430.00	93.60	336.50	225.50
Deficit (-)/Surplus (+)	(-) 259.56	(-) 300.16	(-) 83.56	(-) 73.56
Grand Total of all Accounts (I+ II)				
Opening Balance	(+) 3616.74	(+)5201.09	(+)5201.09	(+)2667.40
Income	9611.92	8173.59	10153.33	9990.67
Total Income	13228.66	13374.68	15354.42	12658.07
Expenditure	8027.57	9659.30	12687.02	12337.95
Closing Balance	**(+) 5201.09**	**(+)3715.38**	**(+)2667.40**	**(+) 320.12**

From the glance of the budget of KU for the last three financial years, it is clear that the financial position of the university is quite sound. The budget has been in surplus for the last four financial years. Haryana Government has been increasing the grant of the university as per its requirements. KU has also generated its resources through self-financing schemes and through other innovative schemes.

5. PU BUDGET AT A GLANCE

(Figures in Lakhs of Rupees)

Current Account	*Estimates for the year 2005-06*		*Estimates for 2006-07*
	Original	*Revised*	
I. Non-Plan			
Revenue Receipts	5,818.22	6,246.80	6,653.66
Less 50% of NRI's income to be transferred to corpus "Foundation for Higher Education and Research" (Corpus Fund)	500	506	527
Total	5,318.22	5,740.80	6,126.16

(*Contd.*)

Expenditure	11,104.82	12,607.04	13,179.24[⊗]
Deficit (Non-Plan)	5,786.60	6,866.24	7.053.08
New and Special Demands	—	—	62.47
Total Deficit including New and Special Demands	5,786.60	6,866.24	7,115.55
II. Plan			
Income: Grants	98.57	761.2	124.26
Expenditure	118.86	684.42	154.17
III. Schemes			
Income (By way of Grants)	1,088.25	1,297.26	1,227.44
Expenditure	12,966.80	1,347.13	1,185.09
Total Income (Parts I, II, III)	6,505.04	7,799.35	7,477.86
Total Expenditure (Parts I, II, III)	12,520.48	14,638.59	14,518.50

[⊗] Includes estimated expenditure for 40% of sanctioned vacant Teaching Positions. (B.O.F.) dated 29.11.2000, item No. 30, VC orders dated 30.1.2006.

A glance of the PU budget for last two financial years reveals that the finances of the university are running in deficit. It may be because the university needed an additional sum of Rs. 10.00 crore for the Pension Scheme for PU Employees introduced in 2005-06. There were also additional provisions sanctioned for the construction of new buildings in PU campus, sectors 15 and 25. The university also made efforts to increase its revenue receipts with the NRI funds.

Observations of Chitleen K. Sethi also deserve to be mentioned here:

> "The Union Budget has once again ignored Panjab University. While the finance minister P. Chidambaram today proposed a special grant of Rs. 50 crore each to Govind Ballabh Pant University of Agriculture and Technology, Pant Nagar, and Tamil Nadu Agriculture University, Coimbatore. Panjab University has been left high and dry in its diamond Jubilee year. Panjab University has a unique status among universities in being both a state and central university. But the university has been paying a price for this status. The Punjab Government tends to ignore the university in terms of grants on the

pretext that it is a central university and the centre has been over the years ignoring the university by not providing it adequate funds. As a result the university here is left to fend for itself."[2]

From the above comparative study of the budgets of all the universities of the sample, different financial position of the universities is quite clear. GNDU, JU and KU are surplus in funds. PU and HPU are running in deficit. HPU is having the worst financial position amongst all the universities of the sample.

10. WORK-CULTURE

System is quite close to total collapse. Most of the employees lack proper motivation. They have a little knowledge of rules and procedures. They do not understand the spirit behind an official task to be done and are always after some self- devised procedure or method to be followed and not for the task to be completed or some target to be achieved. Everybody seems to be groping in the labyrinth of files, struggling in the dinosaurian structure and at a loss what to do and how to tackle this over-powering and all pervasive chaos. Some of the personnel who are interested in doing some worthwhile work are scared by the forbidding rules, regulations and procedures and shy away venturing to save their skins and avoid uncalled for trouble or criticism. Still the system bad, inefficient, chaotic, cracking under it own heavy weight as it is, has some conscientious, ingenuous, devoted persons who keep this system going. They are engaged in some useful research projects, building organizations even with the outdated, cumbersome and forbidding rules, regulations and procedures, unimaginative and frustrating audit objections, pushing the files to their logical ends, and doing all the activities to keep the system alive. These persons complete all the formalities of admissions to various courses, on merit basis or through entrance tests. They also help in the conduct of timely and fair examinations and declarations of results. (It may be mentioned that the university results cannot be seen on internet. They follow the age-old manual procedure of tabulation and totaling.

Computerisation of examination results still is to be done even after creation of some committees for computerization, holding of meetings of the University top brass and tossing of files for more than a decade. Again thanks to the systemic failure in this regard.) It is perhaps because of these persons that the university administrative system is just going on giving a semblance of functioning. So we find some persons and not the system functioning.

Above observations about the work-culture pertain to HPU, but these are more or less true to not only all other universities of the sample but also to other bureaucratic organizations in India. In fact, our organizations are much more rule-oriented than result-oriented.

All sorts of teachers in all the universities were observed. There were some—dedicated, learned, immersed in their scholastic pursuits, busy with research projects, teaching and guiding students. Some others were those who did not teach at all, were busy in politics, intrigues, interested only in promotions, lucrative positions, money making through examination duties, taking classes in paid NRI courses, or even minting money through private coaching. There were others who were making a wise combination of both the above divergent qualities. Similarly, there were students busy in the laboratories, libraries, attending classes, seminars, preparing not only for their university examinations but for other State, UPSC, UGC and other competitive examinations. Then there were others who were busy with merry-making only, avoiding classes, busy with political activities, indulging in mischief-mongering, creating troubles in the campuses, adopting underhand methods for admissions and examinations, and indulging in all sorts of anti-social activities. I do not want to say that all those who were busy with political activities were anti-social elements. There were undoubtedly many good exceptions. But the nexus was there especially when there was instigation from some ex-students.

To sum up, in this chapter a comparative study of the universities of the sample has been made with respect to infrastructure, general satisfaction in the universities, quality of education, objectives of university education as perceived by the university personnel, administrative efficiency, autonomy, violence, criminalization, finances and work-culture. Conclusions and suggestions have naturally been evolved in the next chapters on the basis of the discussion of the above factors.

Notes and References

1. P.R. Dubhashi, Focus on Fundamentals, In M.V. Mathur, Ramesh K. Arora and Meena Sogani, *op. cit.*, 84.
2. Chitleen K. Sethi, Budget funds: Panjab varsity left high and dry, *The Tribune*, March 1, 2007, p. 3.

CHAPTER 7

Conclusions

Usual empirical research methodology has been adopted in the present study. The researcher has laid his hands both on secondary and primary sources. The secondary sources included Ordinances, Handbooks, Rules, Regulations, Reports, routine files, news paper reports, Ph.D. dissertations, books, etc. The primary sources were observation, questionnaires, and interviews. Quantitative information collected through questionnaires has been supplemented with qualitative information in the form of case studies. Information about the case studies has been collected during the visits to the universities of the sample by interviewing the officials, through official records, and news papers reports. Data collected through above methodology may be concluded as follows:

I. INFRASTRUCTURE

Data collected through questionnaires show that in many aspects the situation in all the Universities is quite similar and the differences are not statistically significant. Some universities are better in some aspects whereas some others are better in other aspects. Information collected through Observation-Sheet throws a good deal of light on the campuses and infrastructure of the universities of the sample. A study of the observation-sheets of the universities reveals that PU followed by GNDU is the best as for infrastructural facilities are concerned, whereas HPU is the worst especially with respect to hostels, buildings, library, toilets, internet facilities, etc.

2. LEVEL OF SATISFACTION IN THE UNIVERSITIES

A very high level of satisfaction has been found amongst the university personnel. As high as 90.40% of the teachers in the sample feel teaching interesting and 94.70% of the teachers consider teaching profession respectable. A large majority of students (69.80%) finds class-room teaching interesting and 70.50% of the students consider the syllabus useful. As for non-teaching employees, 75.50% of them find their job interesting as well as respectable.

3. QUALITY OF EDUCATION

As for the quality of education, teachers mostly depend upon lecture method (Teachers point out 90.40% and the students point out 91.40%). They also use other methods like discussion, seminar, project, and tutorial. They also give assignments and take monthly tests. Some of the teachers also use OHP (Teachers point out 29.80 % and the students point out 25.70%) and video-films (Teachers point out 20.20% and the students point out 14.20%) as aids for teaching. Overall picture may not be quite bright and rosy but it is not quite dark as well. 89.40% teachers say that students discuss their academic problems with them, whereas only 52.80% students agree that they discuss their academic problems with their teachers. This wide gap between the opinions of the teachers and students clearly points out the lack of academic interaction between the teachers and their students. 83.00% teachers are in favour of making minimum attendance of classes by the students compulsory, whereas only 65.80% students are in favour of making minimum attendance of classes by the students compulsory. This wide gap between the opinions of the teachers and students clearly points out many of the students are not in favour of attending the classes. A high percentage of teachers (71.30%) and students (59.60%) favouring marking of answer-books by outside examiners clearly underlines the atmosphere of distrust in the fairness and impartiality of the teachers. It is also against the ideal, those who teach must evaluate. Majority of teachers (56.40%) have noticed cheating in the examinations by the students, whereas only 8.90% students have admitted of being indulged in cheating. Cheating as well as lying by the students is a clear message if we read between the percentages of both the teachers and the students. This perhaps is the result of not only of our examination system but that of our education system also. Only 56.40% teachers and 53% students in the total sample get reading material of their interest from their respective University libraries. Difficulties faced by the teachers in pursuing their academic activities certainly hamper their academic growth. 51.10% Teachers in the total sample find it difficult to get the research grant released. Similarly, 37.20% teachers in the total sample find it difficult to settle accounts of National/International Seminars conducted by them. 52.10% teachers, 40.60% students and 52.90% officers in the total sample find the quality of education imparted in their respective Universities comparable to that of advanced countries. 73.40% teachers and 76.50% officers in the total sample say that they have made efforts to improve the quality of education in their respective Universities to make that comparable to the standards of advanced countries.

4. OBJECTIVES OF UNIVERSITY EDUCATION

Objectives of university education as derived from the responses of questionnaires may be mentioned as follows: A small percentage of teachers (25.50%), students (25.90%) and non-teaching staff (21.00%) prefer university education to be limited to a few persons only, whereas a greater percentage is in favour of providing university education to all. In the similar vein, Knowledge Commission appointed by Government of India has also recommended that by 2015 the percentage of the students getting admission in the institutes of higher education should be raised to 15%. For achieving this target the number of the universities has to be raised to 1500 from the present 350 universities. Only a small percentage of teachers (14.90%), students (16%) and non-teaching staff (23.10%) prefer university education for job only. Similarly, a small percentage of teachers (14.90%), students (28.20%) and non-teaching staff (25.10%) prefer university education for self-development only. A large majority of teachers (83.00%), students (85.80%) and non-teaching staff (82.70%) prefer university education both for job as well as for self-development. 58.50% of the teachers and 65.80% of the students in the total sample are in favour of election to Students' Central Association. In KU only 40% of teachers and 41.80% of students are in favour of election to SCA. This small percentage may perhaps be due to the bad consequences of the students' elections.

5. ADMINISTRATIVE EFFICIENCY

Under the heading Administrative Efficiency, topics like VCs and their tenures, employees and their habits in doing the official work, training they received, difficulties they find in dealing with different persons in the universities, pressures on the officers, difficulties different persons in the universities find in getting administrative work done, percentage of the persons finding university administration sympathetic and quick in redressing their grievances, difficulties experienced by the people in getting the clearance of their bills from LAD, and effectiveness of the Internal Audit of the universities in the sample have been included.

Close relationship between the longevity of the tenure of a VC and his administrative efficiency has been observed. For example, HNB Garhwal University known for its bad administration and unrest had 10 VCs in ten years. Out of 10 VCs, only Prof. K.P. Nautiyal could complete his tenure. "But, if the circumstances do not allow them (VCs) to complete their tenure and leave the chair in between, the planning and execution of the university developmental work is bound to suffer, as the whole thing has to be revised afresh, said Mr. Chander Singh Mehta, the registrar of the university. He has worked with four VCs within two years."[1] In HPU and KU, VCs have been frequently changed. Average tenure of VCs was 1.80

years in HPU and 2.00 years in KU. However, PU is the best with 5.80 years, and GNDU and JU are quite good with the average of 5.43 and 4.31 respectively. In these three universities included in the sample, VCs were not changed with the change of the Government. However, in HPU, not only VCs but Registrars were also changed equally frequently. Changing of PVCs, Deans, Hostel Chief Wardens, Wardens, and even the HODs with the change of Government has also become an established practice for more than a decade. Resigning and threatening to resign by above high officials like Deans, Hostel Chief Warden and Wardens in wake of students' agitations or some other pressures are also day-to-day stories. Same is the case with KU. In KU also, VCs and other high officers have to resign with the change of the Government. In Haryana, all the VCs except one were removed with the change of the last Government.

It may be mentioned that none of the universities has Pro-Vice-Chancellor at present. HPU and KU had this official earlier. Relations between the VC and PVC were rarely cordial. By developing another centre of power in the universities, the PVCs have done more harm than good to the university system. Haryana, Punjab, and Himachal have abolished this post. PU and JU never had the post of PVC.

Only 47.80% of the employees in the total sample say that they keep weekly/monthly diaries of their official work. 66.60% of the employees say that they make planning for doing their official work. Only 38.30% of the employees say that they have received training for doing their official work. 38.30% employees find difficulties in dealing with their seniors. Next in the difficulty level are teachers and students both with 17.30% each. In HPU, 46.10% of the employees find difficulties in dealing with their seniors and 25.50% of the employees find difficulties in dealing students. In JU, 66.70% of the employees find difficulties in dealing with the teachers. Above high percentage of employees pointing out their difficulties in dealing with the groups is an indication of the conflict in the groups. 58.50% of teachers, 35.30% of officers, 66.10% of students, and 30.50% of the employees in the total sample find difficulties in getting their administrative work done. Employees with 30.50% are the best placed. Percentage of teachers and students finding difficulties is very high. Position in HPU is the worst where 75% teachers, 70% officers, 66% students and 35.30% employees find difficulties in getting their administrative work done. However, the position in PU is the worst in case of students where the highest percentage of the students (78.50%) in the total sample finds difficulties in getting their administrative work done. 52.10% of teachers, 70.60% of officers, 45.50% of students, and 48.40% of the employees in the total sample find the administration of their respective universities sympathetic to them. Position in HPU is the worst where only 25% of teachers, 40% of officers, 36.10% of students and 37.30% of employees find university administration sympathetic to them. Strangely enough amongst the officers who constitute part of administration themselves, only 40% find it sympathetic to them. May be this explains the spate of resignations by officers which was noticed during 2005-06. Only 38.30% of teachers, 58.80% of officers, 34.80% of students, and 44.10% of the employees in the total sample find the administration of their respective universities quick in redressing their grievances. Here again position in HPU is the worst where only 28.60% of teachers, 20% of officers, 27.80% of students and 30.40% of employees find university administration quick in redressing their grievances. Strangely enough amongst the officers who constitute part of administration themselves, the lowest percentage, i.e., only 20% find university administration quick in redressing their grievances. It means the officers are feeling the pinch much more than what the teachers, students and employees are feeling. Some drastic steps are needed to ameliorate this condition.

57.40% of teachers, 35.30% of officers and 41.80% of the employees in the total sample find difficulties in getting the clearance of their bills from LAD. Here again position in HPU is the worst where as many as 78.60% teachers, 80% officers and 63.70% employees find difficulties in getting the clearance of their bills from LAD. It may be mentioned here that in the chapter relating to case studies, we have discussed the conflict between audit officials and the university personnel in detail. This conflict is reflected in the answers given by teachers, officers and employees here also. Overall situation of the teachers is the worst with 57.40% facing difficulties in the clearance of their bills from the LAD. Only 39.40% of teachers, 47.10% of officers and 39.80% of the employees in the total sample find Internal Audit System effective. Here again, position in HPU is the worst where only 32.10% teachers, 40% officers and 45.10% employees find Internal Audit effective. It may be mentioned here that the HPU employees got Internal Audit after a long battle against the LAD, and still ironically only a small percentage of university personnel are finding it effective. It means the persons posted in the Internal Audit Section of the HPU are not trained and also there are some basic flaws with the audit system of the university itself. Moreover, persisting conflict due to lack of clarity at many points in the instructions issued on the division of work between the Internal Audit Section and the LAD also hampers the smooth functioning of the Internal Audit Section.

6. AUTONOMY

Under the heading Autonomy, opinions of teachers and employees of the universities of the sample have been discussed. Only 44.70% of teachers and 49.30% of employees say that their universities enjoy autonomy in the appointments. Overall position of PU is the best with the 75% of teachers and 66.70% of employees mentioning that their university enjoys autonomy in the appointments. Overall position of HPU is the worst with only 21.40% of teachers and 38.20% of employees saying that their university enjoys autonomy in the appointments. However, in KU a slightly lower percent of employees, i.e., 37.60% say that their university enjoys autonomy in the appointments. Only 51.0% of teachers and 54.50% of employees say that their universities enjoy autonomy in the promotions. Overall position in JU and PU is the best and worst in HPU and KU. 53.20% of teachers and 55% of employees say that their universities enjoy autonomy in appointing officers in their universities. Overall position of PU is the best with the 75% of teachers and 93.30% of employees mentioning that their university enjoys autonomy in appointing officers in their universities. Only 54.30% of teachers and 61.40% of employees have the faith that they will get promotion on merit/whenever it is due to them. Overall position of JU and PU is the best. In KU only 40% and in HPU 53.60% have the faith that they will get promotion on merit/whenever it is due to them. As sequel to the case of "Question Papers Printing Scam" in HPU the State Legislative Assembly amended the Himachal Pradesh University Act, 1970 by including "Section 35-A Creation of Posts, etc". This gave another blow to the university autonomy which was already working as a State Government Department even without the above amendment.

7. PREVALENCE OF VIOLENCE

In the present context, violence included sexual harassment, eve-teasing, ragging, using abusive language, group clashes, murder, and destruction of university property. Differences in the perception of teachers and students with respect to sexual harassment have been found. 9.60% teachers and 20% of students have noticed sexual harassment of female students by male students. Similarly, 14.90% teachers and 17.30% students have noticed sexual harassment of female students by male teachers. 14.90% teachers have noticed sexual harassment of female teachers by male teachers. As for employees, 18.20% employees have noticed sexual harassment of female employees by male employees.

Cases of eve-teasing have been observed in KU. News paper reports with respect to GNDU writing about frequent quarrels even among senior officers and faculty members alleging threats to life from colleagues, beating up of even Head of a Department, conviction of a coach in a case of sexual harassment, verbal abuses, charges and counter-charges paint a poor picture of the university. In HPU, murders of two students' leaders by the rival political groups, usual violence during and after the SCA elections, etc. are painful pointers to imminent educational fiasco. In JU too, some stray cases of students' violence of a very small scale have been reported. In PU also, students have been observed resorting to strikes for getting their grievances redressed, but surprisingly in a very peaceful manner.

8. INCIDENCE OF CRIMINALISATION

Next to violence, criminalization too has entered some of the universities of the sample in a big way. As observed in the case studies, entrance test mafia has spread its tentacles in HPU. Connection of the HPCPMT paper leak has been found with Punjab, Uttar Pradesh, Uttrakhand, Bihar, and New Delhi. Irregularities in financial matters and conduct of examinations have also been found. Fake degree and fake certificate cases have also come to light. Murders and instigation to suicide have also occurred. These crimes are mostly related to conduct of examinations, financial irregularities, and political rivalries.

9. FINANCES

Financial position of the universities of a sample presents an interesting study. It has been observed that the financial health of a university depends upon the factors like the quantum of funds given by the respective state governments, internal resources of a university depending upon the infrastructure it has got, additional requirements of a university according to the emerging needs, etc. The above factors are clear from the financial position of the universities given below.

Financial position of the GNDU university is quite sound. Its budget has been running in surplus for the last four financial years. Though the Punjab Government has been continuously reducing the maintenance grant, the university, however, has increased its revenue receipts from the self-financing courses. The university is well equipped with the required infrastructure for starting self-financing courses.

Financial position of the HPU is not sound. It has been in considerable deficit for the last three years. Himachal Pradesh Government has reduced the grant-in-aid to the non-plan budget of the beleaguered and impoverished university to a considerable extent. Efforts of the university to increase its domestic receipts added only a few chips and did not make much difference to its financial health. Combination of both plan and non-plan budget also makes addition to the deficit.

Financial position of the JU is quite sound. The budget has been in surplus for the last four financial years. State

Government has been increasing the grant of the university as per its requirements. University receipts have also increased.

Financial position of KU is quite sound. The budget has been in surplus for the last four financial years. Haryana Government has been increasing the grant of the university as per its requirements. KU has also generated resources through self-financing schemes and through other innovative schemes. By making a combined comparative study of the political interference and financial positions of HPU and KU, a conclusion can easily be drawn that Haryana Government with its interference is providing sufficient funds to KU, whereas the Himachal Pradesh Government with its tight rope control is not giving the required funds to HPU to flourish and function efficiently.

PU budget is in deficit for last two financial years. It may be because the university needed additional funds for the Pension Scheme for PU Employees introduced in 2005-06 and for the construction of new buildings in PU campus, sectors 15 and 25. The university also made efforts to increase its revenue receipts with the NRI funds. The proposals of the PU worth Rs. 250 crore sent by its VC Professor R.C. Sobti to the Central Government for expansion and up-gradation of infrastructure have borne little fruits so far.

To sum up, PU and GNDU have the best and HPU the worst infrastructure. A very high level of satisfaction has been found amongst the university personnel. Teachers mostly depend upon lecture method. Majority of the university personnel prefer university education both for job as well as for self-development. Close relationship between the longevity of the tenure of a VC and his administrative efficiency has been observed. Financial health of a university depended upon the factors like the quantum of funds given by the respective state governments, and internal resources of a university.

Note and Reference

1. Indu, Khandoori, HNB Varsity: 10 VCs in 10 yrs., *Hindustan Times*, 20.9.2003, p. 6.

CHAPTER

8

Suggestions

Conclusions have been drawn in the previous chapter by analyzing and interpreting the data collected through usual empirical research methodology in the present study. Following suggestions thus naturally emerged out of the conclusions:

1. IMPROVE INFRASTRUCTURAL FACILITIES

Investment in education is undoubtedly investment in the future of a country. Universities should be provided with better infrastructural facilities. They should be fully equipped with modern computers and internet facilities to enable the teachers and students to come up to international standards. HPU cries for special attention in this respect. Hostels and toilets in HPU need to be overhauled immediately. Computer and internet facilities in HPU, JU and KU need to be upgraded.

2. MOTIVATE TEACHERS, STUDENTS AND NON-TEACHING EMPLOYEES

A very high level of satisfaction of the university personnel has been found in the universities of the sample. As high as 90.40% of the teachers in the sample feel teaching interesting and 94.70% of the teachers consider teaching profession respectable. A large majority of students (69.80%) finds class-room teaching interesting and 70.50% of the students consider the syllabus useful. As for non-teaching employees, 75.50% of them find their job interesting as well as respectable. These highly satisfied people can certainly create a climate of excellence. All that is needed is the world-class infrastructure and high motivation.

3. IMPROVE THE QUALITY OF EDUCATION

Lots of efforts are required to improve the quality of education imparted in the universities of the sample to make it comparable to the standards of advanced countries. Dependency mainly on lecture method has to be given up and other interactive methods like discussion, assignment, seminar, project and tutorial have to be adopted. OHP and video-films have to be used as teaching aids to make teaching-learning process interesting. This will increase much needed academic and intellectual interaction between teachers and students, develop original ideas in the students, enlighten their minds and brighten their personalities. This will also save the Chairpersons of the University Departments from the wrath of agitating and misbehaving students who indulge in many sorts of mischief to get the required percentage of lectures. Teaching-learning and evaluation process has to be made simultaneous by resorting to assignment and presentation in classroom-seminars to get rid of the fear and dependence only on annual/ semester system of examination. This way many of the maladies of our education system, which ironically is mainly examination and entrance-test centered and not learning centred, can be removed or mitigated. For this teachers have to raise their intellectual and moral statures to be able to assess the assignments and presentations of the students. The key to success is with the teachers. They have to rise to the occasion to inspire confidence in the students about their fairness and impartiality. Libraries, no doubt, have to be equipped with the latest reading material to cater to the needs of the readers.

Libraries have also to be fully computerized and provided with internet facilities to make searching of information and data convenient and efficient. Administrative and audit system has to streamlined to save the teachers from the difficulties they face with respect to release of research grants and settling the accounts of the National/International Seminars organised by them.

4. EXTEND COVERAGE OF UNIVERSITY EDUCATION AND IMPART IT BOTH FOR JOB AS WELL AS FOR SELF-DEVELOPMENT

In India only 7% of the students go in for higher education. In view of the essentiality of higher education for the national development, efforts have to be made to bring more number of persons in its fold. Recommendations of the Knowledge Commission appointed by Government of India that by 2015 the percentage of the students getting admission in the institutes of higher education should be raised to 15% and the number of the universities be raised to 1500 from the present 350 universities deserve to be implemented earnestly in this respect. However, before adding new universities, the already existing universities need to be equipped with proper infrastructure to provide world class quality education. Mere adding of more universities without adequate infrastructure will not serve the purpose.

More than 80% of the teachers, students and non-teaching staff in the sample favour university education to be imparted both for job as well as for self-development. In view of this opinion, the course contents in the universities have to be designed both for providing job and catering to self-development. Course contents in the universities should be reoriented in consultation with the industry to suit its requirements and thereby increase employability. With the introduction of subjects like computers, commerce, economics, environment, management, etc., subjects in the faculty of languages and social sciences should not be ignored. These subjects are very much essential for self-development and harmonious development of the society. In a democratic society, we cannot disallow elections to any section of people. Elections to the SCA will help in providing future leaders to the nation, but in order to ward-off the harmful effects of these results on the quality of higher education, guidelines provided by the Lyngdoh Committee should be strictly adhered to.

5. MANY PRONGED ACTIONS ARE REQUIRED FOR INCREASING ADMINISTRATIVE EFFICIENCY

Following actions are suggested for increasing administrative efficiency:

(i) *Appointment of Competent Vice-Chancellors*: Long tenure of a Vice-Chancellor, rightly called the kingpin of university system, is essential for the development of a University. Frequent changes of VCs disturb the academic atmosphere of a University and hamper its development. VCs are generally changed because of the charges of corruption, favouritism, financial irregularities, violation of university rules, and political interferences, etc. Changing of VCs with the change of the Government has also become a practice in many of the universities. A VC is required to provide academic leadership and efficient administration to a university. Selection/appointment of a VC should, therefore, be guided by these criteria only. Appointing a VC on considerations like political, caste, religious and regional affiliations, not only fails to inspire confidence in his calibre, but also leads to unnecessary agitations in a university. Some universities have three year duration for a VC. Perhaps, this is not a right tenure, in as much as in such a situation a VC takes first year of the tenure in understanding the university and last year in appeasing his political masters/appointing authorities for one more extension. Thus, practically he is left with only one year to concentrate on a sincere developmental work. A five year duration for a VC is required if we expect him to do something worthwhile and leave some visible footprints on the sand of time. All the capable and renowned VCs of PU and GNDU whom we remember with respect have spent five and more years in their universities to make memorable contributions in the field of higher education. All the State Governments should follow the good practice of PU and GNDU where VCs are appointed for a longer duration and are not changed with the change of Government. After appointing persons of known integrity and calibre in academic and administrative fields for five years, the appointing authorities should give them a free hand in administering the university. Political interference in the matter of appointments leads to recruitment of substandard teachers and officials which not only makes the university inferior, but also gives birth to agitations, spoils the academic atmosphere by the poor quality of teaching, learning and research, and develops a culture of political patronage. This justifies the slogan of a students' organisation, "When politics decides your future, you decide your politics". As a natural corollary to it, politicization of the university is justified.

(ii) *Decentralisation of Decision-making*: It has been observed beyond any doubt that VCs concentrate all the powers in themselves. Even the most insignificant routine files go to them for signatures. This way their time is consumed in the trifles and they are left with a little time to devote to the developmental work where their dynamism and leadership is really required. They should decentralize as much as they can by developing a trusted team of devoted and capable colleagues not the coteries. Routine matters should be decided at the lower levels and only matters which call for some new policy-making should come to the VC. Proper use of democratically constituted academic and administrative bodies should be made. Decision-making should be left to them only. Involvement of teachers, non-teaching staff and students in decision-making will not only increase transparency, openness and fairness but also develop acceptability, practicability and successful implementation of the decisions. VC should no doubt provide his leadership and should influence decision-making through his leadership qualities and not through his discretionary powers.

(iii) *Training of Non-Teaching Employees*: Success of the institutions of higher education depends to a great extent on the efficient working of the non-teaching employees. However, training is woefully missing in these institutions Therefore, well planned training efforts are needed for running these institutions and keeping the personnel abreast with the modern management techniques. They should be educated about the role of the university, its administration, the faculties, the departments, the units of the university, the art of handling the students, teachers, and public in general, the decision-making and problem-solving processes, modern management techniques, as well as the various rules, regulations and bye-laws of the university. Efforts should be made to sensitise employees and high-level officers to be sympathetic in their behaviour in dealing with the students, teachers, and all those who come to them for the solutions of their problems. They should also be trained in redressing the grievances quickly. Some mechanism should also be developed where employees of a section/branch meet and discuss their problems relating to the expediting the office procedures/routines. This will help them to learn from each other and come to some standardized procedures/routines and remove some of the bottlenecks/impediments/frustrations/irritations. It will also create healthy and congenial social environment essential for effective working. The Japanese organisational system of obtaining and acting upon the suggestions at the grassroots can also be applied to the non-teaching employees of the institutions of higher education. A well-designed training programme is needed for the Non-Teaching Staff. In addition to induction training, they should be provided training at different stages of their career. Orientation and refresher courses should be meticulously and carefully designed for them.

> These programmes in addition to making them methodical and efficient, will remove many of the difficulties they face in dealing with their seniors, colleagues, teachers and students. Detailed instructions with respect to daily routine and procedure should also be given to them to save their time and temper. Training institutes on the pattern of UGC administrative staff colleges should be established for imparting training to the non-teaching employees of the institutions of higher education. To begin with, existing administrative staff colleges can be assigned the job of preparing training modules for the non-teaching staff also and executing the same accordingly.

LAD personnel have to be made conversant with the aims and objectives of higher education. They have to be explained the difference between the general administration and university administration. Before their postings in a university they should be given orientation training in auditing the university accounts. Teachers should be given detailed instructions about the organisation of seminars and conduct of research projects. These instructions should be liberal and should not hurt the dignity of the teachers. It will be perhaps wiser and more productive if the funding agencies give direct and lump-sum financial assistance to the teachers themselves without the involvement, say interference, of the university auditors. UGC perhaps is aware of the complaints of the teachers about getting the funds from the university personnel/ auditors with all their shackles, curbs and irritants. Let the teachers be audited for their research products and not for mere observance of rules. No doubt, rules need to be observed, but these should not be as stringent as one finds them these days. As for Internal Audit staff, they should be given training in the university audit before their posting in the audit section.

There should be a clear cut policy for the promotion of employees. Promotions and punishments should be clearly defined and applied. They should be ensured at least three promotions in their total career. This will help in avoiding unnecessary agitations, bickering and politicization by the employees and at the same time lead to administrative efficiency on their part.

(iv) *Proper Coordination between Academic Programmes and Administrative Work*: Dichotomy and not unity has been observed between the academic and administrative wings of the institutions of higher education. At times we find them in different warring groups. This situation certainly hampers the working the institutions. Therefore, proper coordination between the academic and administrative wings of institutions of higher education is very much essential for their good governance. "Administrative roles should only be instrumental in promoting the academic work in the university, and should not assume unnecessary importance so as to become a competing system within the university. Since the primary functions of the university are providing good teaching and ensuring research of excellent quality, these functions, therefore, should assume priority. If non-academic roles are given too much importance, parallel empires are built in universities which threaten and obstruct academic functions. This does not mean that non-academic roles are not important at all. They may be given importance to the extent they facilitate the functioning of the university and its various sub-systems."[1]

6. HARMONIOUS COMBINATION OF AUTONOMY AND ACCOUNTABILITY IS REQUIRED

Autonomy provides the much needed blood supply to the veins of university system. Following steps are needed for enriching and strengthening the universities to play their roles effectively:

(i) *Allowing Universities Sufficient Autonomy*: Uprightness, vision, and commitment to university autonomy especially with respect to non-interference in the matters of appointment, promotion and posting on the part of political bosses are the pre-requisites for good governance in a university system. Lack of faith in the teachers and employees about their appointment and promotion is harmful for the growth and development of a university. If the teachers and employees do not have the faith that they will get promotion according to their merit/whenever it is due to them, they will not be able to put their heart and soul in the work. If they rightly or wrongly believe that the officers in the university have been appointed not on the basis of their merit but on the basis of their connections, they will not give the due respect to them which will ultimately lead to insubordination and indiscipline. For making universities institutions of excellence autonomy is very much essential.

(ii) *University Administration Needs a Different Treatment*: Arguments in favour of this different treatment are given below: Administering a university is different as well as much more difficult than administering a state government department. A university cannot be administered by general administrative rules or financial rules of any state or central government. This has to be realised and university has to be administered accordingly. Professor Amrik Singh has pointed the same concern when he said, "Today a situation has arisen where those who feel committed to high academic standards have no choice except to lament over what has happened. The application of bureaucratic rules on the scale that has happened has been an unmitigated disaster for the university system in India."[2] M.V. Mathur, Ramesh K. Arora and Meena Sogani have rightly pointed out, "The Weberian hierarchical system of bureaucracy cannot function in a university system where specialization, autonomy, initiative and self-actualization are valued. Yet, to do away with the canons of sound administration which inevitably accord credence to the notion of authority based on hierarchy will be inviting organizational chaos and indiscipline. Hence, a sort of "modified hierarchy" would be desirable for the university system, with due importance and leverage to other components and characteristics of an educational administrative system. Mathai, Pareek and Rao argue that the university organization should be as flat as possible; create a synthesis between centralization and decentralization; academicians' role in general administration should increase; and committees should become legitimate channels of participation and influence."[3] P.R. Dubhashi, a retired IAS officer and a former Vice-Chancellor of Pondicherry University, has also made the same point, "The University ought to evolve its own administrative procedures for speedy and efficient discharge of its various functions and the staff needs to be trained in such procedures. The academic and administrative wings of the university should not produce a dichotomy but unity."[4] Dubhashi has further added, "A university is an academocracy and not just a democracy. It is a self-governing institution in which all elements viz., the vice-chancellor, the registrar, the administrative staff and the academicians have to play their role in an objective and impartial manner. The university should be entirely free from outside interference and should have the dignity of an autonomous self-governing institution."[5]

(iii) *Research Grants Without Exacting Controls*: Closely related to treating university administration differently is the point of giving research grants to the university students and teachers without excessive and impeding controls. Audit system and exacting controls have done a great harm to the institutions of higher education by slowing down their academic growth. Let the teachers in the institutions of higher education be given grants directly to work with the innovative ideas and projects. You will surely find wonderful results. Do not mind a small misuse of funds, if it occurs in a few cases. Small misuse of funds will be a little price for the excellent results they are going to produce. To begin with, such an idea may be tried in some reputed institutions of higher education. Even for now, in case of research projects, UGC should provide sufficient financial assistance with liberal financial rules for their execution. The Principal Investigators should in no cases be chained with archaic colonial rules. They should also be provided with the clerical, stenographic, and ministerial help to be able to concentrate only on their research projects. Let there be academic audit through the research-reviews published in journals wherein we can find certification of quality and originality or otherwise by nationally and internationally acclaimed authorities. In physical sciences, it can be done by patenting of the research results.

(iv) *Reconciliation between Autonomy and Accountability*: University autonomy can never be absolute. It has "to be continuously earned and deserved".[6] Universities have to devise their own methods of maintaining high standards of financial and academic accountability. If they maintain high moral and academic standards, no authority can dare to touch them and interfere with their autonomy. In case of any deviation from the accepted standards of morality, financial and academic accountability interference from the society and state that pay the money will certainly be justified. Professor S.N. Mehrotra, who had been a VC of Agra and Jodhpur universities, has rightly pointed out: "In order to safeguard their autonomy, the universities must be squarely accountable to themselves, to the community and to the nation. The proper sphere of university autonomy lies in the selection of students, the appointment and promotion of teachers and the determination of courses of study, methods of teaching and the selection of areas of research. But even in these spheres the universities cannot function as mere ivory towers with total freedom to do what they like. They have to exercise their autonomy within the broad framework of national policies, programmes and priorities."[7]

7. EFFORTS SHOULD BE MADE TO CURB VIOLENCE/CRIMINALISATION

Following efforts are suggested in this direction:

(i) *Regulating Students' Elections to Depoliticise/Decriminalise Universities*: Politicisation and criminalisation are seen hand-in-glove in the universities of the sample also. This unholy combination has given birth to the cancer which is very difficult to cure. The need to depoliticise universities, colleges and other institutions of higher education has been stressed by a large section of parents, guardians, teachers and administrators. A recent murder of Professor Harbhajan Singh Sabbarbal of a college in Ujjain has led many to argue that the "frenzy, finances and fury" that union elections bring with them has to be stopped. The elective principle in the constitutions of the institutions of higher education is the villain in spoiling their academic climate. However, there are others who argue that students should not be denied their democratic rights. But at the same time election-related violence need to be curbed with a heavy hand. The Lyngdoh Committee appointed by the Union Human Resource Development Ministry on the directions of the Supreme Court has made valuable suggestions for the conduct of students' elections in the institutions of higher education. These suggestions would overhaul the higher education system. These need to be implemented strictly.

(ii) *Maintenance of Campus Discipline*: Defective education system has led to campus indiscipline. Factors like unplanned and indiscriminate growth, over emphasis on examination system, politicisation, commercialisation, negative effect of larger society, etc. have contributed to the campus indiscipline. For tackling this challenge of campus indiscipline, following steps deserve mention here:

- Factors responsible for the breakdown of discipline should be studied with great vision and should be prevented and checked accordingly.
- A culture of respect for the teachers, love for knowledge, craving and devotion for excellence has to be created. Teachers and administrators should create and maintain academic ethos which is essential for higher learning.
- Effective machinery for redressing grievances should be developed to nip any evil in the bud.
- Tutorial system and counselling system should be developed to mitigate the fury of campus indiscipline.

8. IMPROVE FINANCIAL HEALTH OF THE UNIVERSITIES

Following suggestions have been given for improving the financial health of the universities:

(i) *Liberal Financial Assistance is Required*: Finance is very important ingredient in the efficient administration of a university, so efforts should be made to improve the financial conditions. Government should extend liberal grants for increasing the effectiveness of universities. Of all the universities in the present sample, HPU has got the poorest infrastructure. Therefore, an additional amount of at least Rs. 50 crore for the university campus at Shimla and an another additional amount of Rs. 25 crore for its Regional Centre at Dharmshala (which may subsequently be developed to a full-fledged university in order to extend the coverage of higher education and also to meet the needs and aspirations of the poor people of the region) be urgently provided by the State/Central Government. A promised grant of total Rs. 10 crore in two installments to HPU by the Prime Minister, Dr. Manmohan Singh was of very little avail so far. Similarly, it has been observed with great concern by the researcher that his *alma mater* Panjab University a premier University of India, the fourth oldest university of India established in 1882 and the most important university beyond Delhi, has slowly been reduced to an ordinary state university. Its stature needs to be enhanced and brought to its old glory. For this Central Government should extend much needed financial support. The proposals of the PU worth Rs. 250 crore sent by its VC Professor R.C. Sobti to the Central Government for expansion and up-gradation of infrastructure should be considered sympathetically to enable this university to play its natural and vital role in the development of the north-western India.

Next to the state governments, University Grants Commission is a prolific source of finances for the universities. The UGC, in addition to providing grants, also looks after the maintenance of standards by the universities. For the last one and a half decade, UGC too has not been providing sufficient grants to the universities. UGC has to provide substantial financial assistance to the universities to equip them with the capacities to function as institutions of academic excellence competent enough to face the global challenges by providing world class education and producing useful research. Banks should also come with attractive scholarship and loan schemes to the poor and brilliant students who can later pay the loans when they get employed.

Following arguments may be given in favour of enhanced grants to universities:

- Expenditure on education is an investment in the future of the nation. So we should not compromise when the future of the nation is involved.
- Better finances will give real autonomy to the universities. Mr. V.S. Kokje, the Chancellor of HPU, in his discussion with the researcher, has stressed the need for a separate Finance

Commission for the Universities in the country so that greater financial autonomy is ensured. He further pointed out that UGC gives money only for research and development and not for the salary and allowances of the staff. Proposed Finance Commission by looking into all the needs of the universities will give autonomy in the real sense.[8]

- The universities are established under an Act of legislature and, hence, the government has to bear the responsibility of supporting them. But, this commitment is often forgotten. The government sometimes takes a niggardly attitude in supporting institutions of higher education. It tries to evolve some 'pattern' of grant-in-aid assistance to the universities. However, the grant-in-aid formula applied to a charitable or welfare institution has no relationship to the grants to be given to universities which have to be treated as mandatory in character. The grants should support the maintenance of the university fully. Having set-up a university, the government cannot escape its financial responsibility. Often, the release of grants is unconsciously delayed, thereby seriously hampering the working of the university. The university officials have the discomfiture and humiliation of having to repeatedly approach even minor officials in government to get the grants released. This is derogatory to the dignity of the university. It is the duty of the government and the departments concerned to ensure timely and orderly release of installments of the budgeted grants.[9]
- Education is essentially a spending sector and it has a legitimate claim over the country's resources both for its survival and development. To leave it to the considerations and grace of the profit-oriented private sector does not seem to be a wise proposition in the long-run. While efforts

may be made to promote community contribution to educational funding, the government cannot absolve itself of its responsibility towards funding of the social sector in general and education in particular. In the interest of long-term gains, of both equity and efficiency, even higher education should not be left to the discretion of private sector funding alone. The present trend of arguments of populism, of reducing subsidy or government's role in higher education need to be viewed with serious caution. Let the country not lose the game of educational development while winning few points of satisfying the populist claims. One should hasten to add here that the really able to pay should be made to pay for their education and community's contribution should also be mobilized. But, let there not be a blanket policy of withdrawal of government from educational funding and leaving the matter entirely to private sector.[10]

(ii) *Self Help is the Best Help*: Universities should keep this motto as their guide and thereby try to generate their own resources. Some methods in this regard may be suggested. Universities should make an annual hike of the fees keeping it according to the inflation level. The practice of keeping the fees and other dues constant for several years and then raising them manifold naturally irritates students. which follows unnecessary agitations and then withdrawal of the hike. Marginal annual increase by taking the students' organisations into confidence can give university additional money every year without facing agitations over fee hikes. Universities can make their library, laboratory, computer, and cyber-cafe services available to outside individuals and organisations on some reasonably high rates. Universities can undertake consultancy work and applied research for some government departments, business and industry. This way, universities can earn a substantial amount. Universities can extend facilities like guest house, conference hall, seminar rooms, classrooms, examination hall, etc. to outside organisations. Universities should establish alumni associations. Current students should be encouraged to have some functions/seminars in which they should invite the ex-students. Ex-students do have some emotional bonds with their *alma mater*. They can also make substantial contribution for the betterment of the universities. Philanthropists, business, and industry should also be encouraged to give sufficient donations to the universities. They can be encouraged to give scholarships to brilliant poor students, sponsor some research projects, or seminars/conferences and other academic activities. Some chairs may be established with their help or on the name of renowned industrialists, social workers, and leaders in different fields. It has also been observed that whatever meager resources the universities have are not utilized by them efficiently and judiciously. Difficulties in getting the research grants released to the students and teachers have become all-pervasive phenomena. Universities have to manage their limited resources wisely and effectively. They have to do away with the old bureaucratic techniques of mindless audit control which leads to financial inefficiency, waste and uselessness. Modern techniques of financial management aiming at getting the results with economy and efficiency need to be adopted by the universities without any delay and further harm to the university system as well as to finances.

(iii) *Universities may trade in Stock-Market*: To improve their financial position and to get much-needed resources, the universities may tap the capital market. Many universities in the developed countries of the world are trading successfully in stock market. Even in the Asian countries, namely, China and North Korea, some universities are applying this idea. India, a highly developing country, too can think of venturing in this area. Recently, in the last week of March 2007, VC of Bombay University, Vijay Khole, put a proposal to the university senate for getting the university listed in the Bombay Stock Exchange (BSE). The VC has also mooted the idea of conducting a feasibility study about getting listed in the BSE by the Bombay University academics. This is a proactive step taken by the university to improve the funding of the university and also to go global in the near future.[11]

SOME ADDITIONAL SUGGESTIONS

In addition to above suggestions emerged out of the conclusions drawn on the basis of data collected in the present study, some other suggestions emerged out of the related studies in higher education relevant from the point of view of the challenges being faced by university administration in India may be mentioned as follows:

Universities are a microcosm of the society, whatever one finds in society is also there in these institutions. We find a lot of degradation in the present Indian society. Politicisation, criminalisation, communalisation, commercialisation, moral degradation, corruption, etc. rampant in society are also therein the universities. When even pious institutions like religions are getting politicised, criminalised, and commercialised, how can one expect institutions of higher education to be solemn upholders of the truth, and refinement and instruments for broadening the minds of the students? A father who is himself a corrupt civil servant cannot discipline his wards to be honest in answering the questions in the annual examination where the marks are connected with their future career. Pt. Jawaharlal Nehru remarked, "If all is well with the universities, all would be well with the nation." Perhaps its reverse would also be true. Education system is bad so it is making the society bad or society is bad so the education system is bad, is like an unanswered long time question like hen or egg—who came first. From where should we start the reform, from society or from the universities? Again, it is a *Yaksheeya* question to be answered only by a person of the calibre of Yudhishthira.

Situation cannot improve, until and unless we think we can improve it. Thoughts and actions are needed to reform any system. We can certainly get order out of chaos. The situation is not beyond redemption. There is always a silver lining in every cloud. Our universities have still got excellent teachers of very high class international standards and also the students who study seriously and achieve excellence in many spheres of life. There is no dearth of talent, sincerity, commitment and devotion in our universities. Only we have to harness this talent and become catalytic agents in igniting the fire of self-actualisation. Following suggestions for strengthening the university administration to enable it to meet the challenges deserve mention here:

1. Strong Political Will

Strong political will to improve the governance of the universities for their revitalisation and reform is urgently needed. Political will has been put at the number one since it can set the whole tone of all our institutions. It has been observed that whenever and wherever, the political persons get involved in the universities, they undermine the autonomy of the universities, get their puppets appointed for various posts, the total system generates and ultimately gets destroyed.

2. Overhaul Examination System

Indian education system based on the British model lays undue stress on the external annual/semester examination. This examination system is highly based on rote memory supported by cramming again and again without understanding not to talk of application, refinement, and cultivation. Therefore, Indian examination system which has become the total and ultimate touchstone of the education system need to be overhauled to salvage education and make it an effective instrument of personal, social, economic and spiritual development. Following suggestions are worth trying in this regard:

- Internal assessment need to be given greater importance than the external annual/semester examinations.

- Internal assessment has to be not only for evaluation, but also for advice and help to the students for their improvement in learning.
- The assessment has to be continuous, based on assignments, mid-semester tests, etc.
- Tutorial assistance should be provided to correct the assignments under the supervision of the teachers. These tutors can be from the ranks of senior students and research scholars. They should be paid for this work.
- Open book system should be introduced to get rid of cheating and cramming.
- Grading system should be replaced by marks system.
- Objective type questions and short answer type questions should get precedence over essay type questions.
- Practical accomplishments should be given proper weightage.
- Efforts should be made to make education learner centred and learner-friendly and not examination centred to avoid unnecessary stress in the students.

3. Face Challenge of Globalisation boldly

In order to survive honourably by holding our head high amongst the advanced countries of the world, we have to accept the challenge of globalisation, willy-nilly. Globalization, as engineered by GATS, WTO, World Bank, IMF, and Co., has offered old ideas of *laissez faire* and survival of the fittest theory of Social Darwinism to us to swallow or starve meaning thereby that we have to accept it for our very survival. *Veer Bhogya Vasundhara,* a Sanskrit saying which means 'the Earth can be enjoyed only by the brave', a different version of the survival of the fittest has to be acknowledged and accepted. We have to prepare ourselves to face the challenge of globalization. Globalisation has to be considered not a problem but an opportunity to be seized. By taking all the strengths and weaknesses of higher education in India for global competitiveness into consideration, following steps are urgently required:

- In order to attract foreign students, Universities and institutions imparting higher education should improve their infrastructure by providing good lecture halls, well equipped laboratories, adequate library services, sports facilities, recreation facilities, hostel facilities, etc.
- The procedure for the admission of foreign students should be simplified. Government should set-up a single-window mechanism, in the form of Task Force consisting of representatives of different bodies like the UGC, All India Council for Technical Education (AICTE), and Medical Council of India (MCI), for admitting students for different professional programmes. Universities could get their foreign students' applications cleared through Task Force.
- Government and its statutory bodies should allow greater autonomy and flexibility to the Universities and institutes of higher education in dealing with the admission of foreign students, in entering into collaboration with foreign institutions, and in establishing off-shore campuses. Procedural impediments to opening of campuses in foreign countries by the Indian institutes should be removed.
- Some percentage of seats should be reserved for the foreign students or some supernumerary seats should be easily allowed to accommodate foreign students.
- Arrangements should be made through which Indian universities should offer the same academic programmes both in India and in foreign countries.
- Efforts should be made for mutual recognition of degrees and credits.
- The Government should advise Indian Embassies and High Commissions abroad to play a proactive role in providing information regarding the facilities available in the field of higher education in India. They should also help in organizing education fairs and entrance examinations.
- Information regarding various educational programmes, eligibility criteria, admission procedures, tuition fees, career prospects, etc. should

be provided in the web sites by various educational institutions.

- India should update the course contents of various courses in its universities and institutes of higher learning so that foreign students can be attracted and the Indian students who pass out from these institutes compete well with their counterparts all over the world.
- India should provide quality education through competent teachers and ideal academic culture with an eye on building talent for future needs. This can be done by developing appropriate curricula, method of imparting education and evaluation of students according to the internationally adopted standard practices.
- Students need to be encouraged for entrepreneurship by imparting them industry-friendly education. This can be done by establishing university-industry linkages.
- India should develop internationally relevant long-term as well as short-term courses in Social Sciences, Performing Arts like Indian Music and Dance, Yoga, Ayurveda and other systems of medicine, Indian Philosophy, Vedic Mathematics, Traditional Wisdom and Culture, and in other such areas in which we have got expertise. India can pass this knowledge and wisdom to the world for her own benefit and for that of the whole world.

4. Adopt Students' Charter

Suggestion of the Students' Charter made by Dharm Vir and Mullick to improve the satisfaction of students, parents and public at large deserve mention here. Students' Charter is a document, which aims to set out, as clearly as possible, what standards of service can be expected by students and what the university/institute/college can expect of students in return. Such charters are common features in colleges and universities in the West. It is an expression of close working relationship between the administration, the faculty and the students and their shared commitment to maintaining and enhancing excellence in the educational experience of its students. Such a charter would result in greater transparency and accountability on the part of all stakeholders of an institution, especially its management.[12]

5. Some Other Steps are also Needed for the Good Governance in the Institutions of Higher Education

Participation in creative activities like NSS, NCC, Sports, and Games should be given credit. Regional and national level seminars should be organised so that the students and teachers are abreast with the latest developments in their fields. Study programmes should also be reorganised keeping in view the changes and advancement of knowledge. The courses should be made relevant to the changing needs of the society. Changes suggested by the UGC in this direction are quite useful. These changes should be taken into consideration while redesigning the courses. Research and development programmes should be encouraged to modify curricula and methodologies of teaching and learning to incorporate elements of problem-solving, creativity and relevance. Talent search examinations and scholarships should be instituted at undergraduate and postgraduate levels. All-India tests for admission to research programmes should be introduced. Periodic review of fellowships should be done. Universities should establish networking arrangements with selected institutions from all parts of the country through a computer data network for sharing of information, data banks, library and computation resources, consultancy, and consultation and promotion of inter-action between researchers and academics. All the newly recruited lecturers should be given exposure through specially designed orientation programmes in teaching methodologies, pedagogy, educational psychology, etc. Refresher courses for serving teachers to cover every teacher at least once in 5 years should also be organised. Existing infrastructure should be strengthened and funding of research in universities should be enhanced. Industries should be encouraged to set-up most of their research activities in the university sector. Formal links with various research agencies should be established so that university system can provide guidance to the society and at the same time contribute in some worthwhile and socially useful research.

6. Assign Some Socially Useful Duties

Last but not the least, institutions of Higher Education should be assigned some socially useful duties. These institutions can help meet the challenges facing the society-poverty, environmental degradation, low economic growth, terrorism, etc. and realise the "Vision 2020". So rather than discarding them as whipping boys, we should help them, strengthen them, encourage them, rejuvenate them, and endear them. These institutions have a duty to carry out research that should contribute to solving the most serious problems facing the country. They can successfully discharge these duties. But, how can they do all this when the Governments-Central or State—want them not autonomous excellent institutions but their own bureaucratic departments towing their lines sheepishly. These institutions should be involved in research in budget preparations, solving the problems of various government departments like municipal administration, police, forest, customs, etc. The students, who otherwise create law and order problems, can be roped in finding solution to these problems under the guidance of their teachers. Instead of damaging the public property in senseless agitations, they can contribute for development of the country and earn and learn at the same time. Industry should seek the help of these institutions for upgrading their R&D efforts as is being done in developed countries. Examples can be multiplied where these institutions of higher learning can be engaged in socially useful work. This engagement will certainly give them confidence, help them to perform well in the academic field and help the nation in accelerating the pace of harmonious development.

To sum up, universities play a pivotal role in the development of a country. University administration in India is afflicted with many problems and weaknesses and naturally is not in a position to face the challenges it is surrounded with these days. Good governance is urgently needed for making universities efficient and effective. For the sake of good governance in universities we need a many pronged strategy with a great political will and administrative skill. Suggestions made above are worth trying. Scholars, politicians, educationists, administrators, economists, NGOs' and other enlightened citizens can make significant contributions in this regard. Educational administrators, teachers, students, non-teaching employees and all those interested in the future of the country have to sit together, join heads and work collectively for the success of the university administration. Delay in this concerted action will be detrimental to their interests and to those of the country.

Notes and References

1. R.J. Mathai, U. Pareek and T.V. Rao, Designing an Effective University System, In M.V. Mathur, Ramesh K. Arora and Meena Sogani, *Indian University System*, 99-100.
2. Amrik, Singh, *Fifty Years of Higher Education in India: The Role of the University Grants Commission*, New Delhi, Sage Publications, 2004, p. 238.
3. In M.V. Mathur, Ramesh, K. Arora and Meena Sogani, *op. cit.*, 16
4. P.R. Dubhashi, Focus on Fundamentals, In M.V. Mathur, Ramesh K. Arora and Meena Sogani, *op. cit.* 86,
5. *Ibid.*, p. 87.
6. S. Muthukumaran, University Autonomy, In M.V. Mathur, Ramesh K. Arora, and Meena Sogani, *op. cit.*, 194.
7. S.N. Mehrotra, Autonomy and Accountability of Indian Universities, In M.V. Mathur and Ramesh K. Arora (Eds.). *The Vice-Chancellors Remember*, New Delhi, Associated Publishing House, 1992, p. 342.
8. *Amar Ujala*, 3.12.05, p. 11 and *The Tribune*, 4.12.05, p. 6.
9. P.R. Dubhashi, *op. cit.* pp. 88-89
10. P.R. Panchamukhi, Contribution of Private Sector to Financing of Education, In Jandhyala BG Tilak, (Ed.) *Financing Education in India*, New Delhi, National Institute of Educational Planning and Administration, 2003, p. 282.
11. *The Tribune*, 31st March, 2007, p. 19.
12. Dharm Vir and S.K. Mullick, Enhancing Excellence: Charter as instrument of reform in universities, *The Tribune*, March 25, 2007, p. 12.

APPENDIX I

QUESTIONNAIRES

I. Vice-chancellor/Pro-Vice-chancellor/Registrar

(Please See: Information requested by Professor P.N. Gautam, Principal Investigator, UGC Major Research Project, Department of Public Administration, HP University, Shimla will be kept secret and will be used for research purpose only. Title of the Research Project, Challenges to the University Administration in India: A Study of North-Western Universities. Y stands for yes, N for no and ? for can't say. Please encircle any of these.)

(P.N. Gautam)

Name (Optional)
Qualifications
Age
Sex
Designation
Department
Date Since Working in the University
Date Since Working in the present position

1. Do you enjoy your administrative work Y N ?
2. Do you find dealing with the students' leaders
   - Frustrating Y N ?
   - Challenging Y N ?
   - Enjoyable Y N ?
   - Rewarding Y N ?
3. Do you find dealing with the teachers' leaders
   - Frustrating Y N ?
   - Challenging Y N ?

Enjoyable Y N ?
Rewarding Y N ?

4. Do you find dealing with the employees' leaders
   Frustrating Y N ?
   Challenging Y N ?
   Enjoyable Y N ?
   Rewarding Y N ?
5. Please mention the percentage of the total time you spend on these activities:
   Academic work %
   Routine Administration %
   Political Relationship %
   Arranging Finances %
   Dealing with Students %
   Dealing with Teachers %
   Dealing with Employees %
   Any Other %
   Total 100%
6. Do you face following pressures in the appointment/promotions of teachers:
   Political Y N ?
   Teachers' Unions Y N ?
   Students' Unions Y N ?
7. Do you face following pressures in the appointment/promotions of employees:
   Political Y N ?
   Employees' Unions Y N ?
   Teachers' Unions Y N ?
   Students' Unions Y N ?
8. Do you face following pressures in the appointment of Deans/Directors:
   Political Y N ?
   Employees' Unions Y N ?
   Teachers' Unions Y N ?
   Students' Unions Y N ?
9. Do you face following pressures in your routine administrative work:
   Political Y N ?

Employees' Unions Y N ?
Teachers' Unions Y N ?
Students' Unions Y N ?

10. Should there be elections to the Students' Central Association Y N ?
11. Should there be rotation in headship of various Departments Y N ?
12. Do you get grants easily released from the State Government Y N ?
13. Do you get grants easily released from the UGC Y N ?
14. Do you find grants sufficient to bear the expenses of running the University Y N ?
15. Do you visit the University Departments to meet the students Y N ?
16. Do you visit the University Departments to meet the teachers Y N ?
17. Do you visit the University Branches/Sections to meet the employees Y N ?
18. Do you consider the quality of education imparted in the University comparable to that of the advanced countries Y N ?
19. Have you made efforts to bring the quality of education imparted in the University comparable to that of the advanced countries Y N ?
20. Do you prefer marking of final examination papers by the outside teachers Y N ?
21. Do you think there should be some minimum attendance of classes by the students Y N ?
22. Has any case of sexual harassment of a female student by a male student come to your notice Y N ?
23. Has any case of sexual harassment of a female student by a male teacher come to your notice Y N ?
24. Has any case of sexual harassment of a female teacher by a male teacher come to your notice Y N ?
25. Do you think your University enjoys autonomy in the appointment of teachers Y N ?
26. Do you think your University enjoy autonomy in the promotion of teachers Y N ?
27. Do you think your University enjoys autonomy in the appointment of deans/directors Y N ?

28. Do you think University education should be limited to a few only Y N ?
29. Do you think University education should be for getting job only Y N ?
30. Do you think University education should be for self-development only Y N ?
31. Do you think University education should be both for job and self-development Y N ?
32. Do you consider University administration sympathetic to the demands of teachers, students, and employees Y N ?
33. Do you consider University administration quick in redressing the grievances of the teachers, students, and employees Y N ?
34. Please mention the awards got by you
35. Please mention the achievements/contributions made by you to the administration of your University
36. Out of ten how many marks would you like to give to your University Administration
37. Please mention the strengths of the administration of your university:

____

____

____

____

38. Please mention the weaknesses of the administration of your university:

____

____

____

____

39. Please give your suggestions for the improvement of the administration of your university:

____

____

2. Teachers

(Please See: Information requested by Professor P.N. Gautam, Principal Investigator, UGC Major Research Project, Department of Public Administration, HP University, Shimla will be kept secret and will be used for research purpose only. Title of the Research Project, Challenges to The University Administration in India: A Study of North-Western Universities. Y stands for yes, N for no and ? for can't say. Please encircle any of these.)

(P.N. Gautam)

Name (Optional)

Qualifications

Age

Sex

Designation

Department

Date Since Working in the Department

Are/were you some office bearer of any of University Organisation? Y/N

If yes, please specify

How many a time did you remain office bearer ___________

Please mention your political affiliation, if any ___________

1. Do you find teaching students interesting Y N ?
2. Do you find teaching profession respectable Y N ?
3. Do you conduct monthly tests in the papers you teach Y N?
4. Do you give assignments to the students you teach Y N ?
5. Do you use following teaching methods
   - Lecture Y N ?
   - Discussion Y N ?
   - Seminar Y N ?
   - Project Y N ?
   - Tutorials Y N ?

6. Do you use over-head projector for teaching your students Y N ?
7. Do you use video-films for teaching your students Y N ?
8. Do students discuss their academic problems with you Y N ?
9. Do you discuss your teaching problems with your colleagues Y N ?
10. Do you prefer marking of final examination papers by the outside teachers Y N ?
11. Do you think there should be some minimum attendance of classes by the students Y N ?
12. Should there be elections to the Students' Central Association Y N ?
13. Have you noticed any cheating case in the University examinations Y N ?
14. Do you fill your self-appraisal reports regularly every year Y N ?
15. Are you in favour of rotation in headship in your Department Y N ?
16. Do you find difficulties in getting your administrative work done in the University Y N ?
17. Do you find difficulties in getting the clearance of your bills from your LAD Y N ?
18. Do you find the system of internal audit by the officials effective in the clearance of bills Y N ?
19. Do you easily get the reading material of your academic interests in the library Y N ?
20. Do you find difficulties in getting research grant released Y N ?
21. Do you find difficulties in getting accounts of a National/ International Seminar organized by your Department settled Y N ?
22. Has any case of sexual harassment of a female student by a male student come to your notice Y N ?
23. Has any case of sexual harassment of a female student by a male teacher come to your notice Y N ?
24. Has any case of sexual harassment of a female teacher by a male teacher come to your notice Y N ?
25. Do you think your University enjoys autonomy in the appointment of teachers Y N ?

26. Do you think your University enjoy autonomy in the promotion of teachers Y N ?
27. Do you think your University enjoys autonomy in the appointment of deans/directors Y N ?
28. Do you think you will get promotion on the basis of merit in your University Y N ?
29. Do you think University education should be limited to a few only Y N ?
30. Do you think University education should be for getting job only Y N ?
31. Do you think University education should be for self-development only Y N ?
32. Do you think University education should be both for job and self-development YN ?
33. Do you consider the quality of education imparted in the University comparable to that of the advanced countries Y N ?
34. Have you made efforts to bring the quality of education imparted in the University comparable to that of the advanced countries Y N ?
35. Do you consider University administration sympathetic to your demands Y N ?
36. Do you consider University administration quick in redressing your grievances Y N ?
37. Please mention the number of papers contributed by you to the books

___

___

___

___

38. Please mention the number of articles published by you in the national journals

___

___

___

___

39. Please mention the number of articles published by you in the international journals
40 Please mention the awards got by you

41. Please mention any of your specific achievement/ contribution to the field of teaching

42. Out of ten how many marks would you like to give to your University Administration

43. Please mention the strengths of the administration of your university:

44. Please mention the weaknesses of the administration of your university:

____

____

45. Please give your suggestions for the improvement of the administration of your university:

____

____

____

____

3. Students

(Please See: Information requested by Professor P.N. Gautam, Principal Investigator, UGC Major Research Project, Department of Public Administration, HP University, Shimla will be kept secret and will be used for research purpose only. Title of the Research Project, Challenges to The University Administration in India: A Study of North Western Universities. Y stands for yes, N for no and ? for can't say. Please encircle any of these.)

(P.N. Gautam)

Name

Age

Sex

Class in which Studying

Date Since Studying in the University

Any other Examination Passed from the University Campus

Are/were you some office bearer of any of University Organisation? If yes, please specify

How many a time did you remain office bearer __________

Please mention your political affiliation, if any __________

1. Do you find classroom teaching interesting Y N ?
2. Do you find syllabus useful Y N ?
3. Do you find syllabus interesting Y N ?
4. Do your teachers conduct monthly tests in the papers they teach Y N ?

5. Do your teachers give assignments to you Y N ?
6. Do your teachers use following teaching methods:
   - Lecture Y N ?
   - Discussion Y N ?
   - Seminar Y N ?
   - Project Y N ?
   - Tutorials Y N ?
7. Do your teachers use over-head projector for teaching you Y N ?
8. Do your teachers use video-films for teaching you Y N ?
9. Do you discuss your academic problems with your teachers Y N ?
10. Do you prefer marking of final examination papers by the outside teachers Y N ?
11. Do you think there should be some minimum attendance of classes by the students Y N ?
12. Do you intend to appear in any other examination/test in addition to your University studies Y N ?
13. Do you find difficulties in getting your administrative work done in the University Y N ?
14. Should there be elections to the Students' Central Association Y N ?
15. Have you ever indulged in cheating in the University examinations Y N ?
16. Do you easily get the reading material of your academic interests in the library Y N ?
17. Has any case of sexual harassment of a female student by a male student come to your notice Y N ?
18. Has any case of sexual harassment of a female student by a male teacher come to your notice Y N ?
19. Do you think University education should be limited to a few only Y N ?
20. Do you think University education should be for getting job only Y N ?
21. Do you think University education should be for self-development only Y N ?
22. Do you think University education should be both for job and self-development Y N ?

23. Do you consider the quality of education imparted in the University comparable to that of the advanced countries Y N ?
24. Do you consider University administration sympathetic to your demands Y N ?
25. Do you consider University administration quick in redressing your grievances Y N ?
26. Please mention any of your specific achievement/ contribution to your University
27. Out of ten how many marks would you like to give to your University Administration
28. Please mention the strengths of the administration of your university:

____

____

____

____

____

29. Please mention the weaknesses of the administration of your university:

____

____

____

____

____

30. Please give your suggestions for the improvement of the administration of your university:

____

____

____

____

____

4. Non-Teaching Staff

(Please See: Information requested by Professor P.N. Gautam, Principal Investigator UGC Major Research Project, Department of Public Administration, HP University Shimla will be kept secret and will be used for research purpose only. Title of the Research Project, Challenges to The University Administration in India: A Study of North Western Universities. Y stands for yes, N for no and ? for can't say. Please encircle any of these.)

(P.N. Gautam)

Name

Designation

Department/Branch in which working

Qualification

Age

Sex

Are/were you some office bearer of any of University Organisation? If yes, please specify

How many a time did you remain office bearer ____________

Please mention your political affiliation, if any ____________

1. Do you find your job interesting Y N ?
2. Do you find your job respectable Y N ?
3. Do you maintain weekly/monthly diary of your official work Y N ?
4. Do you make any plan for doing your official work Y N ?
5. Did you receive any training for doing your official work Y N ?
6. Do you find difficulties in dealing with the senior officials Y N ?
7. Do you find difficulties in dealing with your colleagues Y N ?
8. Do you find difficulties in dealing with your subordinates Y N ?
9. Do you find difficulties in dealing with the teachers Y N ?

10. Do you find difficulties in dealing with the students Y N ?
11. Do you find difficulties in getting your administrative work done in the University Y N ?
12. Do you find difficulties in getting the clearance of your bills from your LAD Y N ?
13. Do you find the system of audit by the officials effective in the clearance of bill Y N ?
14. Has any case of sexual harassment of a female employee by a male employee come to your notice Y N ?
15. Do you think your University enjoy autonomy in the appointment of employees Y N ?
16. Do you think your University enjoys autonomy in the promotion of employees Y N ?
17. Do you think your University enjoys autonomy in the appointment of deans/directors Y N ?
18. Do you think you will get promotion whenever it is due Y N ?
19. Do you think University education should be limited to a few only Y N ?
20. Do you think University education should be for getting job only Y N ?
21. Do you think University education should be for self-development only Y N ?
22. Do you think University education should be both for job and self-development Y N ?
23. Do you consider University administration sympathetic to your demands Y N ?
24. Do you consider University administration quick in redressing your grievances Y N ?
25. Please mention any of your specific achievement/contribution to your University

____

____

____

____

26. Out of ten how many marks would you like to give to your University Administration

____

____

____

27. Please mention the strengths of the administration of your university:

____

____

____

____

28. Please mention the weaknesses of the administration of your university:

____

____

____

____

29. Please give your suggestions for the improvement of the administration of your university:

____

____

____

____

5. Deans/Other Officers/HOD/Directors

(Please See: Information requested by Professor P.N. Gautam, Principal Investigator UGC Major Research Project, Department of Public Administration, HP University, Shimla will be kept secret and will be used for research purpose only. Title of the Research Project, Challenges to The University Administration in India: A Study of North-Western Universities. Y stands for yes, N for no and ? for can't say. Please encircle any of these.)

(P.N. Gautam)

Name (Optional)

Qualifications

Age

Sex

Designation

Department

Date Since Working in the University

Date Since Working in the present position

Are you some office bearer of any of University Organisation? If yes, please specify

How many a time did you remain office bearer ____________

Please mention your political affiliation, if any ____________

1. Do you enjoy your administrative work Y N ?
2. Do you find dealing with the students' leaders
   - Frustrating Y N ?
   - Challenging Y N ?
   - Enjoyable Y N ?
   - Rewarding Y N ?
3. Do you find dealing with teachers' leaders
   - Frustrating Y N ?
   - Challenging Y N ?
   - Enjoyable Y N ?
   - Rewarding Y N ?
4. Do you find dealing with the employees' leaders
   - Frustrating Y N ?
   - Challenging Y N ?
   - Enjoyable Y N ?
   - Rewarding Y N ?

5. Please mention the percentage of the total time you spend on these activities:

Academic work	%
Routine Administration	%
Political Relationship	%
Arranging Finances	%
Dealing with Students	%
Dealing with Teachers	%
Dealing with Employees	%
Any Other	%
Total	100%

6. Do you face following pressures in your routine administrative work:

Political	Y N ?
Employees' Unions	Y N ?
Teachers' Unions	Y N ?
Students' Unions	Y N ?

7. Do you visit the University Departments to meet the students Y N ?
8. Do you visit the University Departments to meet the teachers Y N ?
9. Do you visit the University Branches/Sections to meet the employees Y N ?
10. Do you consider the quality of education imparted in the University comparable to that of the advanced countries Y N ?
11. Have you made efforts to bring the quality of education imparted in the University comparable to that of the advanced countries Y N ?
12. Do you consider University administration sympathetic to the demands of teachers, students, and employees Y N ?
13. Do you consider University administration quick in redressing the grievances of the teachers, students, and employees Y N ?
14. Do you find difficulties in getting your administrative work done in the University Y N ?
15. Do you find difficulties in getting the clearance of your bills from your LAD Y N ?
16. Do you find the system of internal audit by the officials effective in the clearance of bills Y N ?

17. Please mention the number of papers contributed by you to the books:

____

____

18. Please mention the number of articles published by you in the national journals:

____

____

19. Please mention the number of articles published by you in the international journals:

____

____

20. Please mention the awards got by you:

____

____

21. Please mention any of your specific achievement/ contribution to the field of teaching/administration

____

____

____

22. Out of ten how many marks would you like to give to your University Administration

____

____

____

23. Please mention the strengths of the administration of your university:

____

____

____

24. Please mention the weaknesses of the administration of your university:

____

____

____

25. Please give your suggestions for the improvement of the administration of your university:

____

____

____

6. Hostel Wardens/Chief Wardens

(Please See: Information requested by Professor P.N. Gautam, Principal Investigator, UGC Major Research Project, Department of Public Administration, HP University, Shimla will be kept secret and will be used for research purpose only. Title of the Research Project, Challenges to The University Administration in India: A Study of North-Western Universities. Y stands for yes, N for no and ? for can't say. Please encircle any of these.)

(P.N. GAUTAM)

Name (Optional)

Qualifications

Age

Sex

Designation

Department

Date Since Working in the University

Date Since Working in the present position

Are you some office bearer of any of University Organisation? If yes, please specify

How many a time did you remain office bearer _______________

Please mention your political affiliation, if any _______________

1. Do you enjoy your administrative work Y N ?
2. Do you find dealing with the students' leaders
   - Frustrating Y N ?
   - Challenging Y N ?
   - Enjoyable Y N ?
   - Rewarding Y N ?
3. Please mention the percentage of the total time you spend on these activities:
   - Academic work %
   - Routine Administration %
   - Political Relationship %
   - Arranging Finances %
   - Dealing with Students %
   - Dealing with Teachers %
   - Dealing with Employees %
   - Any Other %
   - Total 100%
4. Do you face following pressures in your routine administrative work:
   - Political Y N ?
   - Employees' Unions Y N ?
   - Teachers' Unions Y N ?
   - Students' Unions Y N ?
5. Are the students residing in the hostels getting sufficient facilities Y N ?
6. Are the students residing in the hostels often complain about the facilities Y N ?
7. Do you find difficulties in getting the clearance of your bills from your LAD Y N ?
8. Do you find the system of internal audit by the officials effective in the clearance of bills Y N ?
9. Please mention the number of papers contributed by you to the books

   ____

   ____

10. Please mention the number of articles published by you in the national journals

    ____

    ____

11. Please mention the number of articles published by you in the international journals

____

____

12. Please mention the awards got by you

____

____

13. Please mention any of your specific achievement/ contribution to the field of teaching/administration

____

____

____

14. Out of ten how many marks would you like to give to the academic atmosphere of your hostel(s)

____

____

____

15. Out of ten how many marks would you like to give to the residential facilities of your hostel(s)

____

____

____

16. Please mention the strengths of the administration of your hostel(s):

____

____

____

17. Please mention the weaknesses of the administration of your hostel(s):

____

____

____

____

18. Please give your suggestions for the improvement of the administration of your hostel(s):

____

____

____

7. Librarian

(Please See: Information requested by Professor P.N. Gautam, Principal Investigator, UGC Major Research Project, Department of Public Administration, HP University, Shimla will be kept secret and will be used for research purpose only. Title of the Research Project, Challenges to The University Administration in India: A Study of North-Western Universities. Y stands for yes, N for no and? for can't say. Please encircle any of these.)

(P.N. Gautam)

Name (Optional)

Qualifications

Age

Sex

Designation

Department

Date Since Working in the University

Date Since Working in the present position

Are you some office bearer of any of University Organisation? If yes, please specify

How many a time did you remain office bearer ____________

Please mention your political affiliation, if any ____________

1. Do you enjoy your administrative work Y N ?
2. Do you find dealing with the students' leaders

Frustrating	Y N ?
Challenging	Y N ?
Enjoyable	Y N ?
Rewarding	Y N ?

3. Do you find dealing with the teachers' leaders

Frustrating	Y N ?
Challenging	Y N ?
Enjoyable	Y N ?
Rewarding	Y N ?

4. Do you find dealing with the employees' leaders

Frustrating	Y N ?
Challenging	Y N ?
Enjoyable	Y N ?
Rewarding	Y N ?

5. Please mention the percentage of the total time you spend on these activities:

Academic work	%
Routine Administration	%
Political Relationship	%
Arranging Finances	%
Dealing with Students	%
Dealing with Teachers	%
Dealing with Employees	%
Any Other	%
Total	100%

6. Do you face following pressures in your routine administrative work:

Political	Y N ?
Employees' Unions	Y N ?
Teachers' Unions	Y N ?
Students' Unions	Y N ?

7. Are you giving sufficient facilities to your readers Y N ?
8. Are the readers often complain about the facilities in the library Y N ?
9. Do you find difficulties in getting your administrative work done in the University Y N ?

10. Do you find difficulties in getting the clearance of your bills from your LAD Y N ?
11. Do you find the system of internal audit by the officials effective in the clearance of bills Y N ?
12. Do you get sufficient grants from the UGC Y N ?
13. Please mention the number of papers contributed by you to the books
14. Please mention the number of articles published by you in the national journals
15. Please mention the number of articles published by you in the international journals
16. Please mention the awards got by you

____

____

17. Please mention any of your specific achievement/contribution to the field of teaching/administration

____

____

18. Out of ten how many marks would you like to give to your Library:

____

____

19. Please mention the strengths of your Library:

____

____

20. Please mention the weaknesses of your Library:

____

____

21. Please give your suggestions for the improvement of your Library:

____

____

APPENDIX 2

OBSERVATION SHEET FOR THE UNIVERSITIES OF THE SAMPLE

Campus—General Upkeep, Well Marked Boundary Walls, Fountains, Lawns, Roads, Parking Places, Conditions of Buildings, Toilets, General Cleanliness,

University Department, General Upkeep, Roads, Parking Places, Conditions of Buildings, Toilets, General Cleanliness, General Infrastructure, Taking of Classes by the Teachers, Guiding the Students, Consultation of Departmental Libraries by the Students and Teachers, Sitting of the Teachers in their Respective Rooms/Taking of the Classes in the After Noon,

Administrative Block, General Upkeep, Roads, Parking Places, Conditions of Buildings, Toilets, General Cleanliness, Arrangement of Files and Records, General Infrastructure, Punctuality, Attendance, Truancy,

Library, General Upkeep, Roads, Parking Places, Conditions of Buildings, Toilets, General Cleanliness, Arrangement of Stacks, Seating Arrangement, Reading Rooms, General Infrastructure, Library Consultation by the Students, and Teachers,

Laboratories, General Upkeep, Roads, Parking Places, Conditions of Buildings, Toilets, General Cleanliness, General Infrastructure,

Hostel, General Upkeep, Roads, Parking Places, Conditions of Buildings, Toilets, Water, Geysers, General Cleanliness, General Infrastructure, Cubicles, Dormitories, Reading Room, Recreation Room, TV, Radio, Indoor-Games, Availability of Barbers, Laundry, Tailors, PCO, Mess, Canteen, General Provisions,

General Work Culture, Behaviour of the Persons Towards the Opposite Sex, Handbills on the Walls or on the Wooden Boards, Students' Agitations, Strikes, Slogans, Burning of Effigies, Gate Meetings by the Employees, Employees' Agitations, Teachers' Agitations, Tone and Temper of the Speeches of the Persons who Agitate, Reception, Enquiry, Fee-Counters, Public Relations, University Security, Visits to V.C./ Administrative Office.

Bibliography

Asha Gupta, *Education in the 21st Century: Looking Beyond University*, Delhi, Shipra Publications, 2008.

Channa, Karuna (Ed.), *Transforming Links between Higher and Basic Education: Mapping the Field*, New Delhi, Sage Publications, 2004.

Dahiya, Bhim S., *The University Autonomy in India: The Idea and the Reality*, Shimla: Indian Institute of Advanced Study, 2001.

Dongerkery, S.R., *University Education in India*, Bombay: Mamaktalas, 1967.

Goel, Aruna and Goel, S.L., Encyclopaedia of Higher Education in the 21st Century, New Delhi, Deep and Deep Publications (P) Ltd., 2005.

Jeremiah, M.S., *Deteriorating Quality of Higher Education: Owing To Poverty of Resources*, Jaipur, ADB Publishers, 1998.

Kaul, J.N., *Governance of Universities: Autonomy of the University Community*, New Delhi: Abhinav Publications, 1988.

Khan, Fauzia, *Development of University Administration in India*, Delhi, Abhijeet Publications, 2003.

Lewis, Ralph G. and Smith, Douglas H., *Total Quality in Higher Education*, New Delhi: Vanity Books International, 1998.

Malik, S.C. (Ed.), Management and Organization of Indian Universities, Shimla: Indian Institute of Advanced Study, 1971.

Mathur, M.V. Arora, Ramesh K. and Sogani, Meena (Eds.), New Delhi, Wiley Eastern Limited, *Indian University System*, 1994.

Mathur, M.V. and Arora, Ramesh K. (Eds.), *The Vice-Chancellors Remember*, New Delhi, Associated Publishing House, 1992.

Mohanty, Jagannath, *Current Trends in Higher Education*, New Delhi, Deep and Deep Publications (P) Ltd., 2003.

Nanjundappa, D.M., *Working of University Finances*, New Delhi: Sterling Publishers, Private Ltd., 1976.

Noll, Roger G. (Ed.), *Challenges to Research Universities*, Washington, D.C.: Brookings Institution Press, 1998.

Prasad, Anirudh, *University Education Administration and the Law*, New Delhi, Deep and Deep Publications (P) Ltd., 2000.

Ray, Anil Baran, *Students and Politics in India: The Role of Caste, Language and Religion in an Indian University*, Delhi: Manohar, 1977.

Raza, Monis (Ed.), *Higher Education in India: Retrospect and Prospect*, New Delhi: Association of Indian Universities, 1991.

Sethi, J.D., *The Crisis and Collapse of Higher Education in India*. New Delhi: Vikas Publishing House, 1983.

Shah, A.B. (Ed.), *Higher Education in India*, Bombay: Lalvani Publishing House, 1967.

Singh, Amrik (Ed.), *The Higher Learning in India*, Delhi: Vikas Publishing House, 1974.

———, *Asking for Trouble: What it Means to be a Vice-Chancellor Today*, Delhi: Vikas Publishing House Pvt. Ltd., 1984.

———, *Fifty Years of Higher Education in India*, New Delhi, Sage Publications, 2004.

Subbaram, K.V., *Indian Universities and Systemic Ailments*, New Delhi: Harman Publishing House, 1993.

Tickoo, Champa, *Indian Universities: A Historical, Comparative Perspective*, Bombay, Orient Longman, 1980.

Tilak, Jandhyala B.G. (Ed.), *Financing Education in India*, New Delhi, National Institute of Educational Planning and Administration, 2003.

Index